TABLE OF CONTENT

APPETIZERS

Cheese

BRUSCHETTA

Episode: Toast Modern, EA1G17

1 narrow Italian or French loaf of bread	1) Preheat oven on broiler setting. 2) Place a rack approximately 6 inches from broiler. 3) Slice the loaf of bread, on the bias, into 3/4-inch slices. 4) Place bread in oven on sheet pan and broil until golden brown on both sides, approximately 2 minutes for the first side and 1 to 1 1/2 for second side.
1 head garlic, cut in 1/2 crosswise 2 tablespoons extra-virgin olive oil	5) Remove to a platter and rub each slice of bread with the garlic and then brush with olive oil.
Kosher salt and pepper	6) Sprinkle with salt and pepper and serve immediately.

Difficulty: Easy **Prep Time:** 5 minutes **Cook Time:** 4 minutes **Yield:** approximately 32 pieces

FONDUE VUDU

Episode: For Whom The Cheese Melts, EA1B02

1 clove garlic, halved	1) Rub inside of fondue pot or heavy small saucepan with garlic.
1 (12-ounce) bottle hard apple cider	2) Pour cider into pot.
2 tablespoons lemon juice 1 tablespoon brandy Pinch kosher salt	3) Add 1 tablespoon of lemon juice, the brandy and salt and bring to a simmer over medium heat.
5 ounces (2 cups) Gruyere, grated 5 ounces (2 cups) Smoked Gouda, rind removed, grated 1 tablespoon plus 1 teaspoon cornstarch	4) Meanwhile, grate the cheese and toss well with the cornstarch in a large bowl. 5) When the cider just begins to simmer, gradually add the cheese a handful at a time, allowing each addition to melt completely before adding the next. 6) Continue adding cheese and stirring until all cheese is incorporated, about 3 minutes. 7) If mixture starts to bubble, reduce heat to low. The mixture is ready when creamy and easily coats the back of a spoon.
1/4 teaspoon curry powder Several grinds fresh ground black pepper	8) Stir in curry powder and pepper.
<u>Dipping Ingredients:</u> A variety of breads Ex: pumpernickel, rye, bagel chunks Softened vegetables by blanching briefly in boiling water then chilling Ex: cauliflower, broccoli, mushrooms and potatoes. Crisp fruits EX: apples Cooked meats and sausages Soft pretzels	9) If cheese seems stringy, add some or all of the remaining lemon juice. 10) Move fondue pot to alcohol warmer, and keep stirring during service. 11) A variety of breads, from pumpernickel to rye to bagel chunks can be skewered and dipped as can cauliflower, broccoli, mushrooms and potatoes. (Soften all vegetables by blanching briefly in boiling water then chilling.) Crisp fruits such as apples make great fondue fodder, as do cooked meats and sausages. Even soft pretzels make for good dipping. 12) If any fondue is left over, cover with ice water and refrigerate, pour off water and reheat over low heat.

Difficulty: Easy **Yield:** 4 to 6 servings

WELSH RAREBIT

Episode: Toast Modern, EA1G17

Ingredients	Directions
2 tablespoons unsalted butter **2 tablespoons all-purpose flour**	1) In a medium saucepan over low heat, melt the butter and whisk in the flour. 2) Cook, whisking constantly for 2 to 3 minutes, being careful not to brown the flour.
1 teaspoon Dijon mustard **1 teaspoon Worcestershire sauce** **1/2 teaspoon kosher salt** **1/2 teaspoon freshly ground black pepper**	3) Whisk in mustard, Worcestershire sauce, salt, and pepper until smooth.
1/2 cup porter beer	4) Add beer and whisk to combine.
3/4 cup heavy cream	5) Pour in cream and whisk until well combined and smooth.
6 ounces (approximately 1 1/2 cups) shredded Cheddar	6) Gradually add cheese, stirring constantly, until cheese melts and sauce is smooth; this will take 4 to 5 minutes.
2 drops hot sauce	7) Add hot sauce.
4 slices toasted rye bread	8) Pour over toast and serve immediately.

Difficulty: Easy **Prep Time:** 15 minutes **Cook Time:** 10 minutes **Yield:** 4 servings as a side dish

Fruit

MANGO CHUTNEY

Episode: Down and Out in Paradise, EASP02

Ingredients	Directions
4 pounds fresh mangos, ripe but not too soft, peeled	1) Cut the mango flesh away from the pit. The pit is shaped similar to an obelisk, so you'll end up with 2 large pieces and 2 smaller pieces from each mango. Roughly chop the flesh.
3 tablespoons vegetable oil **1 teaspoon chile flakes**	2) In a sauté pan heat the oil and add the chile flakes. Be careful not to burn the chile, just toast to flavor the oil.
2 1/2 cups medium dice red onion	3) Add the onions and sweat until soft.
1/4 cup minced fresh ginger **1 cup small dice red bell pepper**	4) Add the ginger and bell pepper and sauté for 1 to 2 minutes. 5) Finally add the mango and cook for 1 more minute.
8 ounces unsweetened pineapple juice 4 ounces cider vinegar 1/2 cup brown sugar 1 1/2 tablespoons curry powder	6) In a separate bowl, combine the pineapple juice, vinegar, sugar, and curry powder. 7) Add this mixture to the pan. Stir to combine. Bring the mixture to a bare simmer and reduce for about 30 minutes, stirring frequently.
Kosher salt and fresh ground white pepper	8) Season with salt and pepper.
1/2 cup raisins or golden raisins **1/2 cup toasted, roughly chopped macadamia nuts**	9) Add the raisins and the nuts and transfer to another container over an ice bath. I used a mild yellow curry powder, but if you want it hotter go for red.

Difficulty: Medium **Prep Time:** 15 minutes **Cook Time:** 45 minutes **Yield:** about 4 cups

Notes:______________________________

SPICY PINEAPPLE SLICES

Episode: Down and Out in Paradise, EASP02

2 teaspoons kosher salt 1 teaspoon chile powder 3 teaspoons dark brown sugar	1) In a small bowl mix the salt, chile powder, and brown sugar.
6 (1-inch) slices pineapple	2) Sprinkle over both sides of the pineapple slices.
Vegetable oil, for coating the grill or grill pan	3) Place pineapple slices onto a preheated, oiled grill or grill pan on high heat for 1 minute on each side. 4) Reduce heat to low and continue cooking for 2 to 3 minutes per side or until the pineapple has softened and the sugar has caramelized on the edges.

Difficulty: Easy **Prep Time:** 10 minutes **Cook Time:** 8 minutes **Yield:** 6 servings

Pickling

AB'S B & B'S

Episode: American Pickle, EA1C07

1/2 onion, thinly sliced 2 medium cucumbers, thinly sliced	1) Combine onion and cucumber slices in a clean spring-top jar.
1 cup water 1 cup cider vinegar 1 1/2 cups sugar Pinch kosher salt 1/2 teaspoon mustard seeds 1/2 teaspoon turmeric 1/2 teaspoon celery seeds 1/2 teaspoon pickling spice	2) Combine the remaining ingredients in a non-reactive saucepan and bring to a boil. 3) Simmer for 4 full minutes to wake up the flavors of the spices. 4) Slowly pour the hot pickling liquid over the onion and cucumber slice, completely filling the jar. 5) Allow the pickles to cool to room temperature before topping off with any remaining pickling liquid. 6) Refrigerate.

Difficulty: Easy **Yield:** 4 servings

FIRECRACKERS

Episode: American Pickle, EA1C07

1/2 pound mini carrots	1) Place carrots in a spring-top glass jar.
1 cup water 1 cup sugar 1 1/2 cups cider vinegar 1 teaspoon onion powder 1/2 teaspoon mustard seeds 1 1/2 teaspoons kosher salt 1 teaspoon chili flakes	2) Bring the water, sugar, cider vinegar, onion powder, mustard seeds, salt, and chili flakes to a boil in a non-reactive saucepan. 3) Boil for 4 minutes. 4) Slowly pour the hot pickling liquid over the carrots, filling the jar to the top.
2 dried chilies	5) Place the chilies in the jar. 6) Allow the carrots to cool before sealing. 7) Refrigerate for 2 days up to 1 week.

Difficulty: Easy **Yield:** 4 servings

Notes:____

HURRY CURRY CAULIFLOWER

Episode: American Pickle, EA1C07

1 tablespoon canola oil	1) Heat the canola oil in a heavy skillet over medium heat.
1 teaspoon cumin seed **1 teaspoon coriander seed**	2) Crush the cumin seed with the coriander seed and add to the pan.
2 teaspoons curry powder **1 teaspoon fresh ginger, minced** **1 whole clove garlic, smashed**	3) Add the curry powder, ginger, and garlic to the pan. Cook these spices, stirring until the oil colors and the spices are fragrant.
1 head cauliflower, cut into florets	4) Add the cauliflower florets to the pan and toss to coat.
1 cup water **1 cup rice wine vinegar** **1/2 cup cider vinegar** **3 tablespoons sugar** **1 teaspoon pickling salt**	5) In a lidded plastic container, combine the water, rice wine vinegar, cider vinegar, sugar, and pickling salt. Shake to combine. 6) Once the cauliflower is slightly tender, add it to a glass jar. 7) Pour the pickling liquid over the cauliflower, filling to the top of the jar. 8) Cool, chill, and store the pickles for 1 week to allow the flavors to develop thoroughly.

Difficulty: Easy **Prep Time:** 20 minutes **Inactive Prep Time:** 1 week **Cook Time:** 5 minutes **Yield:** 4 servings

KINDA SORTA SOURS

Episode: American Pickle, EA1C07

1/2 onion, thinly sliced **2 medium cucumbers, thinly sliced**	1) Combine the onion and cucumber slices in a clean spring-top jar.
1 cup water **1 cup cider vinegar** **1/2 cup champagne vinegar** **1/2 cup sugar** **2 tablespoons plus 2 teaspoons kosher salt** **1 teaspoon mustard seeds** **1/4 teaspoon turmeric** **1 teaspoon celery seeds** **1 teaspoon pickling spice**	2) Combine the remaining ingredients, with the exception of the garlic, in a non-reactive saucepan. 3) Bring to a boil and simmer for 4 full minutes to wake up the spice flavors.
4 whole garlic cloves, smashed	4) Add the garlic cloves to the jar. 5) Slowly and gently pour the pickling liquid over the onion and cucumber slices, filling to the top of the jar. 6) Cool to room temperature. 7) Top off the pickles with any remaining pickling liquid and refrigerate.

Difficulty: Easy **Yield:** 4 servings

Notes:________________________________

PICKLED BEETS

Episode: Beet It, EA1F16

Roasted Beets, recipe follows	1) Remove the skin from the Roasted Beets and slice thinly.
1 large red onion, frenched	2) Arrange in 1-quart jars alternating layers with the onion.
1 cup tarragon wine vinegar **1 1/2 teaspoons Kosher salt** **1/2 cup sugar** **1 cup water**	3) In a small pot boil the rest of the ingredients and pour over the beets. 4) Tightly lid the jars and place in the refrigerator for 3 to 7 days before serving.
Roasted Beets: **6 medium beets, cleaned with 1-inch stem remaining** **2 large shallots, peeled** **2 sprigs rosemary** **2 teaspoons olive oil**	1) Preheat oven to 400 degrees F. 2) In a large bowl toss all of the ingredients. 3) Place into a foil pouch and roast in the oven for 40 minutes.

Difficulty: Easy **Prep Time:** 30 minutes **Inactive Prep Time:** 3 minutes **Cook Time:** 75 minutes **Yield:** 2 (1-quart) jars

SUMMER FRUITS

Episode: American Pickle, EA1C07

1 Bartlett pear, thinly sliced **1 red plum, seeded and quartered** **1/2 lemon, thinly sliced** **1 tablespoon fresh ginger, slivered**	1) Place the pear, plum, lemon, and fresh ginger in a bowl.
1 cup water **1 cup sugar** **1 cup rice wine vinegar**	2) In a non-reactive saucepan, combine the water, sugar, and rice wine vinegar. 3) Bring the liquid to a simmer and cook until sugar dissolves.
1 sprig fresh mint	4) Place the fruit mixture into a spring-top glass jar and add the sprig of mint to the fruit. 5) Slowly pour the hot pickling liquid over the fruit, filling the jar to the top. 6) Cool the pickles, then refrigerate for 2 days up to 1 week before serving.

Difficulty: Easy **Yield:** 4 servings

Figure 1: USDA Food Pyramid

BREADS

VERY BASIC BREAD

Episode: Dr. Strangeloaf, EA1H15

1 pound bread flour, plus extra for shaping **1 teaspoon instant rapid rise yeast** **2 teaspoons honey** **10 ounces bottled or filtered water**	1) Combine 5 ounces of the flour, 1/4 teaspoon of the yeast, all of the honey, and all of the bottled water in a straight-sided container; cover loosely and refrigerate for 8 to 12 hours.
2 teaspoons kosher salt	2) Place the remaining 11 ounces of flour, remaining yeast, and all the salt into the bowl of a stand mixer, and add the pre-ferment from the refrigerator. 3) Using the dough hook attachment, knead the mixture on low for 2 to 3 minutes just until it comes together. 4) Cover the dough in the bowl with a kitchen towel and allow to rest for 20 minutes. 5) After 20 minutes, knead the dough on medium speed for 5 to 10 minutes or until you are able to gently pull the dough into a thin sheet that light will pass through. The dough will be sticky, but not so sticky that you can't handle it.
2 quarts hot water	6) While the dough is kneading, pour half of the hot water into a shallow pan and place on the bottom rack of your oven.
Vegetable oil, for greasing the rising container	7) Grease the inside of a large straight-sided container with the vegetable oil. 8) Place the dough ball into the container and set on the rack above the pan of water. 9) Allow to rise until doubled in size, approximately 1 to 2 hours. 10) Once the dough has doubled in size, turn it onto a counter top, lightly dust your hands with flour, and press the dough out with your knuckles; then fold 1 side in towards the middle of the mass and then the other, as if you were making a tri-fold wallet. Repeat the folding a second time. 11) Cover the dough with a kitchen towel and allow to rest for another 10 minutes. 12) Flatten dough again with your knuckles and then fold the dough in onto itself, like you are shaping something that looks like a jellyfish. 13) Turn the dough over and squeeze the bottom together so that the top surface of the dough is smooth. 14) Place the dough back onto the counter and begin to roll gently between your hands. Do not grab the dough but allow it to move gently back and forth between your hands, moving in a circular motion.
2 tablespoons cornmeal	15) Move the dough ball to a pizza peel or the bottom of a sheet pan that has been sprinkled with the cornmeal. 16) Cover with the kitchen towel and allow to bench proof for 1 hour, or until you poke the dough and it quickly fills back in where you poked it. 17) Place an unglazed terra cotta dish upside down into the oven and heat the oven to 400 degrees F.
1/3 cup water **1 tablespoon cornstarch**	18) Combine the 1/3 cup of water and the cornstarch in a small bowl. 19) Uncover the dough and brush the surface with this mixture. 20) Gently slash the top surface of the dough ball in several places, approximately 1/3 to 1/2-inch deep. 21) Add more of the hot water to the shallow pan if it has evaporated. 22) Slide the bread onto the terra cotta dish in the oven and bake for 50 to 60 minutes. 23) Once the bread has reached an internal temperature of 205 to 210 degrees F, remove to a cooling rack and allow to sit for 30 minutes before slicing.

Difficulty: Medium **Prep Time:** 30 minutes **Inactive Prep Time:** 12 h ours **Cook Time:** 1 hour **Yield:** 1 loaf bread

PUMPKIN BREAD

Episode: Squash Court, EA1D03

	1) Preheat the oven to 325° F.
2 cups all-purpose flour **2 teaspoons cinnamon** **1 teaspoon baking soda** **1/4 teaspoon baking powder** **1/2 teaspoon salt**	2) Sift the flour, cinnamon, baking soda, baking powder, and salt together.
1 1/2 cups sugar **3/4 cup vegetable oil** **3 large eggs** **1 teaspoon vanilla extract**	3) In a separate bowl, mix the sugar, vegetable oil, eggs, and vanilla.
3 cups shredded fresh pumpkin **1 cup toasted pumpkin seeds**	4) Combine both mixtures and fold in the shredded pumpkin and pumpkin seeds. 5) Once the ingredients are all incorporated pour into a non- stick 9 by 5 by 3-inch loaf pan. If your pan is not non-stick coat it with butter and flour. 6) Bake for 1 hour and 15 minutes. At this point a knife inserted into the middle of the loaf should come out clean. 7) Cool for 15 minutes and turn out onto a cooling rack. Cool completely. 8) For muffins temperature should also be 325° F, but bake for 30 minutes.

Difficulty: Easy **Prep Time:** 20 minutes **Cook Time:** 1 hour 15 minutes **Yield:** 1 loaf or 1 1/2 dozen small muffins

SCONES

Episode: The Dough Also Rises, EA1A07

	1) Heat oven to 375°.
2 cups flour **4 teaspoons baking powder** **3/4 teaspoon salt** **1/3 cup sugar**	2) In a large mixing bowl, combine flour, baking powder, salt and sugar. Mix well.
4 tablespoons butter **2 tablespoons shortening**	3) Cut in butter and shortening.
3/4 cup cream **1 egg**	4) In a separate bowl, combine cream with beaten egg then add to dry ingredients.
Handful dried currants or dried cranberries	5) Stir in fruit. 6) Turn dough out onto a floured surface. 7) Roll dough out and cut into biscuit size rounds. 8) Bake for 15 minutes or until brown.

Difficulty: Easy **Prep Time:** 15 minutes **Cook Time:** 15 minutes **Yield:** 1 dozen

BASIC COOKED WHEAT BERRIES

Episode: Ill Gotten Grains, EA1G07

2 cups wheat berries **4 cups water** **2 tablespoons salt**	1) Place all ingredients into a pressure cooker and cook on high heat until hissing begins and pressure rises. 2) Lower heat to maintain hissing and cook for 45 minutes.

Difficulty: Easy **Prep Time:** 5 minutes **Cook Time:** 50 minutes **Yield:** 4 cups

Notes:

BREAKFAST

Pancakes & Waffles

"INSTANT" PANCAKE MIX

Episode: Flap Jack Do It Again, EA1C09

MIX 6 cups all-purpose flour 1 1/2 teaspoons baking soda (check expiration date first) 3 teaspoons baking powder 1 tablespoon kosher salt 2 tablespoons sugar	1) Combine all of the ingredients in a lidded container. Shake to mix. 2) Use the mix within 3 months. 3) Heat an electric griddle or frying pan to 350° F. 4) Heat oven to 200° F.

Difficulty: Easy **Yield:** 3 batches of pancakes

PANCAKES

Episode: Flap Jack Do It Again, EA1C09

2 eggs, separated 2 cups buttermilk	5) Whisk together the egg whites and the buttermilk in a small bowl.
4 tablespoons melted butter	6) In another bowl, whisk the egg yolks with the melted butter.
2 cups Mix, recipe above	7) Combine the buttermilk mixture with the egg yolk mixture in a large mixing bowl and whisk together until thoroughly combined. 8) Pour the liquid ingredients on top of the pancake mix. 9) Using a whisk, mix the batter just enough to bring it together. Don't try to work all the lumps out. 10) Check to see that the griddle is hot by placing a few drops of water onto to the griddle. The griddle is ready if the water dances across the surface.
1 stick butter, for greasing the pan	11) Lightly butter the griddle. Wipe off thoroughly with a paper towel. (No butter should be visible.)
2 cups fresh fruit such as blueberries, if desired	12) Gently ladle the pancake batter onto the griddle and sprinkle on fruit if desired. 13) When bubbles begin to set around the edges of the pancake and the griddle-side of the cake is golden, gently flip the pancakes. 14) Continue to cook 2 to 3 minutes or until the pancake is set. 15) Serve immediately or remove to a towel-lined baking sheet and cover with a towel. Hold in a warm place for 20 to 30 minutes.

Difficulty: Easy **Yield:** 12 pancakes

Food Related Phobias

Alcohol:	Potophobia	**Garlic:**	Alliumphobia
Chickens:	Alektorophobia	**Heat:**	Thermophobia
Cooking:	Mageirocophobia	**Ice:**	Pagophobia
Dining:	Deipnophobia	**Meat:**	Carnophobia
Drinking:	Dipsophobia	**Shellfish:**	Ostraconophobia
Eating or Swallowing:	Phagophobia	**Taste:**	Geumaphobia
Fish:	Ichthyophobia	**Vegetables:**	Lachanophobia
Food or Eating:	Sitophobia	**Wine:**	Oenophobia
Peanut butter sticking to the roof of the mouth:	Arachibutyrophobia		

BASIC WAFFLE

Episode: The Waffle Truth, EA0909

<table>
<tr><td colspan="2">Vegetable spray, for waffle iron</td></tr>
<tr><td>4 3/4 ounces all-purpose flour, approximately 1 cup
4 3/4 ounces whole-wheat flour, approximately 1 cup
1/2 teaspoon baking soda
1 teaspoon baking powder
1 teaspoon salt
3 tablespoons sugar</td><td>1) Preheat waffle iron according to manufacturer's directions.
2) In a medium bowl whisk together the flours, soda, baking powder, salt, and sugar.</td></tr>
<tr><td>3 whole eggs, beaten
2 ounces unsalted butter, melted
16 ounces buttermilk, room temperature</td><td>3) In another bowl beat together eggs and melted butter, and then add the buttermilk.
4) Add the wet ingredients to the dry and stir until combined. Allow to rest for 5 minutes.
5) Ladle the recommended amount of waffle batter onto the iron according to the manufacturer's recommendations.
6) Close iron top and cook until the waffle is golden on both sides and is easily removed from iron.
7) Serve immediately or keep warm in a 200 degree F oven until ready to serve.</td></tr>
</table>

Difficulty: Easy **Prep Time:** 15 minutes **Inactive Prep Time:** 5 minutes **Cook Time:** 10 minutes
Yield: approximately 6 8-in round waffles

CHOCOLATE WAFFLE

Episode: The Waffle Truth, EA0909

<table>
<tr><td colspan="2">Vegetable spray, for waffle iron</td></tr>
<tr><td>7 ounces all-purpose flour, approximately 1 1/2 cups
1 3/4 ounces sugar, approximately 3 tablespoons
1.5 ounces cocoa powder, approximately 1/2 cup
1 teaspoon baking powder
1 teaspoon salt
1/2 teaspoon baking soda</td><td>1) Preheat waffle iron according to manufacturer's directions.
2) In a medium bowl whisk together the flour, sugar, cocoa powder, baking powder, salt, and baking soda.</td></tr>
<tr><td>3 whole eggs, beaten
2 ounces unsalted butter, melted and slightly cooled
1 teaspoon pure vanilla extract
16 ounces buttermilk, room temperature</td><td>3) In another bowl beat together the eggs and melted butter and vanilla, and then add the buttermilk.</td></tr>
<tr><td>4 ounces chocolate chips, approximately 3/4 cup</td><td>4) Add the wet ingredients to the dry and stir in the chocolate chips just until combined. Allow to rest for 5 minutes.
5) Ladle the recommended amount of waffle batter onto the center of the iron.
6) Close the iron top and cook until the waffle is crispy on both sides and is easily removed from iron.
7) Serve immediately or keep warm in a 200 degree F oven until ready to serve.</td></tr>
</table>

Difficulty: Easy **Prep Time:** 15 minutes **Inactive Prep Time:** 5 minutes **Cook Time:** 10 minutes
Yield: approximately 6 8-in round waffles

Notes:____

PECAN, SOUR CREAM WAFFLES

	1) Heat waffle iron.
1 cup whole milk 1 cup sour cream 2 eggs 3 tablespoons butter, melted 1 teaspoon vanilla	2) Combine wet ingredients and whisk well to combine.
2 teaspoons baking powder 1 1/2 cups all purpose flour 1 teaspoon baking soda 1/2 teaspoon cinnamon Pinch kosher salt	3) Sift dry ingredients into a large bowl and form a well in the center. 4) Add the wet mixture to the well and fold in with the dry. Don't worry if there are a few lumps.
1/2 cup pecans, toasted and chopped fine	5) Stir in pecans just before cooking. 6) When iron is hot, spray lightly with non-stick spray. 7) Spoon 1/2 to 3/4 cup of batter onto the center of the iron and cook until a golden brown crust forms. 8) Serve warm with Burnt Peach Ice Cream.

Difficulty: Easy **Prep Time:** 35 minutes **Yield:** about 12 waffles depending on size

SWEET POTATO WAFFLES

Episode: Potato, My Sweet, EA1G

Special equipment: steamer basket waffle iron	
1 1/2 cups peeled and cubed sweet potatoes	1) Put cubed sweet potatoes in a steamer basket. 2) Place the basket in a large pot of simmering water that is no closer than 2 inches from the bottom of steamer. 3) Allow potatoes to steam for 20 minutes of until fork tender. 4) Mash cooked potatoes and set aside.
2 cups all purpose flour 1 tablespoon baking powder 1/2 teaspoon salt	5) In a large bowl, whisk together flour, baking powder, and salt and set aside.
1 cup milk 1/4 cup firmly packed light brown sugar 1/4 cup butter, melted 1 tablespoon grated orange rind	6) In another bowl combine the sweet potatoes, milk, brown sugar, butter, and grated orange rind. 7) Stir the sweet potato mixture into the flour mixture and thoroughly combine.
6 egg whites, at room temperature	8) Beat egg whites until stiff peaks form. 9) Gradually fold egg whites into batter 1/3 at a time. The batter will be thick.
Vegetable spray, for waffle iron	10) Using a No. 20 disher (scoop), place 2 scoops of batter onto a preheated, oiled waffle iron, and cook until lightly browned, about 5 to 6 minutes.

Difficulty: Easy **Prep Time:** 15 minutes **Cook Time:** 30 minutes **Yield:** 4 8-in waffles

Notes:

SOUTHERN BISCUITS

Episode: The Dough Also Rises, EA1A07

2 cups flour **4 teaspoons baking powder** **1/4 teaspoon baking soda** **3/4 teaspoon salt**	1) In a large mixing bowl, combine flour, baking powder, baking soda and salt.
2 tablespoons butter **2 tablespoons shortening**	2) Using your fingertips, rub butter and shortening into dry ingredients until mixture looks like crumbs. (The faster the better, you don't want the fats to melt.)
1 cup buttermilk, chilled	3) Make a well in the center and pour in the chilled buttermilk. 4) Stir just until the dough comes together. The dough will be very sticky. 5) Turn dough onto floured surface, dust top with flour and gently fold dough over on itself 5 or 6 times. 6) Press into a 1-inch thick round. 7) Cut out biscuits with a 2-inch cutter, being sure to push straight down through the dough. 8) Place biscuits on baking sheet so that they just touch. 9) Reform scrap dough, working it as little as possible and continue cutting. (Biscuits from the second pass will not be quite as light as those from the first, but hey, that's life.) 10) Bake until biscuits are tall and light gold on top, 15 to 20 minutes.

Difficulty: Easy **Prep Time:** 20 minutes **Cook Time:** 20 minutes **Yield:** 1 dozen

MA MAE'S BISCUITS

Episode: The Dough Also Rises, EA1A07

Advice courtesy Mae Skelton: I don't have much use for recipes but the one you get on a bag of White Lily® self-rising flour is hard to beat. And it's a lot easier than the one my crazy grandson dreamed up.

ALTON-ISMS: Common Sayings to Many an Episode.
" ... but that's another show."
" ... we're dealing with a culinary ticking time bomb."
" ... _________ makes great refrigerator Velcro."
" ... and it will bring a lot of flavor to the party."
" ... works and plays well with others ... "
" ... the rest of the hardware ...", " ... now, the software ... "
" ... put the spurs to her/it ... "
"I have told you time and time again that I'm not a nutritional anthropologist."
"Your patience will be rewarded."
"Now, wash those (insert meat here) hands."
"Oh bother."

CRÊPES

Episode: Crepe Expectations, EA1D09

2 large eggs **3/4 cup milk** **1/2 cup water** **1 cup flour** **3 tablespoons melted butter**	1) In a blender, combine all of the ingredients and pulse for 10 seconds.
Butter, for coating the pan	2) Place the crepe batter in the refrigerator for 1 hour. This allows the bubbles to subside so the crepes will be less likely to tear during cooking. The batter will keep for up to 48 hours. 3) Heat a small non-stick pan. Add butter to coat. 4) Pour 1 ounce of batter into the center of the pan and swirl to spread evenly. 5) Cook for 30 seconds and flip. 6) Cook for another 10 seconds and remove to the cutting board. 7) Lay them out flat so they can cool. 8) Continue until all batter is gone. 9) After they have cooled you can stack them and store in sealable plastic bags in the refrigerator for several days or in the freezer for up to two months. 10) When using frozen crepes, thaw on a rack before gently peeling apart.
***Savory Variation:** Add 1/4 teaspoon **salt** and 1/4 cup **chopped fresh herbs, spinach or sun-dried tomatoes** to the egg mixture. ***Sweet Variation:** Add 21/2 tablespoons **sugar**, 1 teaspoon **vanilla extract** and 2 tablespoons of **your favorite liqueur** to the egg mixture.	

Difficulty: Medium **Prep Time:** 5 minutes **Cook Time:** 20 minutes **Yield:** 17 to 22 crepes

CRÊPE QUICHE LORRAINE

Episode: Crepe Expectations, EA1D09

	1) Preheat the oven to 350° F.
2 teaspoons butter **1/2 cup yellow onion, sliced**	2) In a small sauté pan, melt the butter and sweat the onions until translucent.
4 strips cooked bacon, crumbled	3) In a small bowl, mix the onions and crumbled bacon together.
8 eggs **12 ounces milk** **1 teaspoon kosher salt** **1 teaspoon fresh cracked pepper**	4) In a separate bowl, whisk together the eggs and milk, and season with salt and pepper.
6 savory crepes, recipe above **6 ounces cheddar, shredded**	5) In a large, non-stick, 6-cup muffin tin, place one crepe into each cup. Make sure that the edges of the crepes are slightly pleated and overlap the edge of the tin slightly. 6) Spoon the bacon and onion mixture into each cup. 7) Distribute the cheese evenly into the cups. 8) Pour the egg mixture into each cup so that all of the quiches are the same size. 9) Place into a preheated oven for 15 minutes or until the egg mixture is completely set.

Difficulty: Medium **Prep Time:** 25 minutes **Cook Time:** 15 minutes **Yield:** 6 servings

Notes:____

CRÊPES SUZETTE

Episode: Crepe Expectations, EA1D09

Sweet crepes, recipe above	1) Fold your crepes in half twice, so they are in the shape of a triangle.
½ pound butter, softened	2) In a non-stick pan over medium heat, melt half of the butter.
4 ounces of your favorite liquor **4 tablespoons sugar**	3) When it begins to foam remove from heat and add 2 ounces of the liquor and 2 tablespoons of the sugar. Always add alcohol off of the heat to avoid a jumping flame. 4) Use tongs to gently lay crepes into the pan. Turn the crepes to coat.
4 scoops of vanilla ice cream	5) Lay the crepes out on a plate and top with ice cream. 6) Pour remaining sauce over the ice cream. 7) Serve immediately.

Difficulty: Medium **Prep Time:** 10 minutes **Cook Time:** 25 minutes **Yield:** 4 servings

Eggs

SCRAMBLED EGGS UNSCRAMBLED

Episode: The Egg-Files, EA1A03

5 eggs **5 tablespoons milk**	1) In a small mixing bowl, combine eggs and milk with a fork.
1 pat of butter	2) In a non-stick skillet, melt the butter over medium-low heat until it bubbles.
Kosher salt	3) Stir a pinch of kosher salt into egg mixture then pour into pan, stirring slowly with a heat resistant rubber spatula.
	4) As soon as curds begin to form, increase heat to high and instead of stirring, use the spatula to fold the eggs over themselves while gently shaking the pan with your other hand. As soon as no more liquid is running around the bottom of the pan, remove from the heat and serve.
Ground pepper **Chives or parsley to garnish**	5) Season with fresh black pepper and garnish with fresh chives or parsley.

Difficulty: Easy **Prep Time:** 5 minutes **Cook Time:** 5 minutes **Yield:** 3 to 4 servings

Remember: if they look done in the pan, they'll be over-done on the plate.

OMELET

Episode: The Egg-Files VI: French Flop, EA1G03

3 eggs, warmed in hot water for 5 minutes **Pinch salt**	1) Crack warm eggs into bowl, add salt, and blend with fork. 2) Heat a 10-inch non-stick aluminum pan over medium-high heat.
1 teaspoon room temperature butter, plus 1/2 teaspoon for finishing omelet	3) Once pan is hot add butter and brush around surface of pan. 4) Pour eggs into center of pan and stir vigorously with rubber spatula for 5 seconds. 5) As soon as a semi-solid mass begins to form lift pan and move around until the excess liquid pours off into pan. 6) Using your spatula move around the edge of the egg mixture to help shape into round and loosen edge. 7) Let omelet sit in pan for 10 seconds without touching. 8) Shake pan to loosen from pan. Lift up the far edge of the pan and snap it back toward you. Using your spatula, fold over 1/3 of the omelet. 9) Slide omelet onto plate and fold over so that omelet is a tri-fold.
1/2 teaspoon fresh chopped chives	10) Coat with remaining butter and sprinkle with chives. Serve immediately.

Difficulty: Medium **Prep Time:** 5 minutes **Inactive Prep Time:** 5 minutes **Cook Time:** 5 minutes **Yield:** 1 servings

OMELET FOR A CROWD

Episode: The Egg-Files VI: French Flop, EA1G03

10 eggs, warmed for 5 minutes in hot water **1/4 cup water** **2 heavy pinches salt** **1/4 cup any combination chopped, fresh herbs (chives, parsley, tarragon, dill, or basil)**	1) Add eggs, water, salt, and herbs to blender and combine on high for 5 to10 seconds. 2) Heat a 10-inch non-stick aluminum pan over medium-high heat.
4 teaspoons room temperature butter, plus 2 teaspoons for finishing omelet	3) Once pan is hot add 1 teaspoon butter and brush around surface of pan. 4) Using a 4 1/2-ounce ladle, place 1 ladle full of egg mixture into center of pan and stir vigorously with rubber spatula for 5 seconds. 5) As soon as a semi-solid mass begins to form lift pan and move around until the excess liquid pours off into pan. 6) Using your spatula move around the edge of the egg mixture to help shape into round and loosen edge. Let sit for 10 seconds without touching.
1 cup of any combination sautéed peppers and onions, grated cheese, sautéed mushrooms, cooked and drained spinach	7) Place 1/4 cup of filling onto 2/3 of surface of omelet. 8) Shake pan to loosen from pan. Left up the far edge of the pan and snap it back toward you. Using your spatula, fold over 1/3 of the omelet without filling. 9) Slide omelet onto plate and fold over so that omelet is a tri-fold. 10) Coat with 1/2 teaspoon butter. 11) Repeat process above for remaining 3 servings. Serve immediately.

Difficulty: Medium **Prep Time:** 10 minutes **Inactive Prep Time:** 5 minutes **Cook Time:** 20 minutes **Yield:** 4 servings

EGGS OVER EASY

Episode: The Egg-Files, EA1A03

1 tablespoon unsalted butter	1) Heat a small non-stick skillet over low heat and add butter.
2 eggs (the fresher the better)	2) As soon as the butter stops foaming, crack the eggs into the pan.
	3) Lift the handle about an inch so that the eggs pool in the far corner of the pan. Hold for 30 seconds or until the whites start to set, then lower the handle and give the pan a jiggle just to make sure there's no sticking.
Salt and pepper	4) Season with a pinch of salt and pepper and continue to cook over low heat until the whites become opaque.
	5) Jiggle to loosen the eggs, then lift the pan, holding it about a foot above the heat. 6) Now, flip the eggs over by pushing the pan away and snapping upward simultaneously. Once the eggs start their somersault, raise the pan to meet them so that the exposed yolks experience the softest landing possible. The goal of course is to avoid breaking the yolks. 7) If you succeed, count to 10 slowly then flip the eggs again, slide them onto a plate and serve. 8) If the yolks do break, act like you meant them to, fry for another minute and serve. They'll still taste great.

Difficulty: Easy **Cook Time:** 5 minutes **Yield:** 1 servings

Notes:____

POACHED EGG TIPS

Episode: Mission: Poachable, EA1C13

1) Always use fresh eggs. If you can't see the difference between the "thick" white and the "thin" white, the yolks will probably break in the pan.
2) Always deliver the eggs to the pan with a custard cup or large spoon.
3) Avoid cracking directly into the pan.
4) When using a non-stick skillet cook in no more than an inch of water. If you don't have a non-stick pan, poach in a deep saucepan containing at least 3 inches of water.
5) Always acidulate the poaching liquid with either vinegar or lemon juice (1 tsp. per each cup of water).
6) Bring liquid to a boil, add eggs, then remove from heat and cover. How long you ask? It depends on how many eggs. I like my yolks barely runny so I'll cook 4 eggs for 7 to 8 minutes depending on there size. Since more eggs will absorb more heat from the water, they will take longer to cook, so for large batches always include an extra "test" egg.
7) Always remove eggs with a slotted spoon.
8) Poached eggs can be refrigerated in ice water for up to 8 hours, then reheated in hot water. Do not re-boil.

Difficulty: Easy **Prep Time:** 2 minutes **Cook Time:** 8 minutes **Yield:** 1 servings

FRITTATA

Episode: The Egg-Files VI: French Flop, EA1G03

6 eggs, beaten **1-ounce Parmesan, grated** **1/2 teaspoon black pepper** **Pinch salt**	1) Preheat oven to broil setting. 2) In medium size bowl, using a fork, blend together eggs, Parmesan, pepper, and salt. 3) Heat 12-inch non-stick, oven safe sauté pan over medium high heat.
1 teaspoon butter	4) Add butter to pan and melt.
1/2 cup chopped roasted asparagus **1/2 cup chopped country ham**	5) Add asparagus and ham to pan and sauté for 2 to 3 minutes. 6) Pour egg mixture into pan and stir with rubber spatula. 7) Cook for 4 to 5 minutes or until the egg mixture has set on the bottom and begins to set up on top.
1 tablespoon chopped parsley leaves	8) Sprinkle with parsley. 9) Place pan into oven and broil for 3 to 4 minutes, until lightly browned and fluffy. 10) Remove from pan and cut into 6 servings. Serve immediately.

Difficulty: Easy **Prep Time:** 10 minutes **Cook Time:** 10 minutes **Yield:** 6 servings

BLUEBERRY MUFFINS

Episode: The Muffin Method Man, EA1G06

12 1/2 ounces cake flour **1 teaspoon baking soda** **2 teaspoons baking powder** **Heavy pinch salt**	1) Preheat oven to 380 degrees F. 2) In a large bowl sift together the flour, baking soda, baking powder, and salt and set aside.
1 cup sugar **1/2 cup vegetable oil** **1 egg** **1 cup yogurt**	3) In another large bowl, whisk together the sugar, oil, egg and yogurt. 4) Add the dry ingredients reserving 1 tablespoon of the dry ingredients and toss with the blueberries. 5) Stir mixture for a count of 10.
1 1/2 cups fresh blueberries **Vegetable spray, for the muffin tins**	6) Add 1 cup blueberries to mixture and stir 3 more times. 7) Reserve the 1/2 cup of blueberries. 8) Using a #20 ice cream scoop, add the mixture to greased muffin pans. 9) Sprinkle the remaining 1/2 cup of berries on top of muffins and press down lightly. 10) Place into the oven and increase the temperature to 400 degrees. 11) Bake for 20 to 25 minutes, rotating pan halfway through. 12) Remove from oven and turn out, upside down on tea towel to cool completely. 13) Serve immediately or store in airtight container for 2 to 3 days.

Difficulty: Easy **Prep Time:** 15 minutes **Inactive Prep Time:** 10 minutes **Cook Time:** 25 minutes **Yield:** 12 muffins

ENGLISH MUFFINS

Episode: The Muffin Method Man, EA1G06

Special equipment:
- **electric griddle,**
- **3-inch metal rings, see Cook's Note***

1/2 cup non-fat powdered milk **1 tablespoon sugar** **1 teaspoon salt** **1 tablespoon shortening** **1 cup hot water**	1) In a bowl combine the powdered milk, 1 tablespoon of sugar, 1/2 teaspoon of salt, shortening, and hot water, stir until the sugar and salt are dissolved. Let cool.
1 envelope dry yeast **1/8 teaspoon sugar** **1/3 cup warm water**	2) In a separate bowl combine the yeast and 1/8 teaspoon of sugar in 1/3 cup of warm water and rest until yeast has dissolved. 3) Add this to the dry milk mixture.
2 cups all-purpose flour, sifted	4) Add the sifted flour and beat thoroughly with wooden spoon. 5) Cover the bowl and let it rest in a warm spot for 30 minutes. 6) Preheat the griddle to 300 degrees F. 7) Add the remaining 1/2 teaspoon of salt to mixture and beat thoroughly.
Non-stick vegetable spray	8) Place metal rings onto the griddle and coat lightly with vegetable spray. 9) Using #20 ice cream scoop, place 2 scoops into each ring and cover with a pot lid or cookie sheet and cook for 5 to 6 minutes. 10) Remove the lid and flip rings using tongs. 11) Cover with the lid and cook for another 5 to 6 minutes or until golden brown. 12) Place on a cooling rack, remove rings and cool. 13) Split with fork and serve.

Difficulty: Medium **Prep Time:** 15 minutes **Inactive Prep Time:** 30 minutes **Cook Time:** 12 minutes **Yield:** 8 to 10 muffins

*Cook's Note: Small tuna cans with tops and bottoms removed work well for metal rings.

Notes:______________________________

Oatmeal

OVERNIGHT OATMEAL

Episode: Oat Cuisine, EA1D06

1 cup steel cut oats **1 cup dried cranberries** **1 cup dried figs** **4 cups water** **1/2 cup half-and-half**	1) In a crock-pot, combine all ingredients and set to low heat. 2) Cover and let cook for 8 to 9 hours. 3) Stir and remove to serving bowls. This method works best if started before you go to bed. This way your oatmeal will be finished by morning.

Difficulty: Easy **Prep Time:** 10 minutes **Cook Time:** 9 hours **Yield:** 4 servings

STEEL CUT OATMEAL

Episode: Oat Cuisine, EA1D06

1 tablespoon butter **1 cup steel cut oats**	1) In a large saucepot, melt the butter and add the oats. 2) Stir for 2 minutes to toast.
3 cups boiling water	3) Add the boiling water and reduce heat to a simmer. Keep at a low simmer for 25 minutes, without stirring.
1/2 cup whole milk **1/2 cup plus 1 tablespoon low-fat buttermilk**	4) Combine the milk and half of the buttermilk with the oatmeal.
1 tablespoon brown sugar **1/4 teaspoon cinnamon**	5) Stir gently to combine and cook for an additional 10 minutes. 6) Spoon into a serving bowl and top with remaining buttermilk, brown sugar, and cinnamon.

Difficulty: Easy **Prep Time:** 10 minutes **Cook Time:** 35 minutes **Yield:** 4 servings

Sausage

BREAKFAST SAUSAGE

Episode: A Beautiful Grind, EA1G09

Special equipment **meat grinder**	
2 pounds pork butt (2 1/2 pounds with bone), diced into 1/4-inch pieces **1/2 pound fat back, diced into 1/4-inch pieces** **2 teaspoons kosher salt** **1 1/2 teaspoons freshly ground black pepper** **2 teaspoons finely chopped fresh sage leaves** **2 teaspoons finely chopped fresh thyme leaves** **1/2 teaspoon finely chopped fresh rosemary leaves** **1 tablespoon light brown sugar** **1/2 teaspoon fresh grated nutmeg** **1/2 teaspoon cayenne pepper** **1/2 teaspoon red pepper flakes**	1) Combine diced pork with all other ingredients and chill for 1 hour. 2) Using the fine blade of a grinder, grind the pork. 3) Form into 1-inch rounds. 4) Refrigerate and use within 1 week or freeze for up to 3 months. 5) For immediate use, sauté patties over medium-low heat in a non-stick pan. 6) Sauté until brown and cooked through, approximately 10 to 15 minutes.

Difficulty: Medium **Prep Time:** 30 minutes **Inactive Prep Time:** 1 hour **Cook Time:** 15 minutes **Yield:** 2 lbs. or 16 2-inch patties

Notes:______________________________

ITALIAN SAUSAGE

Episode: A Beautiful Grind, EA1G09

<table>
<tr><td colspan="2">Special equipment:
meat grinder with stuffing attachment or manual stuffer</td></tr>
<tr><td>1 1/2 teaspoons fennel seed</td><td>1) Toast fennel seed in medium sized, heavy sauté pan over medium heat, constantly moving seeds around in pan until they start to turn light brown, about 5 minutes.
2) Set aside to cool.</td></tr>
<tr><td>2 teaspoons kosher salt
1 1/2 teaspoons black pepper
1 tablespoon chopped parsley leaves</td><td>3) Once cool, grind seeds and combine with salt, pepper, and chopped parsley in medium mixing bowl.</td></tr>
<tr><td>2 pounds pork butt (2 1/2 pounds with bone), diced into 1/4-inch pieces
5 feet of 36 millimeter collagen casings (do not allow to get wet at any time)
Shortening, to lubricate nozzle of stuffer</td><td>4) Add pork and blend thoroughly.
5) Refrigerate for 1 hour.
6) Using the fine blade of a grinder, grind the pork.
7) After lubricating stuffer or stuffing attachment with shortening, load casing onto attachment, clipping end with a clothespin.
8) Stuff meat into casings, trying to avoid air pockets.
9) After stuffing is finished lay out on counter and tie off end.
10) Pinch and twist to form 4-inch sausages.
11) Wrap in parchment paper and refrigerate for 2 to 3 hours.
12) Store in refrigerator for use within 2 to 3 days or freeze for up to 3 months.</td></tr>
<tr><td colspan="2">13) If freezing, wrap in aluminum foil.</td></tr>
<tr><td colspan="2">14) If using immediately, sauté over medium heat in a heavy sauté pan with 1/4-inch of water.
15) Bring water to boil, put on lid and cook for 10 minutes.
16) Remove lid and continue cooking over medium heat, turning every 2 to 3 minutes until golden brown. Sausage should reach an internal temperature of 150 to 156 degrees F.</td></tr>
</table>

Difficulty: Medium **Prep Time:** 50 minutes **Inactive Prep Time:** 1 hour **Cook Time:** 15 minutes
Yield: 2 lbs. or 10 to 12 4-inch sausage links

Yogurt

FRESH YOGURT

Episode: Good Milk Gone Bad, EA1F04

<table>
<tr><td>1 quart 2-percent milk
1/2 cup powdered milk
1 to 2 tablespoons honey</td><td>1) Pour milk into small saucepan and whisk in powdered milk and honey.
2) Place over medium heat and bring to 120° F on an instant read thermometer.</td></tr>
<tr><td>1/2 cup plain yogurt, room temperature</td><td>3) Once milk has reached 120° F, pour into a cylindrical plastic container, reserving 1/2 cup.
4) Whisk in the reserved 1/2 cup into the yogurt and add back to the milk mixture.
5) Place container into a narrow wine bucket, lined with a heating pad. Set the heating pad to medium. Let the mixture ferment for 3 to 12 hours making sure the temperature stays as close to 115° F as possible.
6) After fermentation is complete place into the refrigerator overnight.</td></tr>
</table>

Difficulty: Medium **Prep Time:** 10 minutes **Cook Time:** 10 minutes **Yield:** 1 quart

> **"When proteins get hot they tend to tangle up tighter than teenagers at a dance. And when they bond up tight enough, they over coagulate. And when they over coagulate, they can curdle. And any cook or parent will tell you that leads to trouble."**
>
> **Alton Brown, Good Eats, "Good Milk Gone Bad"**

LEMON-GINGER FROZEN YOGURT

Episode: Good Milk Gone Bad, EA1F04

8 cups plain yogurt	1) Place yogurt in a cheesecloth-lined colander set over a bowl. Cover and refrigerate for 12 hours. 2) At end of 12 hours, discard the liquid and cheesecloth.
1/2 cup light corn syrup 3/4 cup granulated sugar 3 tablespoons fresh lemon juice 2 teaspoons finely grated lemon peel 1 tablespoon minced fresh ginger	3) In a bowl combine the drained yogurt, corn syrup, sugar, lemon juice, lemon peel, and fresh ginger. 4) Transfer mixture to ice cream maker and process per manufacturer's instructions, about 25 minutes.
1/4 cup sliced crystallized ginger	5) Transfer frozen yogurt to an airtight container, fold in crystallized ginger and freeze for 2 hours.

Difficulty: Easy **Prep Time:** 15 minutes **Yield:** 1 quart

Other

10 MINUTE APPLE SAUCE

Episode: Apple Family Values, EA1B03

3 Golden Delicious apples, peeled, cored, and quartered 3 Fuji apples, peeled, cored, and quartered 1 cup unfiltered apple juice 2 tablespoons cognac or brandy 2 tablespoons butter 3 tablespoons honey 1/2 teaspoon ground cinnamon	1) In a sealable microwave-safe container, combine apples with all other ingredients. 2) Close lid, leaving one corner of lid open to allow steam to escape. 3) Microwave on high for 10 minutes. 4) Using a hand blender or potato masher, blend to desired consistency. 5) Serve hot immediately or chill for later use.

Difficulty: Easy **Prep Time:** 10 minutes **Cook Time:** 10 minutes **Yield:** 1 quart

CHEESE GRITS

Episode: True Grits, EA1H01

2 cups whole milk 2 cups water 1 1/2 teaspoons kosher salt	1) Place the milk, water, and salt into a large, heavy-bottomed pot over medium-high heat and bring to a boil.
1 cup coarse ground cornmeal	2) Once the milk mixture comes to a boil, gradually add the cornmeal while continually whisking. 3) Once all of the cornmeal has been incorporated, decrease the heat to low and cover. 4) Remove lid and whisk frequently, every 3 to 4 minutes, to prevent grits from sticking or forming lumps; make sure to get into corners of pot when whisking. 5) Cook for 20 to 25 minutes or until mixture is creamy.
1/2 teaspoon freshly ground black pepper 4 tablespoons unsalted butter	6) Remove from the heat, add the pepper and butter, and whisk to combine.
4 ounces sharp Cheddar, shredded	7) Once the butter is melted, gradually whisk in the cheese a little at a time. Serve immediately.

Difficulty: Easy **Prep Time:** 5 minutes **Cook Time:** 30 minutes **Yield:** 4 servings

FRENCH TOAST

Episode: Toast Modern, EA1G17

Ingredients	Directions
1 cup half-and-half **3 large eggs** **2 tablespoons honey, warmed in microwave for 20 seconds** **1/4 teaspoon salt**	1) In medium size mixing bowl, whisk together the half-and-half, eggs, honey, and salt. You may do this the night before. 2) When ready to cook, pour custard mixture into a pie pan and set aside. 3) Preheat oven to 375 degrees F.
8 (1/2-inch) slices day-old or stale country loaf, brioche or challah bread	4) Dip bread into mixture, allow to soak for 30 seconds on each side, and then remove to a cooling rack that is sitting in a sheet pan, and allow to sit for 1 to 2 minutes.
4 tablespoons butter	5) Over medium-low heat, melt 1 tablespoon of butter in a 10-inch nonstick sauté pan. 6) Place 2 slices of bread at a time into the pan and cook until golden brown, approximately 2 to 3 minutes per side. 7) Remove from pan and place on rack in oven for 5 minutes. 8) Repeat with all 8 slices. 9) Serve immediately with maple syrup, whipped cream or fruit.

Difficulty: Easy **Prep Time:** 10 minutes **Cook Time:** 24 minutes **Yield:** 4 servings

SAVORY POLENTA

Episode: True Grits, EA1H01

Ingredients	Directions
2 tablespoons olive oil, plus extra for grilling or sautéing if desired	1) Preheat oven to 350 degrees F. 2) In a large, oven-safe saucepan heat the olive oil over medium heat.
3/4 cup finely chopped red onion **1 1/2 teaspoons kosher salt**	3) Add the red onion and salt and sweat until the onions begin to turn translucent, approximately 4 to 5 minutes.
2 cloves garlic, finely minced	4) Reduce the heat to low, add the garlic and sauté for 1 to 2 minutes, making sure the garlic does not burn.
1 quart chicken stock or broth	5) Turn the heat up to high, add the chicken stock, bring to a boil.
1 cup coarse ground cornmeal	6) Gradually add the cornmeal while continually whisking. 7) Once you have added all of the cornmeal, cover the pot and place it in the oven. Cook for 35 to 40 minutes, stirring every 10 minutes to prevent lumps.
3 tablespoons unsalted butter **1 1/2 teaspoons kosher salt** **1/4 teaspoon freshly ground black pepper**	8) Once the mixture is creamy, remove from the oven and add the butter, salt, and pepper.
2 ounces Parmesan, grated	9) Once they are incorporated, gradually add the Parmesan. 10) Serve as is, or pour the polenta into 9 by 13-inch cake pan lined with parchment paper. Place in the refrigerator to cool completely. 11) Once set, turn the polenta out onto a cutting board and cut into squares, rounds, or triangles. 12) Brush each side with olive oil and sauté in a nonstick skillet over medium heat, or grill.

Difficulty: Easy **Prep Time:** 10 minutes **Cook Time:** 50 minutes **Yield:** 4 to 6 servings

Notes:____

TURKEY RE-HASH

Episode: Behind the Bird, EA1C14

8 ounces breakfast sausage	1) Add the sausage to a heavy skillet over medium high heat and cook until the sausage begins to render some of its fat, about 2 to 3 minutes.
1/2 onion, chopped **1/2 jalapeño, minced** **1/2 cup red peppers, chopped**	2) Add the onions, jalapeño and peppers to the sausage and cook until soft and translucent.
1 1/2 cups red bliss potatoes, cubed and cooked	3) Add the potatoes to the skillet and increase the heat to high. Cook until the potatoes have browned lightly.
1 1/2 cups cooked black beans **2 cups "Good Eats" Corn Bread Pudding, cubed, recipe above** **1 to 2 cups cooked turkey, cubed**	4) Add the black beans, pudding, and turkey and stir occasionally. Cook until the hash is thoroughly heated.
Dash cayenne pepper **Salt and pepper, to taste**	5) Season with cayenne, salt, and pepper.

Difficulty: Easy **Prep Time:** 25 minutes **Cook Time:** 10 minutes **Yield:** 4 servings

DRINKS

Cold

COCOA SYRUP

Episode: Art of Darkness, EA1D08

1 1/2 cups water **3 cups sugar** **1 1/2 cups Dutch-processed cocoa** **1 tablespoon vanilla extract** **1/4 teaspoon kosher salt** **2 tablespoons light corn syrup**	1) In a small pot, bring water and sugar to a boil and whisk in cocoa, vanilla, salt, and corn syrup. 2) Whisk until all of the solids have dissolved. 3) Reduce sauce until slightly thickened. 4) Strain and cool to room temperature. 5) Pour into squeeze bottles. 6) Squeeze into cold milk and stir for delicious chocolate milk or serve on your favorite ice cream. And, hey, it's fat free!

Difficulty: Easy **Prep Time:** 5 minutes **Cook Time:** 15 minutes **Yield:** 5 cups

SWEET TEA

Episode: True Brew II, EA1D04

1-ounce loose black tea **1 quart hot water**	1) Infuse loose tea into hot water for 4 to 5 minutes.
1 quart room temperature water	2) Strain tea into room temperature water. 3) Sweeten with simple syrup if desired.
Simple Syrup: **5 cups sugar** **3 cups cold water**	4) For simple syrup, in a small non-reactive pot combine 5 cups of sugar and 3 cups of cold water. 5) Slowly bring to a boil and add 6 sliced lemons and a few sprigs of fresh mint. 6) Remove from heat. Allow to cool 10 minutes and strain.

Difficulty: Easy **Prep Time:** 10 minutes **Cook Time:** 5 minutes **Yield:** 8 to 10 servings

TALL & TANGY TOFU THANGY

Episode: Tofuworld, EA1C01

1 (8 1/4-ounce) can fruit cocktail in light syrup, frozen **1 teaspoon instant lemonade mix** **6 ounces cranberry juice** **1 block silken tofu**	1) Combine all ingredients in a blender and blend until smooth.

Difficulty: Easy **Prep Time:** 5 minutes **Inactive Prep Time:** x minutes **Cook Time:** x minutes **Yield:** 2 servings

Notes:____

GOOD BREW: Beer

Episode: Amber Waves, EA1F10

Hardware: **1 large pot that will hold at least 3 gallons water** **Probe thermometer** **Colander** **Metal mesh strainer** **Cheesecloth** **2 (7-gallon) fermenters,** **1 with a spigot and** **1 with an air lock** **6 feet of plastic tubing that will fit the spigot** **Bottling tube** **2 cases plus a couple of bottles of 20-ounce Grolsh style bottles** **Bottle brush** **Long metal spoon** **Unscented household bleach**	1) It is very important to sterilize all equipment that will come into contact with the beer. 2) Also the hops, yeast, and Irish moss need to be kept refrigerated until use. 3) Begin by sterilizing your equipment that you will use to boil the mash; the pot, metal spoon, probe of the probe thermometer, colander and strainer, including the fermenter. To sterilize everything put 2 ounces of non-scented household bleach and 3 to 4 gallons of water into the fermenter. Place other smaller items in the solution to soak. The items that are too large to fit into the fermenter can be sterilized by pouring the solution in the fermenter into and over these items and then thoroughly rinsing all equipment, including the fermenter.
4 gallons plus 1 pint spring water **1/2 pound crystal grain, milled**	4) After sterilization is complete you can begin brewing beer by adding 2 gallons of spring water as well as the 1/2 pound milled grain to your pot and turn the burner on to medium high. 5) Place the probe thermometer into the pot and set the temperature to 155 degrees; once the liquid reaches 155 degrees set a timer for 30 minutes.
7 pounds light liquid malt extract	6) In the meantime soak the container of liquid malt extract in warm water; it will aid in removing it from the container. 7) After the grain has cooked for 30 minutes, add 1 gallon of water and the liquid malt extract and bring to a boil stirring so that the extract does not burn on the bottom until dissolved. 8) The liquid will foam up to the top; when it does this, turn the heat off and let it settle then turn the heat back on and bring to a boil. Let it foam again and turn the heat off, let it settle and turn the heat back on and add the hops.
1-ounce Cascade hops **1 3/4 ounces Kent Goldings hops**	9) Add 1-ounce of the Cascade hops and 3/4-ounce of Kent goldings hops and boil for 10 minutes.
1/2 teaspoon Irish moss	10) Next add 1/2 teaspoon Irish moss and boil for 5 minutes. 11) Now add the last hops, 1-ounce Kent Goldings, cover, turn off the heat and let sit for 5 minutes.
1 (7-pound) bag of ice	12) Meanwhile put the last gallon and 1 pint of water as well as the bag of ice into the fermenter and fit the top with the colander and mesh strainer. 13) Strain the mash into the fermenter and allow to cool to 80 degrees before pitching the yeast.
1 vial British Ale yeast	14) Once the mash is cooled to 80 degrees it is now safe to add the yeast, shake the vial until the liquid is well mixed and then add to the fermenter. 15) Cover with the lid and put airlock in place. Put into cool dark place to ferment for 7 to 10 days. 16) Attach the siphon on the spigot and transfer beer from one fermenter to the second one.
3/4 cup Priming sugar, boiled with 1 pint water for 5 minutes	17) Add the sugar/water mixture. 18) Bottle using the wand. 19) Cap and place into a cool dark place for another 10 to 14 days. 20) Open and enjoy.

Difficulty: Easy **Prep Time:** 1 hour **Inactive Prep Time:** 7 to 20 days **Cook Time:** 1 hours 25 minutes **Yield:** 5 gallons

COFFEE: BLACK, NO CHASER

Episode: Crust Never Sleeps, EA1B04

Brewing a simply perfect cup of Joe can be perfectly simple, if you stick to some basic guidelines:

Buy quality whole beans from a reliable purveyor (preferably a roaster). If you don't have a grinder at home, ask a salesperson to grind whole beans for you rather than settling for pre-ground.

Purchasing bulk (un-packaged) beans from a specialty shop is okay as long as the bins or jars are relatively small and refilled regularly. Large vats hold a lot of beans and therefore don't need frequent filling. That means that beans can hang around for a long time being exposed to light and air. That can mean stale beans, and staleness is not a desirable attribute.

Purchase pre-packaged whole beans only when sealed in a foil-style bag featuring a one-way valve. The dime-shaped plastic valve is usually integrated into the packaging so that it will be as unobtrusive as possible, so check carefully. The absence of a valve means that the coffee probably sat and "gassed out" before it was packaged. That means it could be stale. Stale, again, is not a good thing. And remember: paper bags with twist tops are temporary transportation vessels, not storage devices.

Try to purchase only a week's worth of beans at a time. If you live where this is impractical, purchase several small sealed packages rather than one large one. Unopened one-way valve bags will keep coffee fresh for approximately three months. If you buy bulk coffee (not sealed with one-way valves) in large amounts, divide into weekly batches, seal in Mason-style jars and freeze. Transfer these small batches to counter top storage as needed (see below).

Store opened or bulk coffee in an airtight, opaque container and store at room temperature for up to a week.

Grind coffee as close to brewing time as possible. For drip method, grind in blade style grinder for 15 to 20 seconds. For French presses, grind for only 10 to 12 seconds.

Regardless of method, brew using 2 heaping tablespoons of coffee for each 6 ounces of clean (filtered or bottled), cool water. If you prefer a milder cup, brew to full strength, and then dilute with hot water. Brewing with too little coffee will result in over-extraction, and that means bitterness.

If you really want to taste the subtle nuances of regional coffees, consider a gold mesh filter.

When purchasing a coffee maker (either manual or electric), look for a model that brews into a thermal carafe rather than a glass pot designed to sit on a heating element. Continuous heating of coffee leads to bitterness.

Quality decaffeinated coffees usually cost more than regular beans.

HOT COCOA

Episode: Art of Darkness, EA1D08

2 cups powdered sugar **1 cup cocoa (Dutch-process preferred)** **2 1/2 cups powdered milk** **1 teaspoon salt** **2 teaspoons cornstarch** **1 pinch cayenne pepper, or more to taste** Hot water	1) Combine all ingredients in a mixing bowl and incorporate evenly. 2) In a small pot, heat 4 to 6 cups of water. 3) Fill your mug half full with the mixture and pour in hot water. Stir to combine. 4) Seal the rest in an airtight container, keeps indefinitely in the pantry. This also works great with warm milk.

Difficulty: Easy **Prep Time:** 5 minutes **Yield:** 5 1/2 cups dry mix

PERFECT CUP OF TEA

Episode: True Brew II, EA1D04

4 heaping teaspoons loose tea 4 cups water	Place loose tea leaves into a warmed tea kettle. Pour heated water over loose tea leaves. Let steep. Strain tea and serve. *Note: For Oolong and Green tea, water should simmer at 200 degrees F. and 180 degrees F. *For Irish and English tea bring water to a full boil. *Black tea should soak for 3 to 5 minutes. Oolong tea should soak for 4 to 7 minutes. Green Tea should soak for 2 to 3 minutes.

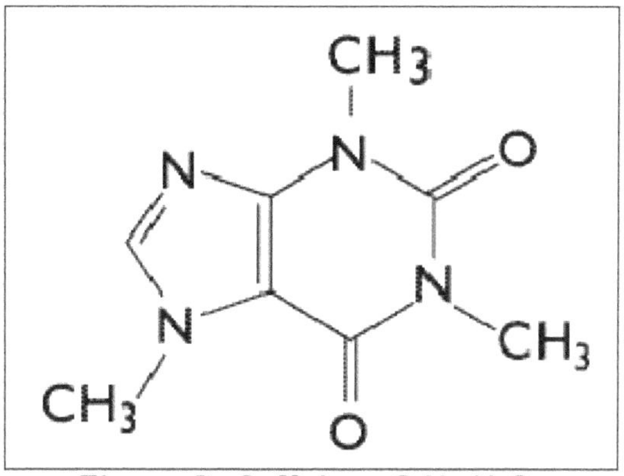

Figure 3: Caffeine: $C_8H_{10}N_4O_2$

Caffeine Content found in Coffee and Drinks (source: Wikipedia 11.26.2005

All fluid ounces are U.S. fluid ounces.

Coffee

- Coffee, brewed (drip) - 4 to 20 mg/floz
- Coffee, decaffeinated - 0.4 to 0.6 mg/floz
- Coffee, instant - 4 to 12 mg/floz
- Espresso Arabica - ~40 mg/floz
- Espresso Robusta - ~100 mg/floz

Teas and other infusions

- Black tea, brewed (USA) - 2.5 to 11 mg/floz
- Black tea, brewed (other) - 3 to 14 mg/floz
- Black tea, canned iced - 2 to 3 mg/floz
- Black tea, instant - 3.5 mg/floz
- Oolong, 3.75 mg/floz (12 to 55 mg per tea bag, i.e. one serving)
- Green tea, 2.5 mg/floz (8 to 30 mg per tea bag, i.e. one serving)
- White tea, 2.0 mg/floz (6 to 25 mg per tea bag, i.e. one serving)
- Decaf, 0.5 mg/oz (1 to 4 mg per tea bag, i.e. one serving)
- Tisanes (i.e. Herbal teas) - caffeine content depends on the herb, e.g. Chamomile and Rooibos "teas" have no caffeine while Yerba mate and Guarana do contain varying quantities. Many tea drinkers characterize herbal tea simply as that which, unlike black or green tea, contains no caffeine.

DESSERTS

Cakes, Custards & Curds

ANGEL FOOD CAKE

Episode: Let Them Eat Foam, EA1D08

	1) Preheat oven to 350° F.
1 3/4 cups sugar	2) In a food processor spin sugar until it is superfine.
1/4 teaspoon salt **1 1/2 teaspoons cream of tartar**	3) Sift half of the sugar with the salt and the cream of tartar, setting the remainder aside.
12 egg whites (the closer to room temperature the better) **1/3 cup warm water** **1 teaspoon orange extract (or extract of your choice)**	4) In a large bowl, use a balloon whisk to thoroughly combine egg whites, water and orange extract. 5) After 2 minutes, switch to a hand mixer. 6) Slowly sift the reserved sugar, beating continuously.
1 cup cake flour, sifted	7) Once you have achieved medium peaks, sift in enough flour to dust the top of the foam. 8) Using a spatula fold in gently. Continue until all of the flour is incorporated. 9) Carefully spoon mixture into an ungreased, two part 10-inch tube pan. 10) Bake for 35 minutes before checking for doneness with a wooden skewer. (When inserted halfway between the inner and outer wall, the skewer should come out dry). 11) Cool upside down on cooling rack for at least 1 hour before removing from pan.

Difficulty: Easy **Prep Time:** 20 minutes **Cook Time:** 35 minutes **Yield:** 1 cake

Cook's Note: Since they're easier to separate, use the freshest eggs you can get.

AUNT VERNA'S ORANGE CAKE

Episode: Pantry Raid IV: Comb Alone, EA1D13

	1) Preheat oven to 350° F.
1 cup orange blossom honey **4 large eggs**	2) In a large bowl, whisk together honey and eggs until thoroughly integrated.
1 tablespoon orange zest	3) Stir in orange zest.
1 1/2 cups all-purpose flour **1 teaspoon baking powder** **1 pinch baking soda**	4) Sift together flour, baking powder, and baking soda.
Butter, for greasing	5) Add butter slowly to egg mixture. 6) Lightly grease a loaf pan with butter. 7) Add the mixture to the pan and bake. 8) After 30 minutes check for doneness with a wooden skewer. (If it comes out clean, you are done. If not, give it another 5 minutes and check it again).

Difficulty: Easy **Prep Time:** 15 minutes **Cook Time:** 20 minutes **Yield:** 6 to 8 servings

Notes:______________________________

CARROT CAKE

Episode: A Taproot Orange, EA1H16

Unsalted butter, for the pan **12 ounces, approximately 2 1/2 cups, all-purpose flour, plus extra for pan**	1) Preheat oven to 350 degrees F. 2) Butter and flour a 9-inch round and 3-inch deep cake pan. 3) Line the bottom with parchment paper. Set aside.
12 ounces grated carrots, medium grate, approximately 6 medium	4) Put the carrots into a large mixing bowl and set aside.
1 teaspoon baking powder **1 teaspoon baking soda** **1/4 teaspoon ground allspice** **1/4 teaspoon ground cinnamon** **1/4 teaspoon freshly ground nutmeg** **1/2 teaspoon salt**	5) Put the flour, baking powder, baking soda, spices, and salt in the bowl of a food processor and process for 5 seconds. 6) Add this mixture to the carrots and toss until they are well-coated with the flour.
10 ounces sugar, approximately 1 1/3 cups **2 ounces dark brown sugar, approximately 1/4 cup firmly packed** **3 large eggs** **6 ounces plain yogurt**	7) In the bowl of the food processor combine the sugar, brown sugar, eggs, and yogurt.
6 ounces vegetable oil	8) With the processor still running drizzle in the vegetable oil. 9) Pour this mixture into the carrot mixture and stir until just combined. 10) Pour into the prepared cake pan and bake on the middle rack of the oven for 45 minutes. 11) Reduce the heat to 325 degrees F and bake for another 20 minutes or until the cake reaches 205 to 210 degrees F in the center. 12) Remove the pan from the oven and allow cake to cool 15 minutes in the pan. 13) After 15 minutes, turn the cake out onto a rack and allow cake to cool completely.
Cream Cheese Frosting, found elsewhere	14) Frost with cream cheese frosting after cake has cooled completely.

Difficulty: Easy **Prep Time:** 40 minutes **Inactive Prep Time:** 1 hour **Cook Time:** 1 hr 10 minutes **Yield:** 1 9-in cake

FREE RANGE FRUITCAKE

Episode: It's a Wonderful Cake, EA1B01

1 cup golden raisins **1 cup currants** **1/2 cup sun dried cranberries** **1/2 cup sun dried blueberries** **1/2 cup sun dried cherries** **1/2 cup dried apricots, chopped** **1/4 cup candied ginger, chopped** **Zest of one lemon, chopped coarsely** **Zest of one orange, chopped coarsely**	1) Combine dried fruits, candied ginger and both zests.
1 cup gold rum	2) Add rum and macerate overnight, or microwave for 5 minutes to re-hydrate fruit.
1 cup sugar **5 ounces unsalted butter (1 1/4 sticks)** **1 cup unfiltered apple juice** **4 whole cloves, ground** **6 allspice berries, ground** **1 teaspoon ground cinnamon** **1 teaspoon ground ginger**	3) Place fruit and liquid in a non-reactive pot with the sugar, butter, apple juice and spices. 4) Bring mixture to a boil stirring often, then reduce heat and simmer for 5 to 10 minutes. 5) Remove from heat and cool for at least 15 minutes. (Batter can be completed up to this point, then covered and refrigerated for up to 2 days. Bring to room temperature before completing cake.) 6) Heat oven to 325°.
1 3/4 cups all purpose flour **1 1/2 teaspoons salt** **1 teaspoon baking soda** **1 teaspoon baking powder**	7) Combine dry ingredients and sift into fruit mixture.
2 eggs **1/4 to 1/2 cup toasted pecans, broken**	8) Quickly bring batter together with a large wooden spoon, then stir in eggs one at a time until completely integrated, then fold in nuts. 9) Spoon into a 10-inch non-stick loaf pan and bake for 1 hour. 10) Check for doneness by inserting toothpick into the middle of the cake. 11) If it comes out clean, it's done. If not, bake another 10 minutes, and check again. 12) Remove cake from oven and place on cooling rack or trivet.
Brandy for basting and/or spritzing	13) Baste or spritz top with brandy and allow to cool completely before turning out from pan. 14) When cake is completely cooled, seal in a tight sealing, food safe container. 15) Every 2 to 3 days, feel the cake and if dry, spritz with brandy. The cake's flavor will enhance considerably over the next two weeks. If you decide to give the cake as a gift, be sure to tell the recipient that they are very lucky indeed.

Difficulty: Easy

Yield: 10 slices

Notes:______________________________

FUNNEL CAKE

Episode: Choux Shine, EA1F09

1 cup water **3/4 stick butter (6 tablespoons)** **1 tablespoon sugar** **1/8 teaspoon salt**	1) Boil water, butter, sugar, and salt together in a saucepan.
1 cup flour	2) Add flour and work it in until it is all incorporated and dough forms a ball. 3) Transfer mixture to the bowl of a standing mixer and let cool for 3 to 4 minutes.
1 cup eggs, about 4 large eggs and 2 whites	4) With mixer lowest speed, add eggs, 1 at a time, making sure the first egg is completely incorporated before continuing. 5) Once all eggs have been added and mixture is smooth, put dough in a piping bag fitted with a number 12 tip.
Vegetable oil, for frying	6) Heat about 1 1/2 inches of oil in a heavy pan. 7) Pipe dough into oil, making a free-form lattice pattern; cook until browned, flipping once.
Powdered sugar, for topping	8) Remove cake from oil, drain on paper towels, and top with powdered sugar. 9) Continue until all of the batter is used.

Difficulty: Easy **Prep Time:** 10 minutes **Cook Time:** 10 minutes **Yield:** 10 cakes

GOLD CAKE

Episode: A Cake on Every Plate, EA1F13

3/4 cup butter flavored vegetable shortening, 140 grams **1 1/4 cup sugar, 300 grams**	1) Preheat the oven to 350 degrees F. 2) Grease 2 (9-inch) cake pans with shortening and set aside. 3) Cream together the shortening and the sugar.
2 1/2 cups cake flour, sifted, 300 grams **3 teaspoons baking powder, 14 grams** **1/4 teaspoon salt**	4) Combine the flour, baking powder, and salt.
8 egg yolks, beaten, 130 grams **3/4 cup milk, 180 grams**	5) Slowly alternate adding the egg yolks and milk with the dry ingredients and mix until well combined.
1 teaspoon vanilla	6) Add the vanilla and mix well. 7) Pour into the prepared pans, about 550 grams of batter for each cake. 8) Bake for 18 to 20 minutes. 9) Remove from oven and cool on a rack. See *Cocoa Whipped Cream* recipe for the Icing paired with this cake in the show

Difficulty: Easy **Prep Time:** 20 minutes **Cook Time:** 20 minutes **Yield:** 2 layers

LEMON CURD

Episode: The Egg-Files, EA1A03

	1) Add enough water to a medium saucepan to come about 1-inch up the side. 2) Bring to a simmer over medium-high heat.
5 egg yolks **1 cup sugar**	3) Meanwhile, combine egg yolks and sugar in a medium size metal bowl and whisk until smooth, about 1 minute.
4 lemons, zested and juiced	4) Measure citrus juice and if needed, add enough cold water to reach 1/3 cup. 5) Add juice and zest to egg mixture and whisk smooth. 6) Once water reaches a simmer, reduce heat to low and place bowl on top of saucepan. (Bowl should be large enough to fit on top of saucepan without touching the water.) 7) Whisk until thickened, approximately 8 minutes, or until mixture is light yellow and coats the back of a spoon.
1 stick butter, cut into pats and chilled	8) Remove promptly from heat and stir in butter a piece at a time, allowing each addition to melt before adding the next. 9) Remove to a clean container and cover by laying a layer of plastic wrap directly on the surface of the curd. 10) Refrigerate for up to 2 weeks.

Difficulty: Easy **Prep Time:** 15 minutes **Cook Time:** 15 minutes **Yield:** 1 pint

PINEAPPLE UPSIDE-DOWN CORNMEAL CAKE

Episode: True Grits, EA1H01

3/4 cup whole milk	1) Preheat oven to 350 degrees F. 2) In a microwave-proof dish, bring the milk to a boil.
1 cup coarse ground cornmeal	3) Remove the milk from the microwave and add the cornmeal. Stir and let soak at room temperature for 30 minutes. Set aside.
4 ounces unsalted butter	4) Melt the butter in a 10-inch cast iron skillet over medium heat.
8 ounces dark brown sugar, approximately 1 cup	5) Once the butter has melted, add the brown sugar and stir until the sugar dissolves, about 5 minutes.
6 slices canned pineapple in heavy syrup **6 maraschino cherries** **1/3 cup chopped pecans, toasted** **3 tablespoons juice from canned pineapple**	6) Remove the skillet from the heat and carefully place 1 slice of pineapple in the center of the pan. Place the other 5 slices around the center slice in a circle. Place the cherries in the centers of the pineapple slices and sprinkle the nuts evenly over the fruit. Drizzle pineapple juice over top.
4 3/4 ounces all-purpose flour, approximately 1 cup **2 teaspoons baking powder** **1/2 teaspoon salt**	7) Sift the flour, baking powder, and salt into a medium mixing bowl and whisk to combine.
3 whole eggs	8) In a separate mixing bowl, whisk the eggs.
5 3/4 ounces sugar, approximately 3/4 cup	9) Add the sugar to the eggs and whisk to combine.
1/2 cup canola oil	10) Add the canola oil and whisk.
	11) Add the cornmeal and milk mixture to the egg mixture and whisk to combine. 12) Add this to the flour and stir just until combined. 13) Pour the batter over the fruit in the skillet and bake for 40 to 45 minutes. 14) Remove from oven and let cool for 30 minutes in the skillet. 15) Set a platter on top of the skillet and carefully invert the cake. Serve.

Difficulty: Easy **Prep Time:** 30 minutes **Inactive Prep Time:** 30 minutes **Cook Time:** 50 minutes **Yield:** 1 10-in cake

Notes:____

SAVORY CHEESECAKE

Episode: The Trouble with Cheesecake, EA1D04

	1) Preheat the oven to 350° F.
Crust: **3 ounces melted butter** **1 egg white** **1 1/2 cups crushed bagel chips**	2) In a small bowl, combine the melted butter, egg white, and the bagel chips. 3) Press them into the bottom of a 10-inch spring form pan. 4) Bake for 8 minutes to crisp up. 5) Remove from oven and cool. 6) Reduce the heat to 250° F.
24 ounces cream cheese **3 tablespoons cornstarch** **1 teaspoon salt** **4 ounces sour cream**	7) In a mixing bowl fitted with a paddle attachment, blend the cream cheese, cornstarch, salt, and sour cream.
2 large eggs	8) Once combined, add the eggs.
6 ounces smoked trout, diced **1/3 cup chopped chives**	9) Fold in trout and chives. 10) Pour the batter over the cooled crust. Bake for 1 hour. 11) Turn the oven off and leave the cake in the oven for an additional hour without opening the door. 12) Cool on a rack for at least 4 hours. 13) Carefully unmold. 14) Keep refrigerated until ready to serve.

Difficulty: Easy **Prep Time:** 20 minutes **Inactive Prep Time:** 4 hours **Cook Time:** 2 hrs 10 min **Yield:** 8 to 10 servings

SHORTCAKE

Episode: Churn Baby Churn, EA1A06

	1) Heat oven 450°.
2 cups flour **4 teaspoons baking powder** **3/4 teaspoon salt** **1 tablespoon sugar**	2) In a large mixing bowl, combine flour, baking powder, salt and sugar.
2 tablespoons butter **2 tablespoons shortening**	3) Cut in butter and shortening.
3/4 cup half and half	4) Mix in half-and-half. 5) Drop by large spoonfuls onto a baking sheet.
Melted butter to brush shortcakes	6) Brush with melted butter and sprinkle with sugar. 7) Bake for 15 minutes or until brown.
Berries **Ice cream or whipped cream**	8) Cool and eat with berries, ice cream and/or whipped cream.

Difficulty: Easy **Prep Time:** 20 minutes **Cook Time:** 15 minutes **Yield:** 8 servings

SOUR CREAM CHEESECAKE

Episode: The Trouble with Cheesecake, EA1D04

	1) Preheat oven to 300° F.
Crust: **4 ounces (1 stick) unsalted butter, melted, plus additional, for brushing the pan**	2) Brush some of the melted butter around a 9 by 3-inch cake pan. 3) Adhere parchment to the bottom and the sides.
33 graham cracker squares, crumbled **1 tablespoon sugar**	4) In a small bowl, combine crumbled graham crackers, the remaining melted butter, and 1 tablespoon of sugar. 5) Press 2/3 of the mixture into the bottom of the parchment-lined pan. 6) Place remaining crumbs on a sheet pan and bake both the crust and the remaining mixture for 10 minutes. 7) Cool. Reserve additional crumb mixture for sides.
Filling: **1 1/4 cups sour cream**	8) In a mixer with a paddle attachment, beat sour cream for 10 seconds.
20 ounces cream cheese **1 cup sugar**	9) Add the cream cheese and sugar and mix on low for 30 seconds and then turn up to medium. Scrape the bowl.
1 tablespoon vanilla extract **2 eggs** **3 yolks** **1/3 cup heavy cream**	10) In a separate container, combine vanilla, eggs, yolks, and heavy cream. 11) With the mixer on medium, slowly pour the liquid mixture in. 12) When half of it is incorporated, stop and scrape. Continue adding the mixture until the rest of the ingredients are incorporated. 13) Once completely combined, pour into the cooled crust. 14) Lower oven temperature to 250° F. 15) Place cheesecake into a preheated water bath, in the oven for 1 hour. 16) Turn the oven off and open the door for one minute. 17) Close the door for one more hour. 18) Remove the cheesecake from the water bath and place in the refrigerator for 6 hours to completely cool before serving. 19) When ready to serve, place the entire cake pan into a hot water bath for about 15 seconds. 20) Unmold onto a cake round or serving dish. 21) Take the remaining graham cracker mixture and press into the sides of the cake. 22) To slice, place your knife into a hot water bath and wipe dry each time you make a pass through the cake.

Difficulty: Medium **Prep Time:** 25 minutes **Inactive Prep Time:** 6 hours **Cook Time:** 2 hours **Yield:** 8 to 10 servings

Notes:____

TOFFEE LACE CUPS

1 stick (4 ounces) unsalted butter 2/3 cup brown sugar (3 1/2 ounces by weight) 5 fluid ounces dark corn syrup (5 1/2 ounces by weight) Pinch of kosher salt Juice of a quarter lemon	1) Combine all ingredients except flour in a small, heavy saucepan over medium-high heat. 2) Bring to a boil, stirring often. Once mixture is at a boil, stir constantly for 2 minutes.
1 cup flour (4 1/2 ounces by weight)	3) Remove from heat and sift in flour a little at a time, stirring to combine each addition before adding the next. 4) Cool to room temperature or refrigerate for later use. (If refrigerated, allow mixture to come up to room temperature before cooking.) 5) Heat oven to 350°. 6) Cover a backing pan or cookie sheet with parchment paper and spoon out mixture with a metal soup spoon or a number 50 disher. 7) Cookies will spread out like crazy, so place dollops 6 to 8 inches apart. Bake 18 minutes or until deep mahogany brown. 8) To form into cups, use a metal spatula to transfer the hot candy disks to the bottoms of inverted ramekins or custard cups. (Have a ramekin for each disk, or the disks will set before you can get through them all.) 9) Work quickly and the disks will conform to the shape of the cups. 10) Remove when cool and store wrapped with paper towel inside re-sealable plastic bags.

Difficulty: Easy **Prep Time:** x minutes **Inactive Prep Time:** x minutes **Cook Time:** x minutes **Yield:** x servings

Variation: While hot, disks can be cut into shapes with a pizza cutter and used as garnish for other desserts, or left flat and eaten like pralines.

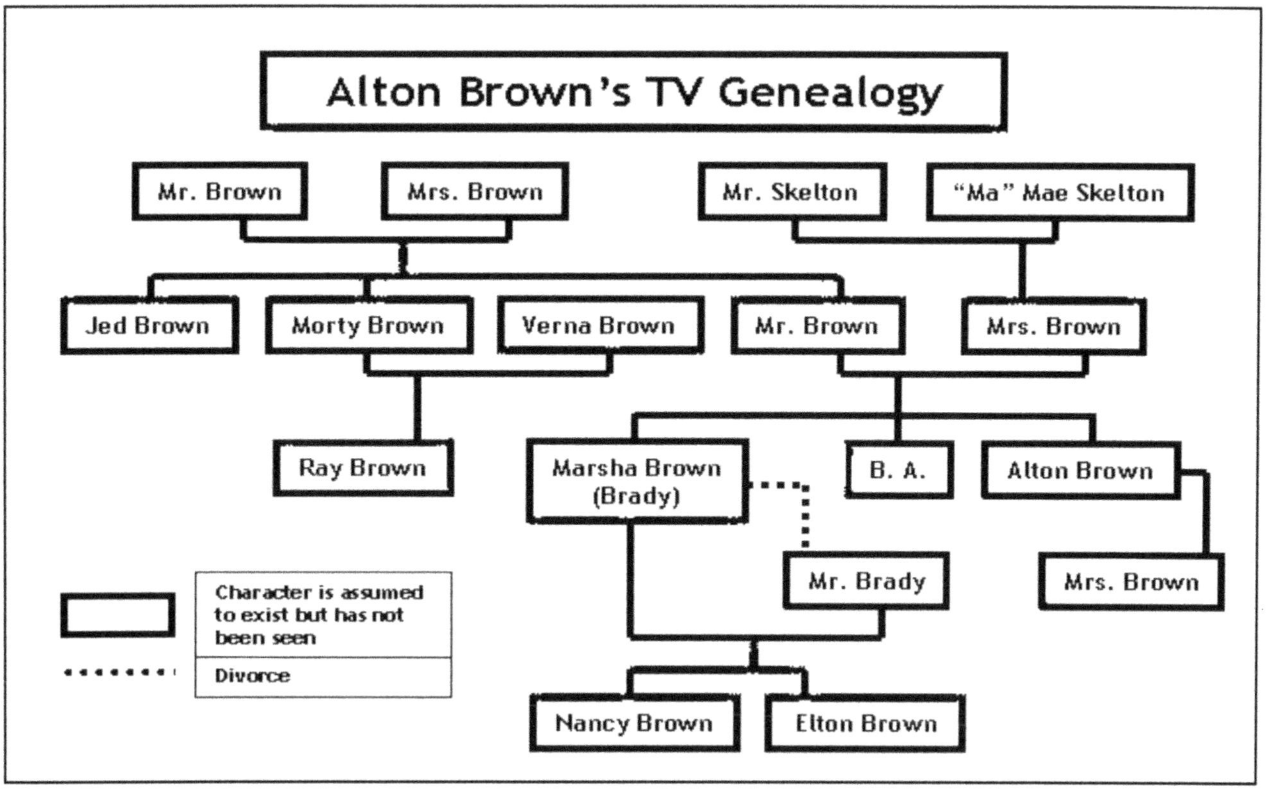

YEAST DOUGHNUTS

Episode: Circle of Life, EA1H04

1 1/2 cups milk	1) Place the milk in a medium saucepan and heat over medium heat just until warm enough to melt the shortening.
2 1/2 ounces vegetable shortening, approximately 1/3 cup	2) Place the shortening in a bowl and pour warmed milk over. Set aside.
2 packages instant yeast **1/3 cup warm water (95 to 105 degrees F)**	3) In a small bowl, sprinkle the yeast over the warm water and let dissolve for 5 minutes. 4) After 5 minutes, pour the yeast mixture into the large bowl of a stand mixer and add the milk and shortening mixture, first making sure the milk and shortening mixture has cooled to lukewarm.
2 eggs, beaten **1/4 cup sugar** **1 1/2 teaspoons salt** **1 teaspoon freshly ground nutmeg** **23 ounces all-purpose flour, plus more for dusting surface**	5) Add the eggs, sugar, salt, nutmeg, and half of the flour. 6) Using the paddle attachment, combine the ingredients on low speed until flour is incorporated and then turn the speed up to medium and beat until well combined. 7) Add the remaining flour, combining on low speed at first, and then increase the speed to medium and beat well. 8) Change to the dough hook attachment of the mixer and beat on medium speed until the dough pulls away from the bowl and becomes smooth, approximately 3 to 4 minutes. 9) Transfer to a well-oiled bowl, cover, and let rise for 1 hour or until doubled in size. 10) On a well-floured surface, roll out dough to 3/8-inch thick. 11) Cut out dough using a 2 1/2-inch doughnut cutter or pastry ring and using a 7/8-inch ring for the center whole. 12) Set on floured baking sheet, cover lightly with a tea towel, and let rise for 30 minutes.
Peanut or vegetable oil, for frying (1 to 1/2 gallons, depending on fryer)	13) Preheat the oil in a deep fryer or Dutch oven to 365 degrees F. 14) Gently place the doughnuts into the oil, 3 to 4 at a time. 15) Cook for 1 minute per side. 16) Transfer to a cooling rack placed in baking pan. 17) Allow to cool for 15 to 20 minutes prior to glazing, if desired.

Difficulty: Medium **Prep Time:** 25 minutes **Inactive Prep Time:** 1 hour 50 minutes **Cook Time:** 12 minutes
Yield: 20 to 25 servings

DOUGHNUT GLAZE

Episode: Circle of Life, EA1H04

1/4 cup whole milk **1 teaspoon vanilla extract**	1) Combine milk and vanilla in a medium saucepan and heat over low heat until warm.
2 cups confectioners' sugar	2) Sift confectioners' sugar into milk mixture. 3) Whisk slowly, until well combined. 4) Remove the glaze from the heat and set over a bowl of warm water. 5) Dip doughnuts into the glaze, 1 at a time, and set on a draining rack placed in a half sheet pan for 5 minutes before serving.

Difficulty: Easy **Prep Time:** 5 minutes **Inactive Prep Time:** 5 minutes **Cook Time:** 3 minutes
Yield: enough glaze for 20 to 25 doughnuts

Notes:____

CHOCOLATE DOUGHNUT GLAZE

Episode: Circle of Life, EA1H04

1/2 cup unsalted butter **1/4 cup whole milk, warmed** **1 tablespoon light corn syrup** **2 teaspoons vanilla extract**	1) Combine butter, milk, corn syrup, and vanilla in medium saucepan and heat over medium heat until butter is melted. 2) Decrease the heat to low, add the chocolate, and whisk until melted.
4 ounces bittersweet chocolate, chopped **2 cups confectioners' sugar, sifted**	3) Turn off heat, add the powdered sugar, and whisk until smooth. 4) Place the mixture over a bowl of warm water and dip the doughnuts immediately. 5) Allow glaze to set for 30 minutes before serving.

Difficulty: Easy **Prep Time:** 7 minutes **Inactive Prep Time:** 30 minutes **Cook Time:** 4 minutes
Yield: enough glaze for 20 to 25 doughnuts

Icing, Frosting, Etc.

AVOCADO BUTTERCREAM FROSTING

Episode: Curious Yet Tasty Avocado Experiment, EA0912

8 ounces avocado meat, approximately 2 small to medium	1) Peel and pit the avocado.
2 teaspoons freshly squeezed lemon juice	2) Place the avocado into the bowl of a stand mixer fitted with the whisk attachment along with the lemon juice and beat until lightened in color, approximately 2 to 3 minutes.
1 pound powdered sugar, sifted	3) Add the powdered sugar a little at a time and beat until smooth.
1/2 teaspoon lemon extract	4) Add the lemon extract and mix to combine. If not using right away, store in the refrigerator.

Difficulty: Easy **Prep Time:** 10 minutes **Yield:** approximately 2 cups of frosting

CREAM CHEESE FROSTING

Episode: A Taproot Orange, EA1H16

8 ounces cream cheese **2 ounces unsalted butter, room temperature**	1) In the bowl of a stand mixer with paddle attachment, combine the cream cheese and butter on medium just until blended.
1 teaspoon vanilla extract	2) Add the vanilla and beat until combined.
9 ounces powdered sugar, sifted, approximately 2 cups	3) With the speed on low, add the powdered sugar in 4 batches and beat until smooth between each addition. 4) Place the frosting in the refrigerator for 5 to 10 minutes before using.

Difficulty: Easy **Prep Time:** 15 minutes **Yield:** approximately 2 cups

GANACHE

Episode: The Icing Man Commeth, EA1F14

3 tablespoons corn syrup **6 ounces heavy cream**	1) In a small saucepan combine the corn syrup and heavy cream.
12 ounces dark chocolate, chopped into small pieces	2) Bring to a simmer and add the chocolate. Stir until smooth.
1/2 teaspoon vanilla extract	3) Remove from the heat and add the vanilla extract.

Difficulty: Easy **Prep Time:** 10 minutes **Cook Time:** 5 minutes **Yield:** 1 1/2 Cups

GANACHE FROSTING

Episode: Art of Darkness III, EA1H06

16 ounces bittersweet chocolate, chopped fine	1) Place the chopped chocolate into the bowl of a food processor.
16 ounces (2 cups) heavy cream	2) Heat the heavy cream in a quart-sized, microwavable container and microwave for 3 to 4 minutes on high, or until it just begins to simmer; be careful not to allow cream to boil over. 3) Pour the cream over the chocolate and let stand for 2 minutes. 4) Process by pulsing several times until chocolate mixture is smooth. 5) Use as is for glazing. 6) If you wish to make a lighter frosting, allow it to come to room temperature, approximately 2 hours. Once at room temperature, place in the bowl of a stand mixer and whisk on high for 2 to 3 minutes.

Difficulty: Easy **Prep Time:** 12x minutes **Inactive Prep Time:** 2 hours **Cook Time:** 4 minutes **Yield:** approx. 3 1/2 cups

BUTTERCREAM

Episode: The Icing Man Commeth, EA1F14

***4 eggs, room temperature**	1) In a large mixing bowl, whip the eggs until light and fluffy.
1/2 cup sugar **1/2 cup dark corn syrup**	2) In a small saucepan bring the sugar and the corn syrup to a boil. 3) Lubricate the inside of a metal baster with a small amount of vegetable oil and dispense it completely. 4) Then use this to drizzle the sugar mixture into the mixing bowl with the eggs. The mixer should be on low speed until you finish drizzling in all of the sugar mixture.
10 ounces butter, cubed and at room temperature	5) Once the entire mixture of the sugar is incorporated, slowly add the butter pieces. 6) Only add more butter when you can no longer see the previously added pieces. 7) It will go fast at first and then slow down. Continue to whip until the mixture is creamy.

Difficulty: Medium **Prep Time:** 25 minutes **Cook Time:** 3 minutes **Yield:** enough for 1 (2-layer) 9-inch cake

***RAW EGG WARNING** The American Egg Board states: "There have been warnings against consuming raw or lightly cooked eggs on the grounds that the egg may be contaminated with Salmonella, a bacteria responsible for a type of food borne illness. Healthy people need to remember that there is a very small risk and treat eggs and other raw animal foods accordingly. Use only properly refrigerated, clean, sound-shelled, fresh, grade AA or A eggs. Avoid mixing yolks and whites with the shell."

WRITING CHOCOLATE

Episode: The Icing Man Commeth, EA1F14

1 cup chocolate chips **2 teaspoons canola oil**	1) In a small bowl or measuring cup combine the chocolate chips and the oil. 2) Heat in the microwave on high for 3 minutes. *Microwaves may vary in power so cooking time may vary.

Difficulty: Easy **Prep Time:** 5 minutes **Cook Time:** 3 minutes **Yield:** 1 cup

Notes:________________________

ROYAL ICING

Episode: The Cookie Clause, EA1G12

3 ounces pasteurized egg whites **1 teaspoon vanilla extract**	1) In large bowl of stand mixer combine the egg whites and vanilla and beat until frothy.
4 cups confectioners' sugar	2) Add confectioners' sugar gradually and mix on low speed until sugar is incorporated and mixture is shiny. 3) Turn speed up to high and beat until mixture forms stiff, glossy peaks. This should take approximately 5 to 7 minutes. 4) Add food coloring, if desired. 5) For immediate use, transfer icing to pastry bag or heavy duty storage bag and pipe as desired. 6) If using storage bag, clip corner. Store in airtight container in refrigerator for up to 3 days.

Difficulty: Easy **Prep Time:** 7 minutes **Yield:** 3 ½ cups

Chocolate

CHOCOLATE COVERED NUTTY COCONUT BALLS (from the Transcript, not Foodtv.com)

Episode: Down and Out in Paradise, EASP02

HARDWARE Parchment Paper or Foil Mixing Bowl Double Boiler or other pan to melt chocolate	
SOFTWARE **1/2 lb. shredded or flaked coconut** **1 cup toasted Macadamia nuts, chopped** **1 cup sweetened, condensed milk** **1 1/2 tsp. almond extract**	1) Mix the coconut, nut, milk and extract together. 2) Form into 3/4" balls. Make them really tight. 3) Leave them out to dry on parchment paper or foil for about 3 to 4 hours or in the refrigerator for 1 hour.
12 oz. bag of semi-sweet chocolate morsels **1 tbs. Shortening**	4) Melt chocolate and shortening together, (probably in a double boiler) 5) Dip coconut balls in chocolate, let extra ooze off and place back on paper or foil to cool and harden.

Difficulty: Easy **Prep Time:** 30 minutes **Inactive Prep Time:** 3 to 4 hours **Cook Time:** 15 minutes **Yield:** ? servings

CHOCOLATE LAVA MUFFINS

Episode: Art of Darkness, EA1A13

	1) Preheat oven to 375°. 2) Place a small metal bowl over a saucepan with simmering water.
8 ounces semisweet chocolate chips **1 stick butter**	3) Melt the chocolate and butter in the bowl.
1/2 teaspoon vanilla extract	4) Stir in vanilla.
1/2 cup sugar **3 tablespoons flour** **1/4 teaspoon salt**	5) In a large mixing bowl, combine sugar, flour and salt. 6) Sift these into the chocolate and mix well with electric hand mixer.
4 eggs	7) Add eggs one at time, fully incorporating each egg before adding the next. 8) Beat at high until batter is creamy and lightens in color, approximately 4 minutes. 9) Chill mixture.
Butter to coat muffin tin	10) Coat the top and each cup of the muffin tin with butter.
1 tablespoon cocoa powder	11) Dust with the cocoa powder and shake out excess. 12) Spoon mixture into pan using a 4-ounce scoop or ladle. 13) Bake for 10 to 11 minutes. Outsides should be cake-like and centers should be gooey.
1 cup vanilla ice cream	14) While muffins are in oven, melt the ice cream in a small saucepan.
1 teaspoon espresso powder	15) Stir in the espresso powder. 16) Serve over warm muffins.

Difficulty: Easy **Yield:** 1 dozen

CHOCOLATE MOUSSE

Episode: Art of Darkness, EA1A13

1 3/4 cups whipping cream	1) Chill 1 1/2 cups whipping cream in refrigerator. 2) Chill metal mixing bowl and mixer beaters in freezer.
12 ounces quality semi-sweet chocolate chips **3 ounces espresso or strong coffee** **1 tablespoon dark rum** **4 tablespoons butter**	3) In top of a double boiler, combine chocolate chips, coffee, rum and butter. 4) Melt over barely simmering water, stirring constantly. Remove from heat while a couple of chunks are still visible. 5) Cool, stirring occasionally to just above body temperature.
1 teaspoon flavorless, granulated gelatin	6) Pour remaining 1/4 cup whipping cream into a metal measuring cup and sprinkle in the gelatin. 7) Allow gelatin to "bloom" for 10 minutes. 8) Then carefully heat by swirling the measuring cup over a low gas flame or candle. Do not boil or gelatin will be damaged. 9) Stir mixture into the cooled chocolate and set aside. 10) In the chilled mixing bowl, beat cream to medium peaks. 11) Stir 1/4 of the whipped cream into the chocolate mixture to lighten it. 12) Fold in the remaining whipped cream in two doses. 13) There may be streaks of whipped cream in the chocolate and that is fine. Do not over work the mousse. 14) Spoon into bowls or martini glasses and chill for at least 1 hour. 15) Garnish with fruit and serve.(If mousses are to be refrigerated overnight, chill for one hour and then cover each with plastic wrap)

Difficulty: Easy **Prep Time:** 10 minutes **Cook Time:** 1 hour 30 minutes **Yield:** 6 to 8 servings

Notes:____

COCOA BROWNIES

Episode: Art of Darkness, EA1D08

	1) Preheat the oven to 300° F.
Soft butter, for greasing the pan **Flour, for dusting the buttered pan**	2) Butter and flour an 8-inch square pan.
4 large eggs	3) In a mixer fitted with a whisk attachment, beat the eggs at medium speed until fluffy and light yellow.
1 cup sugar, sifted **1 cup brown sugar, sifted**	4) Add both sugars.
8 ounces melted butter **11/4 cups cocoa, sifted** **2 teaspoons vanilla extract** **1/2 cup flour, sifted** **1/2 teaspoon kosher salt**	5) Add remaining ingredients, and mix to combine. 6) Pour the batter into a greased and floured 8-inch square pan and bake for 45 minutes. Check for doneness with the tried-and-true toothpick method: a toothpick inserted into the center of the pan should come out clean. 7) When it's done, remove to a rack to cool. Resist the temptation to cut into it until it's mostly cool.

Difficulty: Easy **Prep Time:** 15 minutes **Cook Time:** 1 hour **Yield:** 16 servings

Yield: 16 brownies Prep Time: 15 minutes Cook Time: 1 hour Difficulty: Easy

MOO-LESS CHOCOLATE PIE

Episode: Tofuworld, EA1C01

	1) Place a small metal bowl over a saucepan with simmering water.
2 cups chocolate chips **1/3 cup coffee liqueur**	2) Melt the chocolate and coffee liqueur in the bowl.
1 teaspoon vanilla extract	3) Stir in vanilla.
1 block silken tofu **1 tablespoon honey**	4) Combine the tofu, chocolate mixture, and honey in the blender jar. Liquefy until smooth.
1 prepared chocolate wafer crust	5) Pour the filling into the crust and refrigerate for 2 hours, or until the filling is set.

Difficulty: Easy **Prep Time:** 2 hours 10 minutes **Cook Time:** x minutes **Yield:** 8 servings

Notes:____

> **"You know, being ambisinister I think I'll opt for the more neoteric of the, quintuplet. And although I delectate in discommoding you, I will tarry here no longer. As always, you have been supernumerary."**
>
> Alton Brown speaking to "W", Good Eats, *Art of Darkness II*
> (See the Good Eats Fan Page for a translation)

CHOCOLATE TAFFY

Episode: The Tricks to Treats, EA1G13

2 cups sugar **2/3 cup Dutch process cocoa powder** **1/2 teaspoon salt**	1) In heavy medium saucepan, combine sugar, cocoa powder, and salt. Stir until thoroughly combined.
1 cup light corn syrup **1/4 cup plus 1 tablespoon water** **1 teaspoon white vinegar**	2) Add corn syrup, water, and vinegar to pan and place over medium heat. Stir until sugar and cocoa dissolve, raise heat to high and bring to a boil. 3) Turn heat down to low, clip candy thermometer to side of pan and cook until mixture reaches 260 degrees F.
1 1/2 tablespoons butter, plus additional for greasing pan and hands	4) Remove pan from heat, add the butter and stir. 5) Butter edges of sheet pan, line with silicone baking sheet and pour on taffy. 6) Allow to cool until you are able to handle it. 7) Once you are able to handle the taffy, don vinyl gloves, butter them, and begin to fold taffy in thirds using the silicone mat. Pick up taffy and begin to pull folding the taffy back on itself repeatedly twisting as you go. Taffy is done when it lightens in color, takes on a sheen and becomes too hard to pull. 8) Roll into log, cut into fourths, roll each fourth into a 1-inch wide log, and cut into 1-inch pieces. Make sure to keep pieces separated or they will stick to each other. 9) Wrap individual pieces of candy in waxed paper. 10) Store in airtight container 3 to 5 days.

Difficulty: Medium **Prep Time:** 25 minutes **Inactive Prep Time:** 10 minutes **Cook Time:** 25 minutes **Yield:** about 60 pieces

INSTANT CHOCOLATE PUDDING MIX

Episode: Puddin' Head Blues, EA1H03

3 ounces Dutch-processed cocoa, approximately 1 cup **2 ounces cornstarch, approximately 1/2 cup** **6 ounces confectioners' sugar, approximately 1 1/2 cups** **1 1/2 ounces instant non-fat dry milk, approximately 1/2 cup** **1 teaspoon salt**	1) In a large bowl or plastic container with a lid, combine the cocoa, cornstarch, sugar, instant non-fat dry milk, and salt. 2) Store in an airtight container in the refrigerator for up to 1 month.

Difficulty: Easy **Prep Time:** 5 minutes **Yield:** 3 1/2 cups dry mix

CHOCOLATE PUDDING

Episode: Puddin' Head Blues, EA1H03

1 3/4 cups Instant Chocolate Pudding Mix (recipe elsewhere)	1) Place 1 3/4 cups of dry pudding mix into a medium saucepan.
2 cups milk **2 cups heavy cream**	2) Add milk and heavy cream and whisk to combine. 3) Over medium heat, bring mixture to a boil, continuously whisking gently. 4) Reduce heat to low and cook for 4 minutes while continuing to whisk.
1 teaspoon vanilla extract	5) Remove from heat and stir in vanilla. 6) Pour the mixture through a sieve and into individual dishes or a 1 1/2-quart serving dish. 7) Cover the surface of the pudding with plastic wrap. 8) Place in the refrigerator to chill completely before serving, approximately 4 hours.

Difficulty: Easy **Prep Time:** 10 minutes **Inactive Prep Time:** 4 hrs **Cook Time:** 10 minutes **Yield:** 4 servings

Notes:____________________________________

CHOCOLATE PEPPERMINT PINWHEEL COOKIES

Episode: The Cookie Clause, EA1G12

1 batch Sugar Cookies, recipe in this cookbook **3 ounces unsweetened chocolate, melted** **1 teaspoon vanilla extract**	1) Divide the dough in half and add chocolate and vanilla to 1 half and incorporate with hands.
1 egg yolk **1 teaspoon peppermint extract** **1/2 cup crushed candy canes or peppermint candies**	2) Add egg yolk, peppermint extract, and crushed candy to other half of dough and incorporate with hands. 3) Cover both with plastic and chill for approximately 5 minutes. 4) Roll out doughs separately to approximately 1/4-inch thickness. 5) Place peppermint dough on top of chocolate and press together around the edges. 6) Using waxed paper or flexible cutting board underneath, roll dough into log. 7) Wrap in wax paper and refrigerate for 2 hours. 8) Preheat oven to 375 degrees. 9) Remove dough from the refrigerator and cut into 1/2-inch slices. 10) Place cookies 1-inch apart on greased baking sheet, parchment, or silicone baking mat and bake for 12 to 13 minutes, rotating the pan halfway through cooking time. 11) Remove from oven and let sit on baking sheet for 2 minutes, then move to a wire rack to cool completely. 12) Store in an airtight container for up to 1 week.

Difficulty: Medium **Prep Time:** 45 minutes **Inactive Prep Time:** 2 hours **Cook Time:** 13 minutes **Yield:** about 3 doz.

CHOCOLATE FUDGE

Episode: Fudge Factor, EA1G05

2 3/4 cups sugar **4 ounces unsweetened chocolate** **3 tablespoons butter, plus more for greasing pan** **1 cup half-and-half** **1 tablespoon corn syrup**	1) Grease an 8 by 8-inch pan with butter. 2) In a heavy-bottomed saucepan, combine the sugar, chocolate, 1 1/2 tablespoons of the butter, half-and-half, and corn syrup. 3) Over medium heat, stir with a wooden spoon until sugar is dissolved and chocolate is melted. 4) Increase heat and bring to a boil. 5) Reduce heat to medium-low, cover, and boil for 3 minutes. 6) Remove the cover and attach a candy thermometer to the pot. Cook until the thermometer reads 234 degrees F. 7) Remove from the heat and add the remaining butter. Do not stir. 8) Let the mixture cool for 10 minutes or until it drops to 130 degrees F.
1 tablespoon vanilla extract **1 cup chopped, roasted nuts, optional**	9) Add vanilla and nuts, if desired, and mix until well-blended and the shiny texture becomes matte. 10) Pour into the prepared pan. Let sit in cool dry area until firm. 11) Cut into 1-inch pieces and store in an airtight container for up to a week.

Difficulty: Medium **Prep Time:** 10 minutes **Cook Time:** 30 minutes **Yield:** 64 1-in pieces

CHOCOLATE TRUFFLES

Episode: Art of Darkness III, EA1H06

10 ounces bittersweet chocolate, chopped fine **3 tablespoons unsalted butter**	1) Place the 10 ounces of chocolate and butter in a medium size glass mixing bowl. 2) Microwave for 30 seconds. Remove and stir, and repeat this process 1 more time. Set aside.
1/2 cup heavy cream **1 tablespoon light corn syrup**	3) Heat the heavy cream and corn syrup in a small saucepan over medium heat until simmering. 4) Remove from the heat and pour the mixture over the melted chocolate mixture; let stand for 2 minutes. 5) Using a rubber spatula, stir gently, starting in the middle of bowl and working in concentric circles until all chocolate is melted and mixture is smooth and creamy.
1/4 cup brandy	6) Gently stir in the brandy. 7) Pour the mixture into an 8 by 8-inch glass baking dish and place in the refrigerator for 1 hour. 8) Using a melon baller, scoop chocolate onto a sheet pan lined with parchment paper and return to the refrigerator for 30 minutes.
1/2 cup Dutch process cocoa powder, finely chopped nuts, and/or toasted coconut, for coating truffles	9) Place the cocoa powder, nuts, and/or toasted coconut each in its own in pie pan and set aside.
8 ounces semisweet or bittersweet chocolate, chopped fine	10) In the meantime, place the 8 ounces of chocolate into a medium mixing bowl which is sitting on top of a heating pad lined bowl, with the heating pad set to medium. Depending on the heating pad, you may need to adjust the heat up or down.

11) Stirring the chocolate occasionally, test the temperature of the chocolate and continue heating until it reaches 90 to 92 degrees F; do not allow the chocolate to go above 94 degrees F. If you do, the coating will not have a nice snap to it when you bite into the chocolate. Once you have reached the optimal temperature, adjust the heat to maintain it.
12) Remove the truffles from the refrigerator and shape into balls by rolling between the palms of your hands. Use powder-free vinyl or latex gloves if desired.
13) Dip an ice cream scoop into the chocolate and turn upside down to remove excess chocolate.
14) Place truffles 1 at time into the scoop and roll around until coated.
15) Then place the truffle into the dish with either the cocoa powder, nuts or coconut.
16) Move the truffle around to coat; leave truffle in the coating for 10 to 15 seconds before removing.
17) In the meantime, continue placing the chocolate-coated truffles in the cocoa or other secondary coating.
18) After 10 to 15 seconds, remove the truffle to a parchment lined sheet pan. Repeat until all truffles are coated.
19) Allow to set in a cool dry place for at least 1 hour; or store in an airtight container in the refrigerator. Truffles are best when served at room temperature.

Difficulty: Medium **Prep Time:** 50 minutes **Inactive Prep Time:** 2 hrs 30 min **Cook Time:** 5 minutes **Yield:** 30 to 35 truffles

Notes:____

Cobblers

INDIVIDUAL BERRY CRISPS

Episode: Cobbled Together, EA0904

12 ounces frozen berries (blueberries or raspberries) 1/4 cup sugar 2 teaspoons cornstarch 1/2 cup plus 2 cups crisp topping, recipe follows	1) Preheat oven to 350 degrees F. 2) Place the frozen berries, sugar, cornstarch and 1/2 cup of the crisp topping into a medium mixing bowl and stir to combine. 3) Divide the mixture evenly between 4 (7 to 8-ounce) ramekins. 4) Top each ramekin with 1/2 cup of the remaining crisp topping. 5) Place the ramekins on a sheet pan and bake on the middle rack of the oven for 30 to 35 minutes or until the fruit is bubbling and the topping is browned. 6) Allow the crisps to cool for 15 minutes before serving.
Crisp Topping: 5 ounces all-purpose flour, approximately 1 cup 2/3 cup sugar 1 1/2 cups chopped nuts such as; walnuts, pecans, or almonds 1 1/2 cups crushed crackers, gingersnaps or cereal	1) Place the flour, sugar, nuts and crackers into a large mixing bowl and combine.
4 ounces unsalted butter, cubed and chilled	2) Work the butter into the dry ingredients with your hands until it is crumbly. 3) Store in the refrigerator for up to a week. 4) Use as topping for crisps, cobblers or grunts.

Crisp:
Difficulty: Easy **Prep Time:** 20 minutes **Inactive Prep Time:** 15 minutes **Cook Time:** 35 minutes **Yield:** 4 individual crisps
Crisp Topping: Yield: 4 1/2 cups

RHUBARB PEACH COBBLER

Episode: Cobbled Together, EA0904

9 1/2 ounces all purpose flour, approximately 2 cups **1 ounce sugar, approximately 2 tablespoons, plus 1 cup sugar** **1 tablespoon freshly grated lime zest** **1 teaspoon kosher salt, plus 1/4 teaspoon**	1) Preheat the oven to 375 degrees F. 2) Place a piece of aluminum foil on the bottom rack to catch any drippings. 3) Butter a 9 by 9-inch glass baking dish and set aside. 4) Place the flour, 1-ounce sugar, lime zest, and 1 teaspoon salt into the bowl of a food processor and pulse 3 to 4 times.
4 1/2 ounces unsalted butter, chilled and cut into small pieces, plus extra for dish **1 1/2 ounces lard, chilled and cut into small pieces**	5) Add the butter and lard and pulse until the mixture just becomes crumbly.
1 1/2 ounces ice water, approximately 3 tablespoons	6) Sprinkle or spritz the mixture with the ice water a little at a time and process just until the dough holds together when squeezed in a fist. 7) Place the dough into a 1 gallon zip top bag and form into a disk. 8) Place the dough into the refrigerator for at least 30 minutes, while you prepare the filling.
2 tablespoons cornstarch	9) In a medium mixing bowl whisk together the 1 cup of sugar, cornstarch, and 1/4 teaspoon of salt.
1 pound rhubarb, chopped into 1/2-inch pieces **1 pound sliced peaches, peel on and sliced into 1/2 to 1-inch pieces** **1 tablespoon freshly squeezed lime juice**	10) Stir in the rhubarb, peaches, and lime juice. 11) Remove 1/3 of the dough from the bag, pinch into pieces and distribute evenly in the bottom of the prepared dish. 12) With the remaining dough still in the bag, roll it out to a sheet large enough to cover the top of the dish. 13) Pour the fruit mixture into the dish and top with the dough that has been removed from the bag, pressing the dough into the corners of the dish. 14) Bake, uncovered, for 60 minutes or until the dough is cooked through and starting to turn golden. *If using frozen fruit, increase cooking time to 90 minutes. 15) Change the oven setting to broil and broil until golden brown, approximately 3 minutes. 16) Remove from the oven and allow to stand for 15 to 30 minutes before serving.

Difficulty: Medium **Prep Time:** 20 minutes **Inactive Prep Time:** 30 minutes **Cook Time:** 1 hour **Yield:** 6 to 8 servings

Notes:

BLACKBERRY GRUNT

Episode: Cobbled Together, EA0904

9 1/2 ounces all purpose flour, approximately 2 cups **2 teaspoons baking powder** **1 teaspoon kosher salt** **1/4 teaspoon baking soda**	1) Preheat oven to 400 degrees F. 2) Place a piece of foil on the bottom rack of the oven to catch any drippings. 3) Place the flour, baking powder, salt and baking soda into the bowl of a food processor and process for 3 to 4 pulses.
2 ounces unsalted butter, cut into small pieces and chilled	4) Pour the mixture into a large mixing bowl and, using your hands, work the butter into the flour mixture until about half of the fat disappears and the rest is left in pea-size pieces.
1 cup buttermilk	5) Make a well in the center of the mixture and add the buttermilk and stir with a rubber spatula or wooden spoon just until it comes together. 6) Turn the mixture out onto a piece of parchment or waxed paper that has been lightly dusted with flour, shape into a ball and wrap and store in the refrigerator while you prepare the filling.
1 pound 3 ounces fresh or frozen blackberries, approximately 4 cups **1 cup sugar** **1 cup water** **1/2 teaspoon ground ginger**	7) Combine the blackberries, sugar, water and ginger in a large mixing bowl. 8) Pour the mixture into a 10-inch cast iron skillet and place over medium heat. 9) Bring this to a simmer decrease the heat to medium low and continue to cook, stirring occasionally, for 15 minutes, or until the liquid is thick enough to coat the back of a spoon. 10) Retrieve the dough from the refrigerator and gently drop it on the fruit mixture using a 1-ounce disher or large spoon, evenly distributing it over the top. 11) Bake in the oven for 15 to 20 minutes, or until the top is just starting to brown. 12) Remove from the oven and allow the grunt to cool for 15 to 30 minutes before serving.

Difficulty: Easy **Prep Time:** 25 minutes **Inactive Prep Time:** 30 minutes **Cook Time:** 35 minutes **Yield:** 6 to 8 servings

THE CHEWY

Episode: Three Chips for Sister Marsha, EA1C05

Hardware: Ice cream scooper (#20 disher, to be exact); Parchment paper; Baking sheets; Mixer	
	1) Heat oven to 375° F.
2 sticks unsalted butter	2) Melt the butter in a heavy-bottom medium saucepan over low heat.
2 1/4 cups bread flour **1 teaspoon kosher salt** **1 teaspoon baking soda**	3) Sift together the flour, salt, and baking soda and set aside. 4) Pour the melted butter in the mixer's work bowl.
1/4 cup sugar **1 1/4 cups brown sugar**	5) Add the sugar and brown sugar. 6) Cream the butter and sugars on medium speed.
1 egg **1 egg yolk** **2 tablespoons milk** **1 1/2 teaspoons vanilla extract**	7) Add the egg, yolk, 2 tablespoons milk and vanilla extract and mix until well combined. 8) Slowly incorporate the flour mixture until thoroughly combined.
2 cups semisweet chocolate chips	9) Stir in the chocolate chips. 10) Chill the dough, then scoop onto parchment-lined baking sheets, 6 cookies per sheet. 11) Bake for 14 minutes or until golden brown, checking the cookies after 5 minutes. 12) Rotate the baking sheet for even browning. 13) Cool completely and store in an airtight container.

Difficulty: Easy **Prep Time:** 20 minutes **Cook Time:** 15 minutes **Yield:** 2 1/2 dozen cookies

Notes:______________________________

THE PUFFY

Episode: Three Chips for Sister Marsha, EA1C05

Hardware: Ice cream scooper (#20 disher, to be exact) Parchment paper Baking sheets Mixer	
	1) Heat oven to 375° F.
1 cup butter-flavored shortening **3/4 cup sugar** **1 cup brown sugar**	2) Combine the shortening, sugar, and brown sugar in the mixer's work bowl, and cream until light and fluffy.
2 1/4 cups cake flour **1 teaspoon kosher salt** **1 1/2 teaspoons baking powder**	3) In the meantime, sift together the cake flour, salt, and baking powder and set aside.
2 eggs	4) Add the eggs 1 at a time to the creamed mixture.
1 1/2 teaspoons vanilla extract	5) Then add vanilla. Increase the speed until thoroughly incorporated. 6) With the mixer set to low, slowly add the dry ingredients to the shortening and combine well.
2 cups semisweet chocolate chips	7) Stir in the chocolate chips. 8) Chill the dough. 9) Scoop onto parchment-lined baking sheets, 6 per sheet. 10) Bake for 13 minutes or until golden brown and puffy, checking the cookies after 5 minutes. 11) Rotate the baking sheet for even browning. 12) Cool and store in an airtight-container.

Difficulty: Easy **Prep Time:** 20 minutes **Cook Time:** 15 minutes **Yield:** 2 1/2 dozen cookies

THE THIN

Episode: Three Chips for Sister Marsha, EA1C05

Hardware: Ice cream scooper (#20 disher, to be exact) Parchment paper Baking sheets Mixer	
	1) Heat oven to 375° F.
2 1/4 cups all-purpose flour **1 teaspoon kosher salt** **1 teaspoon baking soda** **Pinch baking soda**	2) Sift together the flour, salt, and baking soda in a mixing bowl.
1 egg **2 ounces milk** **1 1/2 teaspoons vanilla extract**	3) Combine the egg, milk, and vanilla and bring to room temperature in another bowl.
2 sticks unsalted butter	4) Cream the butter in the mixer's work bowl, starting on low speed to soften the butter.
1 cup sugar **1/2 cup brown sugar**	5) Add the sugars. 6) Increase the speed, and cream the mixture until light and fluffy. 7) Reduce the speed and add the egg mixture slowly. 8) Increase the speed and mix until well combined. 9) Slowly add the flour mixture, scraping the sides of the bowl until thoroughly combined.
2 cups semisweet chocolate chips	10) Stir in the chocolate chips 11) Scoop onto parchment-lined baking sheets, 6 cookies per sheet. 12) Bake for 13 to 15 minutes, checking the cookies after 5 minutes. 13) Rotate the baking sheet for more even browning. 14) Remove the cookies from the pans immediately. 15) Once cooled, store in an airtight container.

Difficulty: Easy **Prep Time:** 20 minutes **Cook Time:** 15 minutes **Yield:** 2 1/2 dozen cookies

Notes:____

SUGAR COOKIES

Episode: The Cookie Clause, EA1G12

3 cups all-purpose flour **3/4 teaspoon baking powder** **1/4 teaspoon salt**	1) Sift together flour, baking powder, and salt. Set aside.
1 cup unsalted butter, softened **1 cup sugar**	2) Place butter and sugar in large bowl of electric stand mixer and beat until light in color.
1 egg, beaten **1 tablespoon milk**	3) Add egg and milk and beat to combine. 4) Put mixer on low speed, gradually add flour, and beat until mixture pulls away from the side of the bowl. 5) Divide the dough in half, wrap in waxed paper, and refrigerate for 2 hours. 6) Preheat oven to 375 degrees F. 7) Sprinkle surface where you will roll out dough with powdered sugar.
Powdered sugar, for rolling out dough	8) Remove 1 wrapped pack of dough from refrigerator at a time, sprinkle rolling pin with powdered sugar, and roll out dough to 1/4-inch thick. 9) Move the dough around and check underneath frequently to make sure it is not sticking. If dough has warmed during rolling, place cold cookie sheet on top for 10 minutes to chill. 10) Cut into desired shape, place at least 1-inch apart on greased baking sheet, parchment, or silicone baking mat, and bake for 7 to 9 minutes or until cookies are just beginning to turn brown around the edges, rotating cookie sheet halfway through baking time. 11) Let sit on baking sheet for 2 minutes after removal from oven and then move to complete cooling on wire rack. 12) Serve as is or ice as desired. Store in airtight container for up to 1 week.

Difficulty: Easy **Prep Time:** 15 minutes **Inactive Prep Time:** 2 hours **Cook Time:** 9 minutes **Yield:** 3 dozen 2-1/2 in cookies

Notes:____

Good Eats Theme

Gelatin

CINNAMON CHERRY HEART

Episode: Deep Space Slime, EA1D01

2 packages unflavored powdered gelatin **2 cups cherry flavored juice, (darker juice is the best)**	1) Combine gelatin with one cup of the beverage and bloom for five minutes.
2 teaspoons cinnamon extract	2) In a small saucepan combine the remaining juice and extract and bring to a boil. 3) Combine with gelatin mixture and stir to dissolve solids. 4) Pour into heart shaped mold and refrigerate for four hours. Carefully unmold.

Difficulty: Easy **Prep Time:** 10 minutes **Inactive Prep Time:** overnight **Cook Time:** 5 minutes **Yield:** 4 to 6 servings

PANNA COTTA BRAIN WITH CRANBERRY GLAZE

Episode: Deep Space Slime, EA1D01

3 (12-ounce) cans evaporated milk **5 packages unflavored powdered gelatin**	1) Combine 1 can of evaporated milk with four packages gelatin and bloom for five minutes.
1 1/2 cups heavy cream	2) In a heavy-bottomed saucepan, bring the remaining milk and heavy cream to a boil.
3/4 cup sugar **1 vanilla bean, split** **1 teaspoon salt** **2 ounces bourbon (optional)**	3) Stir in the sugar, vanilla bean, salt, and bourbon.
	4) Combine this mixture with the gelatin mixture and stir until all solids have dissolved. 5) Remove the vanilla bean and pour the mixture into a six-cup brain mold. 6) Refrigerate overnight to fully set.
2 cups cranberry juice	7) For the glaze, combine remaining gelatin with half a cup of cranberry juice. 8) Bring remaining 1 1/2 cups of juice to a boil and stir into gelatin mixture to dissolve any solids. 9) Pour into a squeeze bottle and leave at room temperature until panna cotta brain is set. 10) Unmold the panna cotta and drizzle the glaze over it. The glaze will set up immediately.

Difficulty: Easy **Prep Time:** 15 minutes **Inactive Prep Time:** overnight **Cook Time:** 5 minutes **Yield:** 6 to 8 servings

SPARKLING GINGERED FACE

Episode: Deep Space Slime, EA1D01

1 (750 ml) bottle sparkling wine **9 packages unflavored powdered gelatin**	1) In a non-reactive bowl, combine gelatin and champagne. Bloom for five minutes.
5 cups ginger beer **3 tablespoons sugar**	2) In a small saucepan, bring ginger beer and sugar to a boil. 3) Remove from heat and stir into gelatin mixture to dissolve. 4) Pour into a 9-cup face mold. 5) Refrigerate overnight to set.

Difficulty: Easy **Prep Time:** 15 minutes **Inactive Prep Time:** overnight **Cook Time:** 3 minutes **Yield:** 10 to 12 servings

Notes:____

SPOOKY EDIBLE EYES

Episode: Deep Space Slime, EA1D01

1 1/2 packages of unflavored powdered gelatin **1/2 cup low fat milk**	1) Combine one package of gelatin with the milk and bloom for five minutes.
1 cup water **3 tablespoons sugar** **1/4 teaspoon coconut extract**	2) In a small saucepan, combine half a cup of water with the sugar and coconut extract and bring to a boil. 3) Combine with the gelatin mixture and stir until all solids dissolve.
Oil, for lubricating molds	4) Lubricate molds with oil and pour in gelatin mixture. 5) Refrigerate for one hour. 6) Gently tap and shake to unmold. 7) For the iris, combine remaining gelatin with 1/4 cup of water and bloom for five minutes. 8) In a small saucepan, bring the remaining water to a boil. 9) Remove and gently stir into gelatin mixture until solids dissolve.
Food coloring set (red, yellow, blue, and green)	10) Create the colors of your choice using the food coloring kit. Using an eyedropper, fill the indentation of the eyeballs with the colored gelatin. It will set within moments of contact with the cold gelatin. 11) In a small ramekin, mix one drop of each color to create black for the pupil. 12) Dip a toothpick into the black and paint the center of the iris. 13) To achieve bloodshot eyes, use red food coloring and brush with a cotton swab around the base of each eyeball.

Difficulty: Easy **Prep Time:** 30 minutes **Inactive Prep Time:** overnight **Cook Time:** 5 minutes **Yield:** 8 servings

Fruit

BAKER, BAKER: Oatmeal Filled Apples

Episode: Apple Family Values, EA1B03

3/4 cup oats **3/4 cup flour** **2/3 cup light brown sugar, packed** **1 teaspoon ground cinnamon** **1/2 teaspoon ground ginger** **Pinch kosher salt** **1 stick cold unsalted butter, diced**	1) In a bowl combine all the dry ingredients and diced butter. 2) Rub mixture briskly between finger tips until it forms small moist clumps in a loose sandy mixture. 3) Refrigerate while preparing the apples.
4 Braeburn apples (Fuji will substitute)	4) Cut a small layer off the bottom of each apple to create a flat, stable bottom surface. 5) With a small paring knife, cut a cylindrical cone out of the top of the apple, moving about 1-inch outside of the core, similar to removing the top of a pumpkin when carving a Jack O' Lantern. Remove the top and discard. 6) With a melon baller or a teaspoon, remove the remaining core and seeds taking care not to puncture the base of the apple.
4 teaspoons honey	7) Place apples on a baking sheet or pie dish and fill each center with a teaspoon of honey. 8) Spoon in mixture, packing lightly until heaped and overflowing over sides of the apples. 9) Bake in oven at 350° on the top or middle rack for 40 minutes or until filling is golden brown and the tip of a paring knife can be inserted into the side of the apple with little or no resistance. 10) Let apples stand for 10 minutes before serving.

Difficulty: Easy **Yield:** 4 servings

BANANA SPLITSVILLE

Episode: Citizen Cane, EA1B05

Hardware:	Aluminum foil
Small, heavy saucepan	Cooling rack
Clean soup spoon	Butane torch (available at most hardware stores…darned handy)
Candy thermometer	Safety goggles (see above)
Parchment paper	Plastic squirt bottle (available at most grocery stores)
2 sheet pans or other heatproof surface	

2 cups sugar **1 cup water** **1 tablespoon light corn syrup**	DOODADS 1) Combine the sugar, water and corn syrup in a small, heavy saucepan and place over high heat. 2) As soon as the sugar has dissolved, heat your thermometer under warm tap water (to prevent thermal shock) and attach to side of pan, making sure that the bulb is completely submerged. Do not stir the mixture or agitate the pan at this stage. 3) When the mixture reaches 230°, reduce the heat to medium and allow the sugar to color gradually. 4) As the temperature approaches 300° the color will start to turn to amber. At this point, it's safe to swirl the pan gently to help distribute the heat evenly. 5) As the caramel heads towards 340°, it will reach a deep amber color. Remove the pan from the heat and slowly stir with a metal spoon, allowing it to cool until the caramel falls from the spoon in a solid stream…like a string. When it does, it's doodad time. 6) Form doodads by holding the spoon 12 to16 inches over the caramel and drizzling the patterns on the parchment. (Hint: allow the spoon to "unload" into the pan for a few seconds before attempting doodad. This will allow a narrower stream.) Quick back and forth motions or side to side movements are best. 7) It's all in the wrist. Allow doodads to cool for 15 minutes then peel the paper off (not the other way around). 8) Stack in an airtight container with wax paper between each piece.
1 batch caramel (above) **2 cups heavy cream**	**CARAMEL SAUCE** 9) After making 15 to 20 doodads, you should have sufficient caramel remaining to move on to the sauce phase. So, return the remaining caramel to medium high heat and continue cooking until you see the first sign of smoke. 10) Immediately remove from the heat, and add the cream, all at once, at arms length. (It will boil furiously.) 11) Once the mixture calms down, return to medium heat and boil 3 more minutes, stirring occasionally. 12) Cool to room temperature, move to squirt bottle and refrigerate for up to a week.
4 bananas	**BANANAS BRÛLÉ** 13) To make the bananas brûlé, quarter the bananas (peel on) and rub into sugar to coat thoroughly.
Sugar for coating	14) Remove peel and place on cooling rack over several layers of foil. (Don't try this on your dining room table.) 15) Don your safety goggles and fire up your torch. Hold the torch so that the very tip of the flame barely touches the banana, and move quickly back and forth until the sugar melts, turns brown and bubbles. 16) As soon as it looks like caramel, move on. You know you've got it down when a solid, glasslike sheet of gold (no graininess) has formed on the banana.
Ice cream of your choice	**BANANA SPLITSVILLE** 17) To do the split (so to speak), squirt a pattern of caramel sauce on a chilled plate, top with 4 banana pieces (Lincoln log style), top with the ice cream of your choice (we like our peachy vanilla from "Churn Baby Churn" and finally, a doodad.

Difficulty: Medium **Prep Time:** 1 hour **Cook Time:** 19 minutes **Yield:** x servings

Notes:____

BANANA'S FOSTER

Episode: Top Banana, EA1G18

2 tablespoons unsalted butter	1) Melt butter in a 10-inch heavy skillet over low heat.
1/4 cup (1.75 ounces) dark brown sugar **1/4 teaspoon ground allspice** **1/2 teaspoon freshly ground nutmeg**	2) Add brown sugar, allspice and nutmeg and stir until sugar dissolves.
1 tablespoon banana liqueur	3) Add banana liqueur and bring sauce to simmer.
2 under ripe bananas, sliced in half lengthwise	4) Add bananas and cook for 1 minute on each side, carefully spooning sauce over bananas as they are cooking. 5) Remove bananas from pan to a serving dish.
1/4 cup dark rum	6) Bring sauce to a simmer and carefully add the rum. If the sauce is very hot, the alcohol will flame on its own. If not, using stick flame, carefully ignite and continue cooking until flame dies out, approximately 1 to 2 minutes. 7) If sauce is too thin, cook for 1 to 2 minutes until it is syrupy in consistency.
1/2 teaspoon finely grated orange zest	8) Add orange zest and stir to combine. 9) Immediately spoon the sauce over bananas and serve. 10) Serve with waffles, crepes, or ice cream.

Difficulty: Medium **Prep Time:** 5 minutes **Cook Time:** 7 minutes **Yield:** 2 servings

FRUIT TART

Episode: Puff The Magic Pastry, EA1D07

	1) Preheat oven to 400° F.
1 sheet puff pastry, thawed	2) Crimp seams of puff pastry together with fingertips.
Sugar, for dusting	3) Dust both sides of pastry with sugar. 4) Using a rolling pin, roll pastry in each direction to close seams. 5) Using a sharp pizza cutter (and tracing a small plate) cut out 2 circles of pastry. 6) Place pastry circles on a chilled sheet pan and let cool in the refrigerator for a few minutes.
1 Granny Smith apple, peeled, cored, and quartered	7) Using a vegetable peeler cut wafer thin apple slices.
1 tablespoon lemon juice	8) Put apple slices in lemon-juice-spiked water. 9) Flip pastry circles over on the sheet pans and poke them with a fork to provide an outlet for steam. 10) Put parchment paper on the pan underneath the pastry circles. 11) Sprinkle pastry with sugar and arrange apple slices on top. 12) Bake in the middle of the oven for 15 to 20 minutes. 13) Poke the crust; if it feels soft it needs more time in the oven.
Apricot jam	14) Microwave some apricot jam for 30 seconds. 15) Dab (don't brush) the jam on the tarts. 16) Cool tarts at least 4 hours and seal in a resealable plastic bag. 17) Serve at room temperature or heat in the microwave and top with ice cream.

Difficulty: Easy **Prep Time:** 15 minutes **Cook Time:** 20 minutes **Yield:** 2 servings

Yield: 2 servings Prep Time: 15 minutes Cook Time: 20 minutes Difficulty: Easy

Notes:______________________________

HONEY PLUMS

Episode: Pantry Raid IV: Comb Alone, EA1D13

1/2-3/4 cup wildflower honey	1) Cover the bottom of a sauté pan with honey. 2) Place over low heat to warm the honey.
10 slightly under ripe plums, stones removed, quartered (the plums not the stones)	3) Then add the plums, cut side down. 4) Cook for 5 to 6 minutes or until the cut sides are slightly browned. 5) Turn the plums and cook for another 3 minutes or until the fruit is soft but not mushy. 6) Serve with ice cream.

Difficulty: Easy **Prep Time:** 10 minutes **Cook Time:** 8 minutes **Yield:** 5 servings

MACERATED STRAWBERRIES

Episode: Strawberry Sky, EA1F03

2 pints medium size strawberries, hulled and sliced **1 (750 milliliter) bottle red wine** **1/4 cup orange blossom honey** **1 teaspoon finely chopped lemon zest** **1 teaspoon ground black pepper** **1/2 cup sugar**	1) In a bowl combine all ingredients. Let stand in refrigerator for 2 hours

Difficulty: Easy **Prep Time:** 15 minutes **Inactive Prep Time:** 2 hours **Yield:** 4 servings

DRIED PEAR AND FIG COMPOTE

Episode: Spice Capades, EA1G20

4 ounces (about 3/4 cup) dried figs, roughly chopped **4 ounces (about 1 cup) dried pears, roughly chopped** **1 cup apple cider** **1/2 cup white wine** **2 tablespoons orange blossom honey** **6 whole cloves** **1 stick cinnamon** **1 star anise pod** **1/2 vanilla bean** **1 (1-inch) strip lemon peel** **1 tablespoon fresh lemon juice** **1/2 teaspoon kosher salt**	1) Put all ingredients in medium saucepan, and bring to a simmer over medium heat. 2) Reduce the heat to low, cover, and simmer for 1 to 1 1/2 hours. 3) Remove cloves, cinnamon stick, and star anise. 4) Serve warm or cool. Serve with pork or lamb dishes, or as topping for ice cream. 5) Store in an airtight container with lid in the refrigerator for up to 2 weeks.

Difficulty: Easy **Prep Time:** 15 minutes **Cook Time:** 1 hour 30 minutes **Yield:** about 2 cups

> **"So on one hand, honey is an amazingly sophisticated and efficient food source. On the other hand it's bee backwash."**
>
> Alton Brown, Good Eats, *Pantry Raid IV: Comb Alone*

STRAWBERRY PUDDING

Episode: Strawberry Sky, EA1F03

16 slices stale potato bread	1) Remove both ends from 4 (15-ounce) soup cans. Save 4 of the ends. 2) Using one of the soup cans with the ends removed, cut the potato bread into 16 rounds. To avoid torn bread press straight down, do not twist. Let bread sit for 2 hours to dry out.
1 tablespoon butter, room temperature	3) Butter 1 side of 4 of the bread rounds.
Macerated Strawberries (recipe above)	4) Place the soup cans on a cookie sheet lined with parchment paper. 5) Place the buttered bread round, buttered-side up, in each can. 6) Spoon 2 tablespoons of strawberries with liquid to cover over each round. 7) Dredge 1 side of 4 bread rounds in the strawberry liquid and place over the strawberries. 8) Repeat layering strawberries and dredged bread rounds until you have 3 layers of strawberries and 4 layers of bread. 9) Place reserved ends of soup cans on top of final round and weight with cans of soda. 10) Refrigerate for 8 hours. Remove cans and serve with whipped cream.

Difficulty: Medium **Prep Time:** 30 minutes **Inactive Prep Time:** 10 hours **Yield:** 4 servings

TOASTY COCONUT MACAROONS

Episode: Down and Out in Paradise, EASP02

	1) Preheat oven to 350° F.
4 large egg whites Pinch salt	2) In a mixer fitted with a whip attachment. whip egg whites and salt until they become white and begin to stiffen.
1/2 cup sugar	3) Add sugar in 3 parts. 4) Continue to whip until the egg whites are very stiff.
1 (8-ounce) package sweetened shredded coconut, lightly toasted	5) Using a rubber spatula fold in toasted coconut. 6) On parchment lined cookie sheets, drop a teaspoon of the mixture leaving 1 to 2 inches around each cookie. 7) Place into the oven and bake for 15 to 20 minutes. The outside should be golden brown but the insides should still be moist.

Difficulty: Easy **Prep Time:** 10 minutes **Cook Time:** 20 minutes **Yield:** about 40 cookies

PISTACHIO FRUIT BALLS

Episode: Sometimes You Feel Like A ..., EA1G14

5 ounces (approximately 1 cup) roasted pistachios	1) Put the pistachios in the bowl of a food processor and pulse until finely chopped, but not powdery. 2) Divide in half into 2 separate bowls and set aside.
4 ounces (approximately 1 cup) dried cherries 2 ounces (approximately 1/2 cup) dried apricots 2 ounces (approximately 1/2 cup) golden raisins 2 ounces (approximately 1/2 cup) pitted dates	3) Put the cherries, apricots, raisins, and dates through a food grinder using the medium-grind blade. 4) Add to the bowl with half of the pistachios.
1 tablespoon orange juice 2 tablespoons crème de cassis	5) Add the orange juice and *crème de cassis* to the mixture and combine, using your hands, until the liquid is evenly distributed throughout. 6) Shape the mixture into 24 walnut size balls and roll them in the remaining chopped pistachios. 7) Store in an airtight container in the refrigerator for up to 1 week.

Difficulty: Easy **Prep Time:** 20 minutes **Yield:** 2 dozen balls

Notes:____

VANILLA ICE CREAM

Episode: Churn Baby Churn 2, EA0905

3 cups half-and-half **1 cup heavy cream**	1) Place the half-and-half and the heavy cream into a medium saucepan, over medium heat. 2) Bring the mixture just to a simmer, stirring occasionally, and remove from the heat.
8 large egg yolks	3) In a medium mixing bowl whisk the egg yolks until they lighten in color.
9 ounces vanilla sugar	4) Gradually add the sugar and whisk to combine. 5) Temper the cream mixture into the eggs and sugar by gradually adding small amounts, until about a third of the cream mixture has been added. 6) Pour in the remainder and return the entire mixture to the saucepan and place over low heat. 7) Continue to cook, stirring frequently, until the mixture thickens slightly and coats the back of a spoon and reaches 170 to 175 degrees F. 8) Pour the mixture into a container and allow to sit at room temperature for 30 minutes.
2 teaspoons pure vanilla extract	9) Stir in the vanilla extract. 10) Place the mixture into the refrigerator and once it is cool enough not to form condensation on the lid, cover and store for 4 to 8 hours or until the temperature reaches 40 degrees F or below. 11) Pour into an ice cream maker and process according to the manufacturer's directions. 12) This should take approximately 25 to 35 minutes. 13) Serve as is for soft serve or freeze for another 3 to 4 hours to allow the ice cream to harden.

Difficulty: Medium **Prep Time:** 8 minutes **Inactive Prep Time:** 8 hours **Cook Time:** 10 minutes **Yield:** 1 1/2 servings

"SERIOUS" VANILLA ICE CREAM

Episode: Churn Baby Churn, EA1A06

2 cups half-and-half **1 cup whipping cream** **1 cup minus 2 tablespoons sugar** **2 tablespoons peach preserves (not jelly)** **1 vanilla bean, split and scraped**	1) Combine all ingredients (including the bean and its pulp) in a large saucepan and place over medium heat. 2) Attach a frying or candy thermometer to inside of pan. (see note below) 3) Stirring occasionally, bring the mixture to 170° F. 4) Remove from heat and allow to cool slightly. 5) Remove the hull of the vanilla bean, pour mixture into lidded container and refrigerate mixture overnight to mellow flavors and texture. 6) Freeze mixture in ice cream freezer according to unit's instructions. The mixture will not freeze hard in the machine. 7) Once the volume has increased by 1/2 to 3/4 times, and reached a soft serve consistency, spoon the mixture back into a lidded container and harden in the freezer at least 1 hour before serving.

Difficulty: Easy **Prep Time:** 10 hours **Cook Time:** 1 hour **Yield:** 1 quart

NOTE: If you do not have a thermometer, bring the mixture just barely to a simmer. As soon as you see a bubble hit the surface, remove it from the heat. Do not let it boil.

CHOCOLATE ICE CREAM

Episode: Churn Baby Churn 2, EA0905

1 1/2 ounces unsweetened cocoa powder, approximately 1/2 cup **3 cups half-and-half** **1 cup heavy cream**	1) Place the cocoa powder along with 1 cup of the half-and-half into a medium saucepan over medium heat and whisk to combine. 2) Add the remaining half-and-half and the heavy cream. 3) Bring the mixture just to a simmer, stirring occasionally, and remove from the heat.
8 large egg yolks	4) In a medium mixing bowl whisk the egg yolks until they lighten in color.
9 ounces sugar	5) Gradually add the sugar and whisk to combine. 6) Temper the cream mixture into the eggs and sugar by gradually adding small amounts, until about 1/3 of the cream mixture has been added. 7) Pour in the remainder and return the entire mixture to the saucepan and place over low heat. 8) Continue to cook, stirring frequently, until the mixture thickens slightly and coats the back of a spoon and reaches 170 to 175 degrees F. 9) Pour the mixture into a container and allow to sit at room temperature for 30 minutes.
2 teaspoons pure vanilla extract	10) Stir in the vanilla extract. 11) Place the mixture into the refrigerator and once it is cool enough not to form condensation on the lid, cover and store for 4 to 8 hours or until the temperature reaches 40 degrees F or below. 12) Pour into an ice cream maker and process according to the manufacturer's directions. This should take approximately 25 to 35 minutes. 13) Serve as is for soft serve or freeze for another 3 to 4 hours to allow the ice cream to harden.

Difficulty: Medium **Prep Time:** 8 minutes **Inactive Prep Time:** 8 hours **Cook Time:** 10 minutes **Yield:** 1 1/2 quarts

MINT CHIP ICE CREAM

Episode: Churn Baby Churn 2, EA0905

3 cups half-and-half **1 cup heavy cream**	1) Place the half-and-half and the heavy cream into a medium saucepan, over medium heat. 2) Bring the mixture just to a simmer, stirring occasionally, and remove from the heat.
8 large egg yolks	3) In a medium mixing bowl whisk the egg yolks until they lighten in color.
9 ounces sugar	4) Gradually add the sugar and whisk to combine. 5) Temper the cream mixture into the eggs and sugar by gradually adding small amounts, until about 1/3 of the cream mixture has been added. 6) Pour in the remainder and return the entire mixture to the saucepan and place over low heat. 7) Continue to cook, stirring frequently, until the mixture thickens slightly and coats the back of a spoon and reaches 170 to 175 degrees F. 8) Pour the mixture into a container and allow to sit at room temperature for 30 minutes.
1 teaspoon peppermint oil	9) Add the peppermint oil and stir to combine. 10) Place the mixture into the refrigerator and once it is cool enough not to form condensation on the lid, cover and store for 4 to 8 hours or until it reaches 40 degrees F or below.
3 ounces chocolate-mint candies, coarsely chopped	11) Pour the mixture into an ice cream maker; add the chopped candies and process according to the manufacturers directions. 12) This should take approximately 25 to 35 minutes. 13) Serve as is for soft serve or freeze for another 3 to 4 hours to allow the ice cream to harden.

Difficulty: Medium **Prep Time:** 8 minutes **Inactive Prep Time:** 8 hours **Cook Time:** 10 minutes **Yield:** 1 1/2 quarts

Notes:____

BANANA ICE CREAM

Episode: Top Banana, EA1G18

6 (approximately 2 1/4 pounds) ripe bananas	1) Place bananas in freezer and freeze overnight. 2) Remove bananas from freezer and allow to thaw for 45 minutes to 1 hour.
1 tablespoon fresh squeezed lemon juice	3) Peel bananas and place in bowl of food processor along with the lemon juice. 4) Process for 10 to 15 seconds.
3/4 cup light corn syrup **1 vanilla bean, scraped**	5) Add corn syrup and vanilla bean seeds and turn processor on.
1 1/2 cups heavy cream	6) Slowly pour in the heavy cream. Process until smooth. 7) Chill mixture in refrigerator until it reaches 40 degrees. 8) Transfer mixture to an ice cream maker and process according to manufacturer's instructions. 9) Place mixture in an airtight container and freeze for 3 to 6 hours before serving.

Difficulty: Easy **Prep Time:** 35 minutes **Inactive Prep Time:** 6 hours **Yield:** about 1 quart

AVOCADO ICE CREAM

Episode: Curious Yet Tasty Avocado Experiment, EA0912

12 ounces avocado meat, approximately 3 small to medium	1) Peel and pit the avocados.
1 tablespoon freshly squeezed lemon juice **1 1/2 cups whole milk** **1/2 cup sugar**	2) Add the avocados, lemon juice, milk, and sugar to a blender and puree.
1 cup heavy cream	3) Transfer the mixture to a medium mixing bowl, add the heavy cream and whisk to combine. 4) Place the mixture into the refrigerator and chill until it reaches 40 degrees F or below, approximately 4 to 6 hours. 5) Process the mixture in an ice cream maker according to manufacturer's directions. 6) However, this mixture sets up very fast, so count on it taking only 5 to 10 minutes to process. 7) For soft ice cream, serve immediately. If desired, place in freezer for 3 to 4 hours for firmer texture.

Difficulty: Easy **Prep Time:** 15 minutes **Inactive Prep Time:** 8 hours **Yield:** 1 quart ice cream

BURNED PEACH ICE CREAM

Episode: Cooking Live, CL9349

2 cups half-n-half **1 cup whipping cream** **1/2 cup sugar** **1/2 cup peach preserves (not jelly)** **1 vanilla bean, split and scraped** **Pinch kosher salt** **4 medium peaches, halved, seeded and grilled or broiled until brown**	1) Combine all ingredients (including the bean and its pulp) in a large sauce pan and place over medium heat. 2) Attach a frying or candy thermometer to inside of pan. (see note below) 3) Stirring occasionally, bring the mixture to 170° F. 4) Remove from heat and strain into a lidded container. 5) Cool mixture, then refrigerate mixture overnight to mellow flavors and texture. 6) Freeze mixture in ice cream freezer according to unit's instructions. The mixture will not freeze hard in the machine. 7) Meanwhile, chop peaches roughly. 8) Once the volume has increased by 1/2 and reached a soft serve consistency, add the peaches and continue turning to incorporate. 9) Spoon the mixture back into a lidded container and harden in the freezer at least 1 hour before serving.

Difficulty: Easy **Prep Time:** 8 hours 25 minutes **Cook Time:** 5 hours **Yield:** about 1 1/2 quart

NOTE: If you do not have a thermometer, bring the mixture just barely to a simmer. As soon as you see a bubble hit the surface, remove it from the heat. Do not let it boil.

KEY LIME SORBET

Episode: Churn Baby Churn, EA1A06

1 cup sugar **1 cup key lime preserves** **4 cups lime flavored club soda or seltzer**	1) Combine sugar, preserves and 1 cup of the soda in a medium saucepan and stir over low heat until sugar and preserves are melted.
1 lemon, zested and juiced **1 lime, zested and juiced**	2) Add citrus juice and zest.
Kosher salt	3) Stir in the remaining soda, move to a clean, lidded container and chill thoroughly, 2 to 3 hours. 4) Turn mixture in ice cream maker per maker's instructions or until mixture reaches the consistency of a firm slush. 5) Return mixture to lidded container and harden in freezer 1 hour before serving. 6) If sorbet is to be held frozen for longer than 2 hours, move from freezer to refrigerator for about half an hour before serving. If you'd like a more assertive sorbet, double the amount of citrus zest.

Difficulty: Easy **Prep Time:** 15 minutes **Cook Time:** 3 hours 15 minutes **Yield:** 1 1/2 servings

MELON SORBET

Episode: Melondrama, EA1H01

1 pound, 5 ounces diced watermelon, muskmelon or honeydew	1) Place the melon in the bowl of a food processor and process until smooth.
3 tablespoons freshly squeezed lemon juice **2 tablespoons vodka** **9 ounces sugar, approximately 1 1/4 cups**	2) Add the lemon juice, vodka, and sugar and process for another 30 seconds. 3) Place the mixture into the refrigerator until the mixture reaches 40 degrees F; depending on the temperature of your ingredients and refrigerator, this could take 30 minutes to 1 hour. 4) Pour the chilled mixture into the bowl of an ice cream maker and process according to manufacturer's directions. 5) Transfer the sorbet to an airtight container and place in the freezer for 3 to 4 hours before serving.

Difficulty: Easy **Prep Time:** 15 minutes **Inactive Prep Time:** 4 hrs 30 min **Yield:** 1 quart

COFFEE GRANITA

Episode: Churn Baby Churn, EA1A06

2 cups lukewarm espresso or strong black coffee **1/2 cup sugar** **2 tablespoons coffee flavored liqueur** **1 teaspoon orange or lemon zest**	1) Combine all ingredients and stir until sugar melts. 2) Pour mixture into 9 by 13-inch metal pan and place on level shelf in freezer for half an hour. (Mixture should only come about 1/4-inch up the side of the pan.) 3) Remove and use a dinner fork to scrape any ice crystals that have formed on the side or bottom of the pan. 4) Return to freezer and repeat scraping every 20 to 30 minutes for 3 to 4 hours. 5) Once mixture is thoroughly frozen, fluff with a fork and allow flakes to "dry" in freezer another half hour before serving. 6) When served, the granita should look like a fluffy pile of dry brown crystals. 7) Scoop into goblets and top with barely sweetened whipped cream, add additional citrus zest if desired.

Difficulty: Easy **Prep Time:** 5 minutes **Cook Time:** 5 hours 30 minutes **Yield:** 6 servings

Notes:______________________________

GOOD EATS FUDGEPOPS

Episode: Art of Darkness III, EA1H06

Special Equipment: Icepop molds	
8 ounces bittersweet chocolate, chopped fine	1) Place chopped chocolate into a medium glass mixing bowl. Set aside.
12 ounces (1 1/2 cups) heavy cream **8 ounces (1 cup) whole milk** **2 tablespoons unsweetened cocoa powder**	2) Combine heavy cream, milk, and cocoa powder in a medium saucepan over medium heat. 3) Whisk constantly until cocoa is dissolved and mixture comes to a simmer. 4) Remove from the heat and pour over the chocolate. 5) Let stand for 2 to 3 minutes and then whisk gently until all chocolate is melted.
2 teaspoons vanilla extract	6) Whisk in the vanilla extract. 7) Divide the mixture evenly among the molds and place in the freezer. 8) Freeze for at least 4 hours or until solid. Fudgepops can be held in the freezer for up to 1 week in an airtight container.

Difficulty: Easy **Prep Time:** 15 minutes **Inactive Prep Time:** 4 hours **Cook Time:** 5 minutes
Yield: approximately 8 fudgepops depending on their size

PIE CRUST

Episode: I Pie, EA1G15

3 ounces (6 tablespoons) butter, chilled **1 ounce (2 tablespoons) lard, chilled**	1) Place butter and lard in freezer for 15 minutes. 2) When ready to use, remove and cut both into small pieces.
6 ounces (approximately 1 cup) all-purpose flour, plus extra for rolling dough **1/2 teaspoon table salt**	3) In the bowl of a food processor, combine flour and salt by pulsing 3 to 4 times. 4) Add butter and pulse 5 to 6 times until texture looks mealy. 5) Add lard and pulse another 3 to 4 times.
1/4 cup ice water, in spritz bottle	6) Remove lid of food processor and spritz surface of mixture thoroughly with water. 7) Replace lid and pulse 5 times. 8) Add more water and pulse again until mixture holds together when squeezed. 9) Place mixture in large zip-top bag, squeeze together until it forms a ball, and then press into a rounded disk and refrigerate for 30 minutes. 10) Preheat oven to 425 degrees F. 11) Place 2 metal pie pans in the refrigerator to chill. 12) Remove dough from refrigerator. Cut along 2 sides of the plastic bag, open bag to expose dough, and sprinkle both sides with flour. 13) Cover again with plastic and roll out with a rolling pin to a 10 to 11-inch circle. 14) Open plastic again and sprinkle top of dough with flour. 15) Remove pie pans from refrigerator and set first pan on top of dough. 16) Turn everything upside down and peel plastic from bottom of dough. 17) Place second pan upside down on top of dough and flip again. 18) Remove first pan from atop dough. 19) Trim edges if necessary, leaving an edge for meringue to adhere to. 20) Poke holes in dough and place in refrigerator for 15 minutes.
Approximately 32 ounces of dried beans, for blind baking	21) Place a large piece of parchment paper on top of dough and fill with dry beans. 22) Press beans into edges of dough and bake in the oven for 10 minutes. 23) Remove parchment and beans and continue baking until golden in color, approximately 10 to 15 minutes longer. 24) Remove from oven and place on cooling rack. Let cool completely before filling.

Difficulty: Medium **Prep Time:** 15 minutes **Inactive Prep Time:** 1 hour **Cook Time:** 25 minutes **Yield:** 1 9-in piecrust

Notes:________________________________

MACADAMIA NUT CRUST

Episode: Sometimes You Feel Like A ..., EA1G14

5 ounces (approximately 1 1/4 cups) roasted macadamia nuts, ground **1/2 cup panko (Japanese-style bread crumbs)** **1/4 cup sugar** **2 tablespoons all-purpose flour** **1/4 teaspoon salt**	1) In a medium mixing bowl, combine the nuts, panko, sugar, flour, and salt.
3 tablespoons butter, melted	2) Add the melted butter and stir to combine. 3) Press the mixture into the bottom of a 9 or 10-inch cake, pie, or springform pan as a crust for a cheesecake or cream pie. 4) Bake according to instructions for cheesecake or pie. 5) If baking for a precooked pie filling, preheat the oven to 375 degrees F. Place on the center rack of the oven and bake for 20 to 25 minutes.

Difficulty: Easy **Prep Time:** 10 minutes **Cook Time:** 25 minutes **Yield:** 1 9-to-10-inch pie or cheesecake crust

LEMON MERINGUE PIE

Episode: I Pie, EA1G15

Lemon Filling: **4 egg yolks (reserve whites for meringue)**	1) Adjust the oven rack to the middle position. Preheat oven to 375 degrees F. 2) Whisk egg yolks in medium size mixing bowl and set aside.
1/3 cup cornstarch **1 1/2 cups water** **1 1/3 cups sugar** **1/4 teaspoon salt**	3) In a medium saucepan, combine cornstarch, water, sugar, and salt. Whisk to combine. 4) Turn heat on medium and, stirring frequently, bring mixture to a boil. Boil for 1 minute. 5) Remove from heat and gradually, 1 whisk-full at a time, add hot mixture to egg yolks and stir until you have added at least half of the mixture. 6) Return egg mixture to saucepan, turn heat down to low and cook, stirring constantly, for 1 more minute.
3 tablespoons butter **1/2 cup lemon juice** **1 tablespoon finely grated lemon zest**	7) Remove from heat and gently stir in butter, lemon juice, and zest until well combined.
1 (9-inch) pre-baked pie shell	8) Pour mixture into pie shell and top with meringue while filling is still hot. Make sure meringue completely covers filling and that it goes right up to the edge of the crust.
1 recipe Meringue, recipe follows	9) Bake for 10 to 12 minutes or until meringue is golden. 10) Remove from oven and cool on a wire rack. Make sure pie is cooled completely before slicing.
Meringue Topping: **4 egg whites** **1 pinch cream of tartar** **2 tablespoons sugar**	1) Place egg whites and cream of tartar in the bowl of a stand mixer fitted with the whisk attachment. 2) Beat egg whites until soft peaks form and then gradually add sugar and continue beating until stiff peaks form, approximately 1 to 2 minutes. 3) Use to top lemon filling. Yield: topping for 1 (9-inch) pie

Difficulty: Medium **Prep Time:** 30 minutes **Inactive Prep Time:** 2 hours **Cook Time:** 12 minutes **Yield:** 6 to 8 servings

NO PAN PEAR PIE

Episode: Crust Never Sleeps, EA1B04

2 1/2 cups flour **1/2 cup stone ground cornmeal** **3 tablespoons sugar** **1 teaspoon kosher salt**	<u>For The Dough:</u> 1) Heat oven to 400° F. 2) In a food processor, combine flour, cornmeal, sugar, and salt. Pulse to combine. 3) Place dry ingredients in a mixing bowl and put the bowl into the refrigerator.
8 ounces unsalted butter, diced	4) Remove ½ stick of butter from the refrigerator and allow it to come to room temperature. 5) In a food processor, add the ½ stick of butter to the flour mixture. Pulse until the fat completely disappears. 6) Add the remaining chilled butter in separate batches. Pulse until flour mixture resembles the size of a pea.
3 tablespoons apple juice concentrate **2 tablespoons cold water**	7) Combine the apple juice concentrate and the cold water. 8) Add 1 tablespoon of the juice mixture at a time pulsing as you pour. 9) After 3 tablespoons of the liquid, check the dough for consistency. It should hold together when compressed but remain relatively dry to the touch. If it does not bind, add a little more liquid. 10) Remove from the processor and form the dough into a ball. 11) Wrap the dough in waxed paper or parchment paper and rest in refrigerator for 20 minutes. 12) Heat a cast iron skillet over medium heat.
<u>For the filling:</u> **2 Anjou pears, peeled, cored, and thinly sliced**	13) Add pears to the pan and toss for 2 minutes.
3 tablespoons balsamic vinegar	14) Add the balsamic vinegar and continue to toss for 30 seconds.
4 tablespoons sugar	15) Add sugar and cook until the pears have softened.
1 pinch grated nutmeg **1/4 teaspoon ground cinnamon** **2 tablespoons butter**	16) Add the nutmeg, cinnamon, and the butter and melt slowly.
1 cup blueberries	17) Fold in the blueberries. 18) Remove from heat.
1 teaspoon flour	19) Sprinkle on the flour and combine well. Allow to cool to room temperature. 20) Place dough on a floured piece of parchment and roll out to a 1/4-inch thick disk. 21) Transfer to a baking sheet.
1 1/2 cups pound cake, cubed	22) Place cubed pound cake in the middle of the dough, leaving a 3-inch margin of crust on all sides. 23) Spoon filling over the cake cubes and top the pears with 1-ounce of cubed butter. 24) Lift excess crust onto filling and repeat in a clockwise fashion until a top lip has formed around the edge of the whole tart.
1 egg beaten with 1 tablespoon water **1/2 teaspoon sugar**	25) Brush the tart with the egg wash and sprinkle the crust with the sugar. 26) Bake for 30 to 35 minutes, or until the filling begins to bubble and the crust is golden brown. 27) Remove from the sheet pan immediately and cool on pie rack.

Difficulty: Medium **Prep Time:** 1 hour **Inactive Prep Time:** 20 minutes **Cook Time:** 35 minutes **Yield:** 1 pie

Notes:____

POCKET PIES

Episode: A Pie in Every Pocket, EA0913

Pastry: **9 1/2 ounces all-purpose flour, approximately 2 cups** **2 teaspoons baking powder** **3/4 teaspoon kosher salt**	**Pocket Pie Dough** 1) In the bowl of a food processor, combine the flour, baking powder and salt. 2) Pulse for a few seconds and then pour into a large mixing bowl.
2 1/2 ounces shortening, approximately 6 tablespoons	3) Add the shortening and knead it into the flour with your hands until it is crumbly.
3/4 cup milk **1 egg mixed with 1 to 2 teaspoons water**	4) Add the milk all at once and mix in with a spatula until it begins to come together. 5) Lightly flour your hands and the countertop and turn the dough out onto the countertop. 6) Knead the dough ball, folding over 10 to 20 times. **To Make Pocket Pies** 7) Using a rolling pin roll the dough to 1/3 to 1/2-inch thickness, then cut into rounds using a 2 1/4-inch ring. 8) Roll each round as thinly as possible or to 5 to 6 inches in diameter.
Curried Mango Filling, recipe follows **Chocolate Filling, recipe follows**	9) Spoon 1 to 2 tablespoons of filling onto the dough, brush the edges of half of the dough lightly with the egg wash, fold over and seal the edges together with the tines of a fork, dipping it into flour as needed. 10) Gently press down to flatten and evenly distribute the filling and snip or cut 3 slits in the top of the pie. 11) Dock pies that are going to be deep-fried, instead of snipping or cutting slits.
Vegetable, canola oil or butter, for frying	12) To pan-fry pies, place a medium sauté pan over medium low heat along with 1 to 2 tablespoons vegetable, canola oil or butter. 13) Once heated, place 2 to 3 pies at a time into pan and sauté until golden on both sides, approximately 3 to 4 minutes per side. 14) Allow to cool 4 to 5 minutes before serving. 15) To deep-fry pies, heat vegetable oil in a deep-fryer or a large heavy pot to 375 degrees F. 16) Once hot, add 1 to 2 pies at a time and fry until golden brown, approximately 3 to 4 minutes. 17) To bake pies, preheat the oven to 350 degrees F. 18) Place finished pies onto an ungreased cookie sheet and bake for 25 to 30 minutes or until golden brown.

To Make Toaster Pastries

1) Preheat oven to 350 degrees F.
2) Divide dough in half and roll out to less than 1/8-inch thick.
3) Cut into 4 inch by 5 inch rectangles.
4) Place 1 to 2 tablespoons of filling onto center of one piece of dough.
5) Brush the edges with egg wash and top with second piece of dough.
6) Seal edges by pressing together with tine of fork.
7) Gently press down to flatten and evenly distribute the filling and dock the top of the pie.
8) Repeat with second half of dough.
9) Bake for 20 minutes.
10) Remove from the oven, allow to cool completely and place into zip-top bags until ready to toast.
11) The pies will not be brown until toasted.

Continued →

← Continued from Previous Page

Curried Mango Filling: **4 mangos, peeled and diced, approximately 2 cups or 12 ounces** **1/2 cup brown sugar** **1/2 cup cider vinegar** **2 teaspoons curry powder** **1/4 cup freshly squeezed lime juice**	1) Place all of the ingredients into a small saucepan over high heat and bring to a boil. 2) Reduce the heat to low, cover and simmer for 30 minutes, stirring occasionally. 3) Transfer to a bowl and place in refrigerator to cool completely before using as filling. 4) For each pie place 1 to 2 tablespoons onto the center of the dough. Follow directions above. Yield: enough for 10 to 15 pies
Chocolate Filling: **2 1/2 cups sugar** **1/4 cup plus 1 tablespoon cocoa powder** **Pinch kosher salt** **10 ounces unsalted butter, room temperature**	1) Place the sugar, cocoa powder, salt, and butter into a large zip-top bag and squish to combine. 2) Cut a hole in 1 corner of the bag. 3) For each pie, pipe 1 to 2 tablespoons of mixture onto the center of the dough. Follow directions above. Yield: enough for 10 to 15 pies

Difficulty: Medium **Prep Time:** 40 minutes **Inactive Prep Time:** 2 hours **Cook Time:** 30 minutes **Yield:** 10 to 15 pies or 8 to 10 toaster pastries

Other

ACID JELLIES

Episode: The Tricks to Treats, EA1G13

1 1/4 cups water **8 envelopes gelatin** **1/4 cup freshly squeezed lime juice** **1/2 cup freshly squeezed lemon juice**	1) In small saucepan, combine 1/2 cup of water, gelatin, lime juice, and lemon juice. Set aside.
1 1/4 cups sugar	2) In heavy small saucepan, place over medium heat, combine remaining 3/4 cup of water and 1 cup sugar and stir until sugar dissolves. 3) Bring to a boil, cover and cook for 3 minutes. 4) Remove lid and place candy thermometer on side of pan and cook until it reaches 300 degrees F. 5) Remove from heat, add to gelatin mixture, return pan to low heat and stir constantly in order to dissolve gelatin completely.
2 tablespoons grated lime zest **2 tablespoons grated lemon zest**	6) Add lemon and lime zest and stir to combine.
Non-stick spray, for greasing pan	7) Pour mixture into greased 8-inch by 8-inch pan and cool to room temperature. Do not refrigerate. 8) Once cooled, cut into cubes and toss to coat in the remaining sugar. 9) Store in airtight container for up to 4 days.

Difficulty: Medium **Prep Time:** 20 minutes **Inactive Prep Time:** 4 hours **Cook Time:** 10 minutes **Yield:** 64 1-in servings

Notes:

CHERRY COUSCOUS PUDDING

Episode: Ill Gotten Grains, EA1G07

1/2 cup milk **3 tablespoons sugar** **1/4 cup dried cherries**	1) Heat milk, sugar and cherries in medium saucepan over medium heat. 2) Bring to simmer, remove from heat, cover and let steep for 10 minutes.
1 vanilla bean, pulp scraped	3) Add pulp from vanilla bean to milk and whisk to combine.
1 1/2 cups steamed couscous **1 (8-ounce) container vanilla flavored yogurt**	4) Pour mixture over couscous in bowl and add yogurt. Stir to combine.
1/4 teaspoon ground cinnamon	5) Divide evenly among 4 custard cups, sprinkle with cinnamon and refrigerate for 1 hour.

Difficulty: Easy **Prep Time:** 5 minutes **Inactive Prep Time:** 1 hour **Cook Time:** 10 minutes **Yield:** 4 servings

COCOA WHIPPED CREAM

Episode: A Cake on Every Plate, EA1F13

2 tablespoons water **1 teaspoon gelatin**	1) Place your mixing bowl and whisk into the refrigerator to chill. 2) In a metal measuring cup or a very small saucepan combine the water and the gelatin. 3) Let this sit for 5 minutes then place over low heat for 2 minutes to melt.
2 cups heavy cream **1/2 cup Good Eats Cocoa Mix, (recipe in cookbook)**	4) With your mixer on low combine the cream and the cocoa in the chilled bowl. 5) Drizzle in the melted gelatin.
1 teaspoon vanilla extract	6) Add the vanilla and turn mixer to high and whip to medium peaks.

Difficulty: Easy **Prep Time:** 10 minutes **Cook Time:** 2 minutes **Yield:** enough for a 2 layers, 9-inch cakes

"Find something you're passionate about and keep tremendously interested in it."

Julia Child, The Mother of TV Cooking

August 15, 1912 – August 13, 2004

FLANDANGO

Episode: The Egg Files II: Man with a Flan, EA1C03

Hardware:

Roasting pan large enough to accommodate 8 custard cups with at least 1-inch to spare around 8 custard cups
Glass or stainless steel bowl with a spout
Fine mesh strainer
Small non-reactive saucepan
A kettle boiling water
Whisk

	1) Heat oven to 350° F.
1 1/2 cups whole milk **1 cup half-and- half** **1 teaspoon vanilla extract** **1/2 cup sugar**	2) In the saucepan, combine the milk, half-and-half, vanilla, and sugar. 3) Bring to a bare simmer over medium-low heat.
An assortment of jams, preserves, or dessert sauces such as: **Blueberry jam** **Apricot preserves** **Butterscotch ice cream topping** **Hot fudge ice cream topping**	4) Next, place 1 to 2 tablespoons of each topping into each of the custard cups. The topping should come a few millimeters up the side of the custard cup.
6 eggs	5) Separate 3 of the eggs using the slotted spoon. Reserve the whites. (Note: Freeze the whites in ice trays. After the whites are frozen, place the frozen cubes into zip-top freezer bags. The frozen whites can be frozen up to a year.) 6) Place a mixing bowl on a rubber pad or a wet towel to prevent the bowl from spinning out of control. 7) In a mixing bowl, combine the remaining whole eggs and the yolks. 8) Whip the eggs with a whisk until slightly thickened and lightened in color. 9) While whisking the eggs, drizzle in about a quarter of the hot milk. 10) Now whisk the tempered eggs back into the saucepan with the remaining milk mixture. 11) Place a fine mesh strainer over a glass or stainless steel bowl with a spout. 12) Pour the egg mixture through the strainer in order to catch any curdled egg bits or particles that may be in the mixture. 13) Place the custard cups into the roasting pan. 14) Evenly distribute the custard into the custard cups, going short on the first pass. 15) Place the pan on the middle rack of the oven and pour boiling water into the pan just under the level of the custard. 16) Cook the flans for about 40 minutes, or until they wobble slightly when the pan is wiggled, about 40 minutes. You can also insert a paring knife midway between the edge and the center. If it comes out clean, the flans are done. 17) Using tongs, remove the cups from the pan to a towel-lined sheet pan. 18) Allow the water in the roasting pan to cool before discarding. Cool, cover and chill.

Difficulty: Easy **Prep Time:** 30 minutes **Cook Time:** 2 hours 40 minutes **Yield:** 8 servings

Notes:____

INDIAN RICE PUDDING

Episode: Puddin' Head Blues, EA1H03

1 cup cooked long grain or basmati rice **1 cup whole milk**	1) In a large nonstick sauté pan over medium heat, combine the cooked rice and milk. 2) Heat until the mixture begins to boil. 3) Decrease the heat to low and cook at a simmer until the mixture begins to thicken, stirring frequently, approximately 5 minutes.
1/2 cup heavy cream **3/4 cup coconut milk** **2 ounces sugar, approximately 1/4 cup** **1/4 teaspoon ground cardamom**	4) Increase the heat to medium, add the heavy cream, coconut milk, sugar, and cardamom and continue to cook until the mixture just begins to thicken again, approximately 5 to 10 minutes. Use a whisk to help prevent the cardamom from clumping.
1 1/2 ounces golden raisins, approximately 1/3 cup **1 1/2 ounces chopped unsalted pistachios, approximately 1/3 cup**	5) Once the mixture just begins to thicken, remove from the heat and stir in the raisins and pistachios. 6) Transfer the mixture to individual serving dishes or a glass bowl and place plastic wrap directly on the surface of the pudding. 7) Serve chilled or at room temperature.

Difficulty: Easy **Prep Time:** 10 minutes **Inactive Prep Time:** 1 hour **Cook Time:** 20 minutes **Yield:** 4 servings

PEANUT BRITTLE

Episode: The Tricks to Treats, EA1G13

1 1/2 cups lightly salted, roasted peanuts **1/2 teaspoon cinnamon** **1/2 teaspoon cayenne pepper**	1) In a small bowl combine peanuts, cinnamon, and cayenne. Set aside.
Vegetable oil, for coating the saucepan	2) Brush the inside of a medium sized heavy saucepan with vegetable oil.
3 cups sugar **1 1/2 cups water**	3) Add the sugar and water to the saucepan, cook over high heat, stirring occasionally with a wooden spoon, until it comes to a boil. 4) Stop stirring, cover and cook for 3 minutes. 5) Uncover, reduce heat to medium, and cook until the sugar is a light amber color. 6) Stir in peanuts. This will greatly reduce the temperature of the sugar so work quickly. 7) Once evenly mixed, pour mixture onto a sheet pan lined with a silicone baking mat or buttered parchment paper.
Softened butter for spatula	8) Using a buttered spatula, spread thin. You will have to work quickly when pouring out and spreading the mixture in the pan. If necessary, in order to achieve single layer of peanuts, top with second sheet pan whose underside has been buttered. 9) Cool completely and then break into pieces.

Difficulty: Medium **Prep Time:** 10 minutes **Inactive Prep Time:** 30 minutes **Cook Time:** 20 minutes **Yield:** 4 cups

PEANUT BUTTER FUDGE

Episode: Fudge Factor, EA1G05

1 cup butter, plus more for greasing pan **1 cup peanut butter**	1) Microwave butter and peanut butter for 2 minutes on high. 2) Stir and microwave on high for 2 more minutes.
1 teaspoon vanilla **1 pound powdered sugar**	3) Add vanilla and powdered sugar to peanut butter mixture and stir to combine with a wooden spoon. 4) Pour into a buttered 8 by 8-inch pan lined with waxed paper. 5) Place a second piece of waxed paper on the surface of the fudge and refrigerate until cool. 6) Cut into 1-inch pieces and store in an airtight container for up to a week.

Difficulty: Easy **Prep Time:** 10 minutes **Inactive Prep Time:** 1 hour **Cook Time:** 4 minutes **Yield:** 64 1-in pieces

SWEET OR SAVORY PATE A CHOUX

Episode: Choux Shine, EA1F09

1 cup water **3/4 stick butter (6 tablespoons)** **1 tablespoon sugar plus 1/8 teaspoon salt (for sweet)** **1 teaspoon salt (for savory)**	1) Preheat oven to 425 degrees F. 2) Boil water, butter, and salt or sugar.
5 3/4 ounces flour	3) Add flour and remove from heat. 4) Work mixture together and return to heat. 5) Continue working the mixture until all flour is incorporated and dough forms a ball. 6) Transfer mixture into bowl of a standing mixer and let cool for 3 or 4 minutes.
1 cup eggs, about 4 large eggs and 2 whites	7) With mixer on stir or lowest speed add eggs, 1 at a time, making sure the first egg is completely incorporated before continuing. 8) Once all eggs have been added and the mixture is smooth put dough into piping bag fitted with a round tip. 9) Pipe immediately into golf ball-size shapes, 2 inches apart onto parchment lined sheet pans. 10) Cook for 10 minutes, then turn the oven down to 350 degrees F and bake for 10 more minutes or until golden brown. 11) Once they are removed from the oven pierce with a paring knife immediately to release steam.

Difficulty: Expert **Prep Time:** 5 minutes **Cook Time:** 30 minutes **Yield:** 4 dozen bite-sized cream puffs

Notes:

TAPIOCA PUDDING

Episode: Puddin' Head Blues, EA1H03

3 1/2 ounces large pearl tapioca, approximately 1/2 cup **2 cups cold water**	1) Place tapioca in a medium mixing bowl along with the water, cover, and let stand overnight.
2 1/2 cups whole milk **1/2 cup heavy cream** **Pinch salt**	2) Drain water from tapioca. Place the tapioca into a slow cooker along with the milk, heavy cream, and salt. 3) Cook on high for 2 hours, stirring occasionally.
1 egg yolk **1/3 cup sugar**	4) In a small bowl, whisk together the egg yolk and sugar. 5) Temper small amounts of the tapioca into the egg mixture until you have added at least 1 cup. 6) Then add this back into the remaining tapioca in the slow cooker.
1 lemon, zested	7) Add the lemon zest and stir to combine. 8) Cook for an additional 15 minutes, stirring at least once. 9) Transfer the pudding to a bowl and cover the surface with plastic wrap. 10) Allow to cool at room temperature for 1 hour and then place in the refrigerator until thoroughly chilled.

Difficulty: Medium **Prep Time:** 10 minutes **Inactive Prep Time:** 14 hours **Cook Time:** 2 hrs 15 min **Yield:** 4 servings

VANILLA SUGAR

Episode: The Pouch Principal, EA1G08

1 vanilla bean, whole or scraped **2 cups granulated sugar**	1) If vanilla bean is whole, slice down side of bean with back of knife and scrape seeds into airtight container with the sugar. 2) Bury bean in sugar and seal tightly with lid. 3) Let sit for 1 to 2 weeks. 4) Use as regular, granulated sugar.

Difficulty: Easy **Prep Time:** 5 minutes **Yield:** 2 Cups

ENTREES

Beef

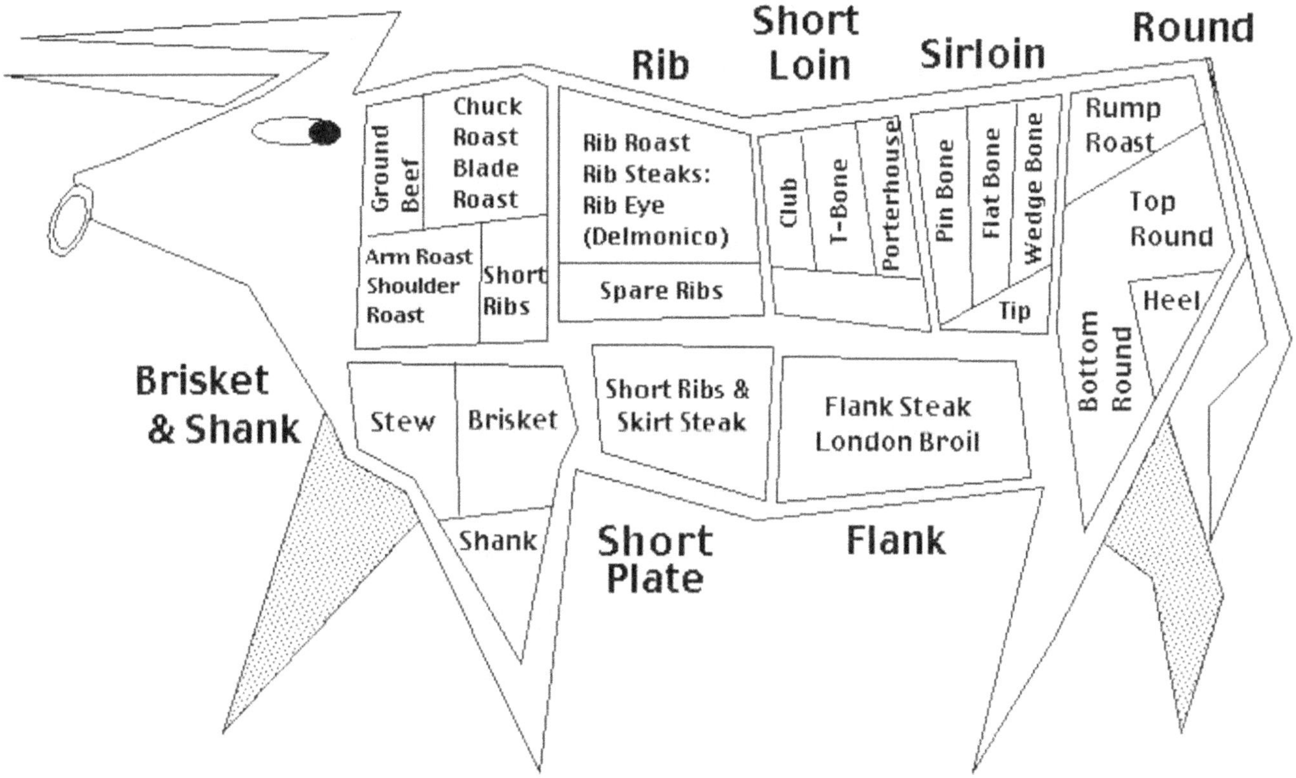

Figure 4: Good Eats Beef Map

BURGER OF THE GODS

Episode: A Grind is a Terrible Thing to Waste, EA1B11

8 ounces chuck, trimmed, cut into 1 1/2-inch cubes **8 ounces sirloin, trimmed, cut into 1 1/2-inch cubes**	1) In separate batches, pulse the chuck and the sirloin in a food processor 10 times.
1/2 teaspoon kosher salt	2) Combine the chuck, sirloin, and kosher salt in a large bowl. Form the meat into 5-ounce patties. 3) Heat a cast iron skillet or griddle over medium-high heat for 2 to 3 minutes. 4) Place the hamburger patties in the pan. 5) For medium-rare burgers, cook the patties for 4 minutes on each side. For medium burgers, cook the patties for 5 minutes on each side. 6) Flip the burgers only once during cooking.

Difficulty: Easy **Prep Time:** 15 minutes **Cook Time:** 10 minutes **Yield:** 3 servings

Notes:____

MINI MAN BURGERS

Episode: The Man Food Show, EA1G16

1/2 teaspoon onion powder **1/2 teaspoon garlic powder** **1/2 teaspoon freshly ground black pepper** **1/2 teaspoon kosher salt**	1) Preheat the oven to 250 degrees F. 2) Preheat a griddle to 350 degrees F. 3) Combine the onion powder, garlic powder, pepper, and salt in a small bowl. Set aside.
1 pound ground chuck	4) Line a jellyroll or sheet pan with parchment paper, and place the ground chuck in the middle of the pan. 5) Cover the meat with a large sheet of plastic wrap. 6) Roll meat with a rolling pin until it covers the surface of the pan; it should be very thin. 7) Remove the plastic wrap, and sprinkle the meat with the seasoning mixture. 8) Fold the meat in half, from side to side, using the parchment paper. 9) Use a pizza wheel to cut the meat into 8 even squares.
8 (3-inch) buns or rolls, split in half	10) Wrap the buns in foil and place in the oven for 5 to 10 minutes. 11) Meanwhile, place the burgers on the griddle and cook for 2 to 3 minutes per side. 12) Remove the buns from the oven.
2 to 3 tablespoons mayonnaise	13) Spread a small amount of mayonnaise on each bun and top with the burger and any other condiments, as desired. Serve immediately.

Difficulty: Easy **Prep Time:** 5 minutes **Cook Time:** 10 minutes **Yield:** 8 burgers

CORN DOGS

Episode: The Man Food Show, EA1G16

Special equipment: **8 sets chopsticks, not separated**	
1 gallon peanut oil	1) Pour oil into a deep fryer or large heavy pot and heat to 375 degrees F.
1 cup yellow cornmeal **1 cup all-purpose flour** **2 teaspoons kosher salt** **1 teaspoon baking powder** **1/4 teaspoon baking soda** **1/2 teaspoon cayenne pepper**	2) In a medium mixing bowl, combine the cornmeal, flour, salt, baking powder, baking soda, and cayenne pepper.
2 tablespoons (approximately 1 large) jalapeno pepper, seeded and finely minced **1 (8.5-ounce) can cream-style corn** **1/3 cup finely grated onion** **1 1/2 cups buttermilk**	3) In a separate bowl, combine the jalapeno, corn, onion, and buttermilk. 4) Add the dry ingredients to the wet ingredients all at once, and stir only enough times to bring the batter together; there should be lumps. Set batter aside and allow to rest for 10 minutes.
4 tablespoons cornstarch, for dredging	5) Scatter the cornstarch into a dry pie pan.
8 beef hot dogs	6) Roll each hot dog in the cornstarch and tap well to remove any excess. 7) Transfer enough batter to almost fill a large drinking glass. Refill the glass as needed. 8) Place each hot dog on chopsticks, and quickly dip in and out of the batter. 9) Immediately and carefully place each hot dog into the oil, and cook until coating is golden brown, about 4 to 5 minutes. 10) With tongs, remove to cooling rack, and allow to drain for 3 to 5 minutes.

Difficulty: Medium **Prep Time:** 20 minutes **Inactive Prep Time:** 15 minutes **Cook Time:** 5 minutes **Yield:** 8 corn dogs

GOOD EATS MEAT LOAF

Episode: A Grind is a Terrible Thing to Waste, EA1B11

	1) Heat oven to 325° F.
6 ounces garlic-flavored croutons **1/2 teaspoon ground black pepper** **1/2 teaspoon cayenne pepper** **1 teaspoon chili powder** **1 teaspoon dried thyme**	2) In a food processor bowl, combine croutons, black pepper, cayenne pepper, chili powder, and thyme. 3) Pulse until the mixture is of a fine texture. Place this mixture into a large bowl.
1/2 onion, roughly chopped **1 carrot, peeled and broken** **3 whole cloves garlic** **1/2 red bell pepper**	4) Combine the onion, carrot, garlic, and red pepper in the food processor bowl. Pulse until the mixture is finely chopped, but not pureed.
18 ounces ground chuck **18 ounces ground sirloin**	5) Combine the vegetable mixture, ground sirloin, and ground chuck with the bread crumb mixture.
1 1/2 teaspoon kosher salt	6) Season the meat mixture with the kosher salt.
1 egg	7) Add the egg and combine thoroughly, but avoid squeezing the meat. 8) Pack this mixture into a 10-inch loaf pan to mold the shape of the meatloaf. 9) Onto a parchment paper-lined baking sheet, turn the meatloaf out of the pan onto the center of the tray. Insert a temperature probe at a 45 degree angle into the top of the meatloaf. Avoid touching the bottom of the tray with the probe. Set the probe for 155°.
1/2 cup catsup **1 tablespoon ground cumin** **Dash Worcestershire sauce** **Dash hot pepper sauce** **1 tablespoon honey**	10) Combine the catsup, cumin, Worcestershire sauce, hot pepper sauce and honey. 11) Brush the glaze onto the meatloaf after it has been cooking for about 10 minutes.

Difficulty: Easy **Prep Time:** 25 minutes **Cook Time:** 45 minutes **Yield:** 6 to 8 servings

BAKED MEATBALLS

Episode: Great Balls of Meat, EA0910

1/2 pound ground pork **1/2 pound ground lamb** **1/2 pound ground round** **5 ounces frozen spinach, thawed and drained thoroughly** **1/2 cup finely grated Parmesan** **1 whole egg** **1 1/2 teaspoons dried basil** **1 1/2 teaspoons dried parsley** **1 teaspoon garlic powder** **1 teaspoon kosher salt** **1/2 teaspoon red pepper flakes** **1/2 cup bread crumbs, divided**	1) Preheat the oven to 400 degrees F. 2) In a large mixing bowl, combine the pork, lamb, ground round, spinach, cheese, egg, basil, parsley, garlic powder, salt, red pepper flakes, and 1/4 cup of the bread crumbs. 3) Using your hands, mix all ingredients until well incorporated. Use immediately or place in refrigerator for up to 24 hours. 4) Place the remaining 1/4 cup of bread crumbs into a small bowl. 5) Using a scale, weigh meatballs into 1.5-ounce portions and place on a sheet pan. 6) Using your hands, shape the meatballs into rounds, roll in the bread crumbs and place the meatballs in individual, miniature muffin tin cups. 7) Bake for 20 minutes or until golden and cooked through.

Difficulty: Easy **Prep Time:** 20 minutes **Cook Time:** 20 minutes **Yield:** 20 meatballs, 4 to 5 servings

Notes:____

SWEDISH MEATBALLS

Episode: Great Balls of Meat, EA0910

2 slices fresh white bread **1/4 cup milk**	1) Preheat oven to 200 degrees F. 2) Tear the bread into pieces and place in a small mixing bowl along with the milk. Set aside.
3 tablespoons clarified butter, divided	3) In a 12-inch straight sided sauté pan over medium heat, melt 1 tablespoon of the butter.
1/2 cup finely chopped onion **A pinch plus 1 teaspoon kosher salt**	4) Add the onion and a pinch of salt and sweat until the onions are soft. 5) Remove from the heat and set aside.
3/4 pound ground chuck **3/4 pound ground pork** **2 large egg yolks** **1/2 teaspoon black pepper** **1/4 teaspoon ground allspice** **1/4 teaspoon freshly grated nutmeg**	6) In the bowl of a stand mixer, combine the bread and milk mixture, ground chuck, pork, egg yolks, 1 teaspoon of kosher salt, black pepper, allspice, nutmeg, and onions. Beat on medium speed for 1 to 2 minutes. 7) Using a scale, weigh meatballs into 1-ounce portions and place on a sheet pan. 8) Using your hands, shape the meatballs into rounds. 9) Heat the remaining butter in the sauté pan over medium-low heat, or in an electric skillet set to 250 degrees F. 10) Add the meatballs and sauté until golden brown on all sides, about 7 to 10 minutes. 11) Remove the meatballs to an ovenproof dish using a slotted spoon and place in the warmed oven.
1/4 cup all-purpose flour	12) Once all of the meatballs are cooked, decrease the heat to low and add the flour to the pan or skillet. 13) Whisk until lightly browned, approximately 1 to 2 minutes.
3 cups beef broth	14) Gradually add the beef stock and whisk until sauce begins to thicken.
1/4 cup heavy cream	15) Add the cream and continue to cook until the gravy reaches the desired consistency. 16) Remove the meatballs from the oven, cover with the gravy and serve.

Difficulty: Easy **Prep Time:** 30 minutes **Cook Time:** 25 minutes **Yield:** approximately 30 meatballs, 4 to 6 servings

PAN SEARED RIB EYE

Episode: Steak Your Claim, EA1A01

1 boneless rib eye steak, 1 1/2-inch thick	1) Place 10 to 12-inch cast iron skillet in oven and heat oven to 500°. 2) Bring steak(s) to room temperature. 3) When oven reaches temperature, remove pan and place on range over high heat.
Canola oil to coat **Kosher salt**	4) Coat steak lightly with oil and season both sides with a generous pinch of salt.
Ground black pepper	5) Grind on black pepper to taste. 6) Immediately place steak in the middle of hot, dry pan. Cook 30 seconds without moving. 7) Turn with tongs and cook another 30 seconds, then put the pan straight into the oven for 2 minutes. 8) Flip steak and cook for another 2 minutes. (This time is for medium rare steaks. If you prefer medium, add a minute to both of the oven turns.) 9) Remove steak from pan, cover loosely with foil, and rest for 2 minutes. 10) Serve whole or slice thin and fan onto plate.

Difficulty: Easy **Prep Time:** 10 minutes **Cook Time:** 5 minutes **Yield:** 1 or 2 servings

POT ROAST

Episode: A Chuck for Chuck, EA1D12

	1) Preheat the oven to 190-200° F. 2) Place a wide, heavy skillet or fry pan over high heat for 2 minutes.
1 (2-pound) blade cut chuck roast **2 teaspoons kosher salt** **2 teaspoons cumin**	3) Meanwhile, rub both sides of meat with the salt and cumin. 4) When the pan is hot (really hot) brown meat on both sides and remove from pan.
Vegetable oil **1 medium onion, chopped** **5 to 6 cloves garlic, smashed**	5) Add just enough vegetable oil to cover the bottom of the pan then add the onion and garlic. Stir constantly until onion is softened.
1 cup tomato juice **1/3 cup balsamic vinegar** **1 cup cocktail olives, drained and broken** **1/2 cup dark raisins**	6) Add the tomato juice, vinegar, olives, and raisins. 7) Bring to a boil and reduce the liquid by half. 8) Create a pouch with wide, heavy-duty aluminum foil. 9) Place half the reduced liquid/chunk mixture on the foil, add the roast, and then top with the remaining mixture. 10) Close the pouch, and wrap tightly in another complete layer of foil. 11) Cook for 3 to 3 1/2 hours or until a fork pushes easily into the meat. 12) Remove from oven and rest (still wrapped) for at least 1/2 hour. 13) Snip off 1 corner of the foil pouch and drain the liquid into a bowl or measuring cup. 14) Add some of the "chunkies" and puree with an immersion blender. 15) Slice meat thinly, or pull apart with a fork. 16) Serve with sauce.

Difficulty: Easy **Prep Time:** 30 minutes **Cook Time:** 4 hours **Yield:** 3 to 6 servings

BRACIOLE: Tied Flank Steak

Episode: Fit to be Tied, EA1F17

3 cups tomato sauce	1) Preheat the oven to 350 degrees F. 2) Place the tomato sauce in a 9 by 13-inch baking dish and place in the oven to heat.
1 1/4 cups flavored croutons **1/3 cup grated Parmesan** **2 eggs** **1 tablespoon chopped fresh parsley** **1 tablespoon chopped fresh oregano** **1 teaspoon finely chopped rosemary** **1 teaspoon finely chopped thyme** **1 clove garlic**	3) In a the bowl of a food processor mix the croutons, cheese, eggs, herbs and garlic until it forms a paste.
1 pound flank steak, pounded to 1/4-inch thick **Olive oil, for brushing** **Salt and pepper**	4) Brush the pounded flank steak with the olive oil and season generously with the salt and pepper. 5) Spread the filling evenly over the meat. 6) Roll tightly and tie with butcher's twine.
Vegetable oil, for searing	7) In a large sauté pan heat 1 to 2 tablespoons of vegetable oil and sear all sides of the rolled meat. 8) Remove from the pan. 9) Add to the hot tomato sauce, cover with a tin foil tent so that the foil is not touching the meat. 10) Braise for 35 minutes or, up to 3 hours.

Difficulty: Medium **Prep Time:** 20 minutes **Cook Time:** 45 minutes **Yield:** 4 to 6 servings

Notes:____

SIRLOIN STEAK

Episode: Raising The Steaks, EA1G10

1 1/2 pounds sirloin steak, 1 to 1 1/4-inches thick **2 teaspoons olive oil** **Salt and freshly ground black pepper**	1) Preheat oven on broiler setting. 2) Make foil 'snake' out of aluminum foil to use to keep oven door slightly ajar so that broiler won't turn off if it gets too hot. 3) Brush steak with oil and salt and pepper, to taste. 4) Place a piece of foil on the bottom rack as a drip pan. 5) Place another rack in the position above this and put the steak directly on this rack. 6) Cook steak in this position for 5 minutes. 7) Flip steak and cook for another 5 minutes. 8) Move rack with steak to top position in oven, moving rack with foil and drippings just underneath, and cook for 3 minutes. 9) Flip 1 last time and cook for another 3 minutes. 10) Transfer steak to wire rack and rest for 3 to 5 minutes.
*The above times are for medium doneness. Adjust cooking times up or down as desired.	

Difficulty: Easy **Prep Time:** 2 minutes **Inactive Prep Time:** 5 minutes **Cook Time:** 16 minutes **Yield:** 4 servings

SKIRT STEAK

Episode: Raising The Steaks, EA1G10

Special equipment: **Blow dryer**	
1/2 cup olive oil **1/3 cup soy sauce** **4 scallions, washed and cut in 1/2** **2 large cloves garlic** **1/4 cup lime juice** **1/2 teaspoon red pepper flakes** **1/2 teaspoon ground cumin** **3 tablespoons dark brown sugar or Mexican brown sugar**	1) Heat charcoal, preferably natural chunk, until grey ash appears. 2) In a blender, put in oil, soy sauce, scallions, garlic, lime juice, red pepper, cumin, and sugar and puree.
2 pounds inside skirt steak, cut into 3 equal pieces	3) In a large heavy duty, zip top bag, put pieces of skirt steak and pour in marinade. 4) Seal bag, removing as much air as possible. 5) Allow steak to marinate for 1 hour in refrigerator. 6) Remove steak from bag and pat dry with paper towels. 7) Using a blow dryer, blow charcoal clean of ash. 8) Once clean of ash lay steaks directly onto hot coals for 1 minute per side. 9) When finished cooking, place meat in double thickness of aluminum foil, wrap, and allow to sit for 15 minutes. 10) Remove meat from foil, reserving foil and juices. 11) Slice thinly across the grain of the meat. 12) Return to foil pouch and toss with juice. 13) Serve with grilled peppers and onions, if desired.

Difficulty: Easy **Prep Time:** 10 minutes **Inactive Prep Time:** 75 minutes **Cook Time:** 2 minutes
Yield: 8 servings as fajita meat, 4 as a main course

STRIP STEAK WITH PEPPER CREAM SAUCE

Episode: Hittin' The Sauce, EA1H01

4 (6 to 8-ounce) strip steaks, 3/4 to 1-inch thick **Kosher salt** **2 teaspoons black peppercorns, coarsely crushed**	1) Preheat oven to 200 degrees F. 2) Sprinkle steaks with kosher salt and crushed black pepper.
2 tablespoons clarified, unsalted butter	3) Heat butter in a 12-inch, heavy bottomed sauté pan over medium heat. 4) Once butter is hot, add steaks and cook until browned on both sides, about 2 minutes per side for medium-rare and 3 minutes per side for medium. 5) Remove steaks from pan and place on a rack set on a sheet pan; place in oven to keep warm.
3/4 cup beef stock or broth	6) Add the stock to the sauté pan and whisk until the crispy bits release from bottom of pan. Allow the liquid to reduce for 3 to 4 minutes over medium-high heat.
3 tablespoons cognac **3/4 cup heavy cream** **1 tablespoon green peppercorns in brine, drained and slightly crushed**	7) Add cognac, heavy cream, and green peppercorns to the pan. 8) Increase heat to high and cook, whisking continually, until sauce thickens slightly, just enough to coat the back of a spoon; this will take 5 to 7 minutes. 9) Season the sauce, to taste, with kosher salt. 10) Place steaks on plates, top with sauce, and serve immediately.

Difficulty: Easy **Prep Time:** 12 minutes **Cook Time:** 18 minutes **Yield:** 4x servings

BEEF PAILLARD

Episode: Flat is Beautiful II, EA1H03

1 pound beef tenderloin, trimmed	1) Place tenderloin in the freezer for 2 hours. 2) Preheat the oven to 200 degrees F. 3) Remove the tenderloin from the freezer. Using an electric knife, cut the beef into 3/8-inch thick slices. 4) Place slices of beef, 1 at a time, between 2 pieces of plastic wrap. 5) Squirt the beef lightly with water and squirt the top of the plastic wrap as well. 6) Pound to no less than 1/8-inch thickness.
Vegetable oil **Kosher salt** **Freshly ground black pepper**	7) Lightly brush each slice of beef on both sides with vegetable oil and season with salt and pepper on both sides. Set aside. 8) Heat a large cast iron skillet over high heat for 3 to 4 minutes. 9) Reduce heat to medium and turn skillet upside down over burner. 10) Brush the pan lightly with oil. 11) Place 2 to 3 slices of beef on the pan at a time and sear for 10 seconds on each side. 12) Remove to an ovenproof platter and keep in warm oven. 13) Repeat until all of the beef has been cooked. Serve immediately.

Difficulty: Easy **Prep Time:** 15 minutes **Inactive Prep Time:** 2 hours **Cook Time:** 10 minutes **Yield:** 4 servings

Notes:____

BEEF TENDERLOIN IN SALT CRUST

Episode: Eat This Rock!, EASP03

Ingredients	Directions
5 cups all-purpose flour **3 cups kosher salt** **3 tablespoons fresh ground black pepper**	1) Place the flour, salt and pepper in a large mixing bowl.
5 egg whites **1 1/2 cups water** **1/2 cup chopped fresh herbs (parsley, thyme, and/or sage)**	2) In another bowl, whisk the egg whites and water and add to the dry ingredients along with 2 tablespoons of the herbs. 3) Combine with a potato masher until the mixture begins to come together. 4) Then knead with your hands for 1 to 2 minutes. 5) Transfer the mixture to a large zip-top bag, seal, and let stand at room temperature for 4 hours, or up to 24 hours. 6) Transfer dough to a floured surface and roll out to 3/16-inch thickness, approximately a 24 by 18-inch rectangle. Trim away extra dough, if necessary. 7) Sprinkle the remaining herbs on the center section of the dough and gently press down. 8) Preheat oven to 400 degrees F.
1 (6 to 7-pound) whole beef tenderloin, trimmed	9) In order to achieve uniform cooking, fold over slender tail end of tenderloin and tie with kitchen twine.
1 tablespoon olive oil	10) Set a large electric griddle at its highest setting; brush the tenderloin with the olive oil and sear on all sides until well browned, approximately 10 minutes. 11) Rest the meat for at least 5 minutes or until it is cool to the touch so as not to melt the dough. 12) Place the tenderloin in the center of the dough. 13) Fold top part of dough over, flipping back about 1-inch of dough onto itself. Repeat with the bottom half of the dough. 14) Press together the 2 flaps of dough and seal. Make sure the dough is not too tight around the tenderloin. 15) At the ends of the tenderloin, press together dough to form a seal and cut away any excess. 16) Transfer to a sheet pan, place in the oven and roast to an internal temperature of 125 degrees F, approximately 25 to 30 minutes. 17) Remove from the oven and allow to rest for 30 minutes or up to 1 hour. 18) The tenderloin will continue to cook 10 to 15 degrees more. 19) Cut salt crust at 1 end and extract meat by pulling out of dough tube. Slice and serve immediately.

Difficulty: Medium **Prep Time:** x minutes **Inactive Prep Time:** x minutes **Cook Time:** x minutes **Yield:** x servings

DRY AGED STANDING RIB ROAST WITH SAGE JUS

Episode: Celebrity Roast, EA1D02

1 (4-bone-in) standing rib roast, preferably from the loin end	1) Remove any plastic wrapping or butcher's paper from the roast. 2) Place the standing rib roast upright onto a half sheet pan fitted with a rack. The rack is essential for drainage. 3) Place dry towels loosely on top of the roast. This will help to draw moisture away from the meat. 4) Place into a refrigerator at approximately 50 to 60 percent humidity and between 34 and 38° F. You can measure both with a refrigerator thermometer. Change the towels daily for 3 days. 5) Place a 16-inch round azalea terra cotta planter into a cold oven. Invert the planter to become a lid over a pizza stone or the bottom of the planter. The oven should be cold to start, to avoid any cracking in the terra cotta pieces. 6) Turn the oven to 250° F.
Canola oil, to coat roast	7) Remove the roast from the refrigerator and rub with canola oil. Remember to rub the bones with oil, as well.
Kosher salt and freshly ground pepper, to cover entire roast	8) Once the roast is completely coated with oil cover the roast with kosher salt, about half a teaspoon per bone. 9) Next, rub with freshly ground pepper to coat the surface. 10) Place the roast over a glass bake-ware dish slightly smaller than the length of the roast. This will catch the drippings needed for the sauce. 11) Finally, place a probe thermometer into the center of the roast and set for 118°. 12) Put the roast and the bake-ware dish onto the pizza stone, cover with the terra cotta pot, and return to the oven. 13) Turn the oven down to 200° F and roast until internal temperature is achieved. 14) Remove the roast and turn oven up to 500° F. 15) Remove the terra cotta lid and recover with heavy-duty foil. 16) Allow the roast to rest until an internal temperature of 130° F. is reached. 17) Place the roast back into the preheated 500 degree F oven for about 10 minutes or until you've achieved your desired crust. 18) Remove and transfer roast to a cutting board. Keep covered with foil until ready to serve.
1 cup water	19) Degrease the juices in the glass pan. Place the pan over low heat and deglaze with 1 cup of water.
1 cup red wine	20) Add the wine and reduce by half.
4 fresh sage leaves	21) Roll the sage leaves in between your fingers to release the flavors and aroma. 22) Add to the sauce and cook for 1 minute. 23) Strain and serve on the side.

Difficulty: Easy **Prep Time:** 35 minutes + 3 days **Cook Time:** 4 hours **Yield:** 10 servings

Notes:

SAUERBRATEN

Episode: Good Wine Gone Bad, EA0908

2 cups water **1 cup cider vinegar** **1 cup red wine vinegar** **1 medium onion, chopped** **1 large carrot, chopped** **1 tablespoon plus 1 teaspoon kosher salt, additional for seasoning meat** **1/2 teaspoon freshly ground black pepper** **2 bay leaves** **6 whole cloves** **12 juniper berries** **1 teaspoon mustard seeds**	1) In a large saucepan over high heat combine the water, cider vinegar, red wine vinegar, onion, carrot, salt, pepper, bay leaves, cloves, juniper, and mustard seeds. 2) Cover and bring this to a boil, then lower the heat and simmer for 10 minutes. Set aside to cool.
1 (3 1/2 to 4-pound) bottom round **1 tablespoon vegetable oil**	3) Pat the bottom round dry and rub with vegetable oil and salt on all sides. 4) Heat a large sauté pan over high heat; add the meat and brown on all sides, approximately 2 to 3 minutes per side. 5) When the marinade has cooled to a point where you can stick your finger in it and not be burned, place the meat in a non-reactive vessel and pour over the marinade. 6) Place into the refrigerator for 3 days. If the meat is not completely submerged in the liquid, turn it over once a day. 7) After 3 days of marinating, preheat the oven to 325 degrees F.
1/3 cup sugar	8) Add the sugar to the meat and marinade, cover and place on the middle rack of the oven and cook until tender, approximately 4 hours. 9) Remove the meat from the vessel and keep warm. 10) Strain the liquid to remove the solids. 11) Return the liquid to the pan and place over medium-high heat.
18 dark old-fashioned gingersnaps (about 5 ounces), crushed	12) Whisk in the gingersnaps and cook until thickened, stirring occasionally. 13) Strain the sauce through a fine mesh sieve to remove any lumps.
1/2 cup seedless raisins, optional	14) Add the raisins if desired. 15) Slice the meat and serve with the sauce.

Difficulty: Easy **Prep Time:** 30 minutes **Inactive Prep Time:** 3 days **Cook Time:** 4 hrs 20 min **Yield:** 4 to 6 servings

SPICY BEEF KABABS

Episode: Dis-Kabob-Ulated, EA0903

Special equipment: 4 (12-inch) metal skewers	
1 1/2 to 2 pounds boneless beef sirloin	1) Cut the beef into 1 1/2 to 1 3/4-inch cubes and place into a large mixing bowl. Set aside.
3 cloves garlic, minced **2 teaspoons smoked paprika** **1/2 teaspoon ground turmeric** **1 teaspoon ground cumin** **1 teaspoon kosher salt** **1/2 teaspoon freshly ground black pepper** **1/3 cup red wine vinegar** **1/2 cup olive oil**	2) In the bowl of a food processor combine the garlic, paprika, turmeric, cumin, salt, pepper and red wine vinegar. 3) With the processor running drizzle in the olive oil. 4) Pour the marinade over the meat and toss to coat. 5) Place in the refrigerator in an airtight container or a sealable plastic bag and allow to marinate for 2 to 4 hours. 6) Preheat the grill to medium-high heat. 7) Thread the meat onto the skewers leaving about 1/2-inch in between the pieces of meat. 8) Place on the grill and cook, with lid lowered, 2 to 3 minutes per side, 8 to 12 minutes in all (8 minutes for rare and 12 for medium). 9) Remove from the heat to aluminum foil, wrap and allow to rest for 2 to 3 minutes prior to serving.

Difficulty: Easy **Prep Time:** 20 minutes **Inactive Prep Time:** 2 hours **Cook Time:** 12 minutes **Yield:** 4 servings

CITY HAM

Episode: Ham I Am, EA1D06

	1) Heat oven to 350° F.
1 city style (brined) ham, hock end*	2) Remove ham from bag, rinse and drain thoroughly. 3) Place ham, cut side down, in a roasting pan. 4) Using a small paring knife or clean utility knife set to the smallest blade setting, score the ham from bottom to top, spiraling clockwise as you cut. (If you're using a paring knife, be careful to only cut through the skin and first few layers of fat). 5) Rotate the ham after each cut so that the scores are no more than 2-inches across. 6) Once you've made it all the way around, move the knife to the other hand and repeat, spiraling counter clockwise. The aim is to create a diamond pattern all over the ham. (Don't worry too much about precision here.) 7) Tent the ham with heavy duty foil, insert a thermometer, and cook for 3 to 4 hours or until the internal temperature at the deepest part of the meat registers 130° F. 8) Remove and use tongs to pull away the diamonds of skin and any sheets of fat that come off with them.
1/4 cup brown mustard	9) Dab dry with paper towels, then brush on a liberal coat of mustard, using either a basting brush or a clean paint brush (clean as in never-touched paint).
2 cups dark brown sugar	10) Sprinkle on brown sugar, packing loosely as you go until the ham is coated.
1-ounce bourbon (poured into a spritz bottle) **2 cups crushed ginger snap cookies**	11) Spritz this layer lightly with bourbon, then loosely pack on as much of the crushed cookies as you can. 12) Insert the thermometer (don't use the old hole) and return to the oven (uncovered). 13) Cook until interior temperature reaches 140° F, approximately 1 hour. 14) Let the roast rest for 1/2 hour before carving.

Difficulty: Easy **Prep Time:** 15 minutes **Cook Time:** 6 hours **Yield:** 10 to 15 portions, depending on beginning weight

*Cook's note: A city ham is basically any brined ham that's packed in a plastic bag, held in a refrigerated case and marked "ready to cook", "partially cooked" or "ready to serve". Better city hams are also labeled "ham in natural juices".

Notes:____

COUNTRY HAM

Episode: Ham I Am, EA1D06

1 country (dry cured) ham	1) Unwrap ham and scrub off any surface mold (if you hung in a sack for 6 months you'd have mold too). 2) Carefully remove hock with hand saw. (If this idea makes you eye your first aid kit, ask your butcher to do it. But make sure you keep the hock, it's the best friend collard greens ever had.) 3) Place ham in cooler and cover with clean water. (As long as it's not too dirty you can use what southerners call the "hose pipe"). 4) Stash the cooler in the bushes. If it's summer, throw in some ice. If it's freezing out, keep the cooler inside. 5) Change the water twice a day for two days turning the ham each time. 6) Preheat oven to 400° F.
1 liter Dr. Pepper	7) Place ham in a large disposable turkey-roasting pan and add enough Dr. Pepper to come about halfway up the side of the ham.
1 cup sweet pickle juice, optional	8) Add pickle juice if you've got it and tent completely with heavy-duty foil. 9) Cook for 1/2 hour then reduce heat to 325° F, and cook another 1 1/2 hours. 10) Turn the ham over, insert an oven safe thermometer (probe-style is best) and cook another 1 1/2 hours, or until the deepest part of the ham hits 140° F (approximately 15 to 20 minutes per pound total). 11) Let rest 1/2 hour then slice paper-thin. Serve with biscuits or soft yeast rolls.

Difficulty: Easy **Prep Time:** 48 hours **Cook Time:** 4 hours 30 minutes **Yield:** 20 portions

Cooks note: Even after soaking, country ham is quite salty, so thin slicing is mandatory. If you're a bacon fan, however, cut a thicker (1/4-inch) slice and fry it up for breakfast.

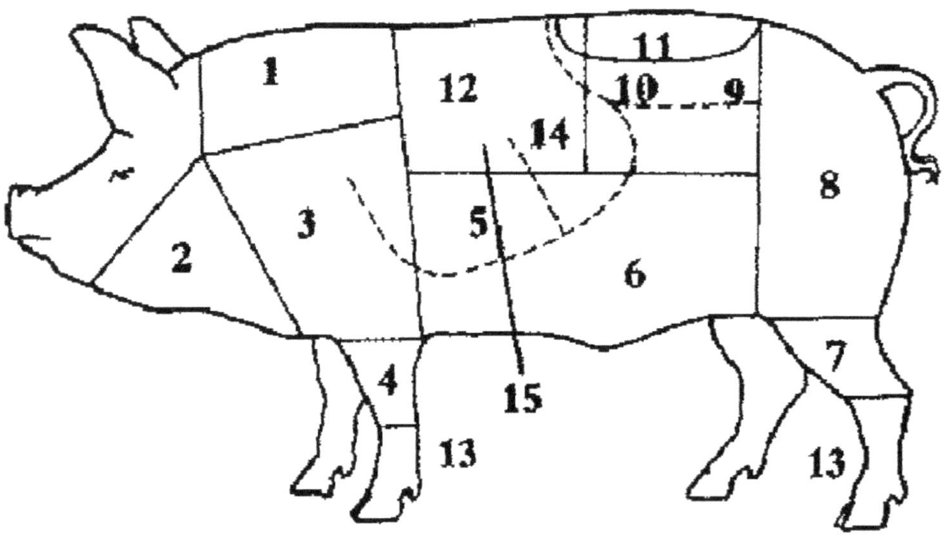

1-CHINE, NECK	**6-BELLY, LEAN**	**11-FILLET**
2-PORK CHEEK	**7-HINDLEG**	**12-CUTLET**
3-SHOULDER	**8-HAM, HIND QUARTER**	**13-FOOT**
4-FORELEG	**9-LOIN**	**14-MIDDLE PORK RIB**
5-FORERIB	**10-PORK CUTLET WITH FILLET**	**15-LARD, PORK FAT**

Figure 5: Pork Primals

SCRAP IRON CHEF'S BACON

Episode: Scrap Iron Chef - Bacon Challenge, EA1D12

Ingredients	Directions
1/2 gallon (2 quarts) water **1 cup sugar** **1 cup salt** **8 ounces molasses**	1) In a large non-reactive pot, bring half the water, 1 cup of sugar, salt, and 8 ounces molasses to a boil. Stir to dissolve the sugar.
1/2 gallon (2 quarts) apple cider	2) Pour into a large container with the remaining water, and the apple cider. 3) Place in the refrigerator and cool to 40° F.
2 tablespoons course ground black pepper **1 (5 pound) piece raw pork belly from the lion end**	4) Press the black pepper into the pork belly. 5) Once the brine has cooled place the peppered pork belly into the mixture until completely submerged. 6) Refrigerate for three days. 7) After three days have passed, remove the pork from the brine and pat dry with paper towels. 8) Lay on a rack over a sheet pan and place in front of a fan for 1 hour to form a pellicle. 9) Lay the pork in the protein box of a cold smoker and smoke for 4 to 6 hours. 10) Chill the meat in the freezer for 1 hour to stiffen for easy slicing into strips of bacon. 11) Slice what you need and keep the remainder in a freezer safe bag in the refrigerator or freezer. 12) Place the strips of bacon onto a sheet pan fitted with a rack and place into a cold oven. 13) Turn the oven to 400° and cook for about 12 to 15 minutes, depending on how crispy you like your bacon. 14) Remove from rack and drain on paper towels. 15) Enjoy.

Difficulty: Expert **Prep Time:** 10 minutes **Cook Time:** 6 hours **Yield:** approximately 4 pounds of bacon

> **"Slicing a warm slab of bacon is a lot like giving a ferret a shave. No matter how careful you are, somebody's going to get hurt."**
>
> **Alton Brown, Good Eats, *Scrap Iron Chef: Bacon Challenge***

Notes:____

SWEET AND SOUR PORK

Episode: Down and Out in Paradise, EASP02

2/3 cup soy sauce **2 teaspoons minced garlic** **1 tablespoon minced ginger** **1/4 cup flour, plus seasoned flour for dredging** **1/4 cup cornstarch**	1) In a large non-reactive bowl, combine soy, garlic, ginger, flour, and cornstarch.
1 pound pork butt, cut into 1-inch cubes **Kosher salt and pepper**	2) Season the pork generously with salt and pepper. 3) Place the pork in the bowl and toss to cover. 4) Marinate in the refrigerator overnight. 5) Drain off any excess marinade and dredge the pork in flour seasoned with salt and pepper.
Vegetable oil, for frying	6) In a large frying pan heat 1-inch of oil to 350° F. 7) Fry the pork in batches, until golden brown. 8) Drain on paper towels. Reserve on a warm plate.
1 cup ketchup **1/4 cup sugar** **1/4 cup red wine vinegar** **1 ounce honey**	9) In a separate bowl, combine the ketchup, sugar, vinegar, and honey. Whisk to blend.
1 tablespoon vegetable oil **1/2 tablespoon sesame oil**	10) In a small roasting pan heat the canola and sesame oils.
1/3 cup large diced Vidalia onion **1/3 cup large diced celery** **1/3 cup carrots sliced 1/4-inch thick, on a bias** **1/3 cup large diced red bell pepper** **1/3 cup large diced green bell pepper** **1 cup fresh pineapple, cut into 1-inch cubes**	11) Place the pork and vegetables into the pan and cover with the ketchup mixture. 12) Bring to a simmer and cook until the pork is tender.

Difficulty: Medium **Prep Time:** 30 minutes **Inactive Prep Time:** 12 hours **Cook Time:** 30 minutes **Yield:** 4 to 6 servings

STUFFED GRILLED PORK CHOPS

Episode: Chops Ahoy, EA1F07

1 cup salt **1 cup brown sugar** **1 tablespoon black peppercorns** **1 tablespoon mustard powder**	1) In a plastic container put the salt, sugar, peppercorns, and mustard powder.
2 cups cider vinegar, heated	2) Add the hot vinegar and swirl to dissolve. Let mixture sit for 5 to 10 minutes to develop flavor.
1 pound ice cubes	3) Add ice cubes and shake to melt most of the ice.
4 double thick bone-in loin end pork chops	4) Add chops and cover with brine. Refrigerate for 2 hours. 5) Remove chops from container and rinse. 6) Cut horizontal pockets in each pork chop for stuffing.
1 1/2 cups cornbread, crumbled **2 tablespoons golden raisins** **1/4 cup walnuts, roughly chopped** **1/4 cup dried cherries, halved** **1/4 cup buttermilk** **1/2 teaspoon ground pepper** **2 teaspoons fresh sage, thinly sliced** **1/2 teaspoon kosher salt**	7) Combine rest of ingredients, and put into piping bag that is not fitted with a tip. 8) Pipe each chop full with cornbread mixture. 9) Grill the chops on medium high heat for 6 minutes on each side. 10) Turn each chop 45 degrees after 3 minutes to mark.

Difficulty: Medium **Prep Time:** 15 minutes **Inactive Prep Time:** 12 minutes **Cook Time:** 12 minutes **Yield:** 4 servings

WHO LOVES YA BABY-BACK?: Ribs

Episode: Pork Fiction, EA1B14

	1) Preheat oven to 250°.
<u>Dry Rub:</u> **8 parts light brown sugar, tightly packed** **3 parts kosher salt** **1 part chili powder** **1/6 part ground black pepper** **1/6 part cayenne pepper** **1/6 part jalapeño seasoning** **1/6 part Old Bay Seasoning** **1/6 part rubbed thyme** **1/6 part onion powder**	2) In a bowl, combine all dry ingredients and mix well.
2 whole slabs pork baby back ribs	3) Place each slab of baby back ribs on a piece of heavy-duty aluminum foil, shiny side down. 4) Sprinkle each side generously with the dry rub. Pat the dry rub into the meat. 5) Refrigerate the ribs for a minimum of 1 hour. 6) In a microwavable container, combine all ingredients for the braising liquid. Cook for 1 minute. 7) Place the ribs on a baking sheet.
<u>Braising Liquid:</u> **1 cup white wine** **2 tablespoons white wine vinegar** **2 tablespoons Worcestershire sauce** **1 tablespoon honey** **2 cloves garlic, chopped**	8) Open one end of the foil on each slab and pour half of the braising liquid into each foil packet. 9) Tilt the baking sheet in order to equally distribute the braising liquid. 10) Braise the ribs in the oven for 2 1/2 hours. 11) Transfer the braising liquid into a medium saucepot. 12) Bring the liquid to a simmer and reduce by half or until of a thick syrup consistency. 13) Brush the glaze onto the ribs. 14) Place under the broiler just until the glaze caramelizes lightly. 15) Slice each slab into 2 rib bone portions. 16) Place the remaining hot glaze into a bowl and toss the rib portions in the glaze.

Difficulty: Easy **Prep Time:** 1 hr 10 min **Cook Time:** 3 hours 25 minutes **Yield:** 2 slabs ribs

Notes:____

PULLED PORK

Episode: Q, EA1G04

Brine: **8 ounces or 3/4 cup molasses** **12 ounces pickling salt** **2 quarts bottled water**	1) Combine molasses, pickling salt, and water in 6 quart Lexan.
6 to 8 pound Boston butt	2) Add Boston butt making sure it is completely submerged in brine, cover, and let sit in refrigerator for a minimum of 8 hours. 12 hours is ideal.
Rub: **1 teaspoon whole cumin seed** **1 teaspoon whole fennel seed** **1 teaspoon whole coriander**	3) Place cumin seed, fennel seed, and coriander in food grinder and grind fine.
1 tablespoon chili powder **1 tablespoon onion powder** **1 tablespoon paprika**	4) Transfer to a small mixing bowl and stir in chili powder, onion powder, and paprika. 5) Remove Boston butt from brine and pat dry. 6) Sift the rub evenly over the shoulder and then pat onto the meat making sure as much of the rub as possible adheres. More rub will adhere to the meat if you are wearing latex gloves during the application. 7) Preheat smoker to 210 degrees F. 8) Place butt in smoker and cook for 10 to 12 hours, maintaining a temperature of 210 degrees F. Begin checking meat for doneness after 10 hours of cooking time. Use fork to check for doneness. Meat is done when it falls apart easily when pulling with a fork. 9) Once done, remove from pot and set aside to rest for at least 1 hour. 10) Pull meat apart with 2 forks and serve as sandwich with coleslaw and dressing as desired.

Difficulty: Easy **Prep Time:** 20 minutes **Inactive Prep Time:** 13 hours **Cook Time:** 11 hours **Yield:** 8 to 10 servings

Notes:

PERFECT POTSTICKERS

Episode: Wonton Ways, EA1H05

1/2 pound ground pork **1/4 cup finely chopped scallions** **2 tablespoons finely chopped red bell pepper** **1 egg, lightly beaten** **2 teaspoons ketchup** **1 teaspoon yellow mustard** **2 teaspoons Worcestershire sauce** **1 teaspoon light brown sugar** **1 1/2 teaspoons kosher salt** **1/2 teaspoon freshly ground black pepper** **1/4 teaspoon cayenne pepper**	1) Preheat oven to 200 degrees F. 2) Combine the first 11 ingredients in a medium-size mixing bowl (pork through cayenne). Set aside.
35 to 40 small wonton wrappers **Water, for sealing wontons**	3) To form the dumplings, remove 1 wonton wrapper from the package, covering the others with a damp cloth. 4) Brush 2 of the edges of the wrapper lightly with water. 5) Place 1/2 rounded teaspoon of the pork mixture in the center of the wrapper. 6) Fold over, seal edges, and shape as desired. 7) Set on a sheet pan and cover with a damp cloth. 8) Repeat procedure until all of the filling is gone. 9) Heat a 12-inch sauté pan over medium heat.
3 to 4 tablespoons vegetable oil, for frying	10) Brush with vegetable oil once hot. 11) Add 8 to 10 potstickers at a time to the pan and cook for 2 minutes, without touching.
1 1/3 cups chicken stock, divided	12) Once the 2 minutes are up, gently add 1/3 cup chicken stock to the pan, turn the heat down to low, cover, and cook for another 2 minutes. 13) Remove wontons to a heatproof platter and place in the warm oven. 14) Clean the pan in between batches by pouring in water and allowing the pan to deglaze. 15) Repeat until all the wontons are cooked. Serve immediately.

Difficulty: Medium **Prep Time:** 50 minutes **Cook Time:** 20 minutes **Yield:** 35 to 40 potstickers

Notes:______________________________

SILENCE OF THE LEG O' LAMB

Episode: Grill Seekers, EA1C06

Ingredients	Directions
Paste **4 cloves garlic**	1) Roughly chop the garlic cloves in the food processor.
8 fresh mint leaves	2) Add the mint and repeat.
1 tablespoon brown sugar **1 tablespoon kosher salt** **2 teaspoons black pepper** **5 tablespoons strong mustard, such as Dijon** **2 tablespoons canola oil**	3) Add the brown sugar, salt, pepper, mustard, and oil and blend to a paste.
1 sirloin end leg of lamb, boned, and trussed	4) Spread the paste evenly on the meat side of the roast. 5) Roll the leg into a roast shape and tie with cotton butcher's twine. 6) Fire 2 quarts (1 chimney's worth) of charcoal (natural chunk is best). 7) When charcoal is lightly covered with gray ash, split the coals into 2 piles and move them to the far sides of the cooker. 8) Close the lid and allow the grate to heat. 9) Then, place the lamb, skin side up, on the middle of the hot grate.
2 sprigs fresh rosemary	10) Add the rosemary sprigs to the charcoal briquettes and close the lid and grill. 11) After 20 minutes, flip the roast and rotate it 180°. 12) Insert the probe thermometer into the roast and continue to grill until it reaches an internal temperature of 135°, about 25 to 30 minutes. 13) Remove the roast at 135°. 14) Remove the butcher's twine from the roast. 15) Cover with foil and rest it for 15 minutes before serving.

Difficulty: Easy **Prep Time:** 45 minutes **Cook Time:** 1 hour **Yield:** 6 servings

GYRO MEAT WITH TZATZIKI SAUCE

Episode: My Big Fat Greek Sandwich, EA1H017

1 medium onion, finely chopped or shredded	1) Process the onion in a food processor for 10 to 15 seconds and turn out into the center of a tea towel. 2) Gather up the ends of the towel and squeeze until almost all of the juice is removed. Discard juice.
2 pounds ground lamb **1 tablespoon finely minced garlic** **1 tablespoon dried marjoram** **1 tablespoon dried ground rosemary** **2 teaspoons kosher salt** **1/2 teaspoon freshly ground black pepper**	3) Return the onion to the food processor and add the lamb, garlic, marjoram, rosemary, salt, and pepper and process until it is a fine paste, approximately 1 minute. 4) Stop the processor as needed to scrape down sides of bowl.

To cook in the oven as a meatloaf, proceed as follows:

5) Preheat the oven to 325 degrees F.
6) Place the mixture into a loaf pan, making sure to press into the sides of the pan.
7) Place the loaf pan into a water bath and bake for 60 to 75 minutes or until the mixture reaches 165 to 170 degrees F.
8) Remove from the oven and drain off any fat.
9) Place the loaf pan on a cooling rack and place a brick wrapped in aluminum foil directly on the surface of the meat and allow to sit for 15 to 20 minutes, until the internal temperature reaches 175 degrees F.
10) Slice and serve on pita bread with tzatziki sauce, chopped onion, tomatoes and feta cheese.

To cook on a rotisserie, proceed as follows:

11) Form the meat mixture into a loaf shape and place on top of 2 overlapping pieces of plastic wrap that are at least 18 inches long.
12) Roll the mixture in the plastic wrap tightly, making sure to remove any air pockets.
13) Once the meat is completely rolled in the wrap, twist the ends of the plastic wrap until the surface of the wrap is tight.
14) Store in the refrigerator for at least 2 hours or up to overnight, to allow the mixture to firm up.
15) Preheat the grill to high.
16) Place the meat onto the rotisserie skewer. Place a double-thick piece of aluminum foil folded into a tray directly under the meat to catch any drippings.
17) Cook on high for 15 minutes.
18) Decrease the heat to medium and continue to cook for another 20 to 30 minutes or until the internal temperature of the meat reaches 165 degrees F.
19) Turn off the heat and allow to continue to spin for another 10 to 15 minutes or until the internal temperature reaches 175 degrees.
20) Slice and serve on pita bread with tzatziki sauce, chopped onion, tomatoes, and feta cheese.

Tzatziki Sauce: **16 ounces plain yogurt**	1) Place the yogurt in a tea towel, gather up the edges, suspend over a bowl, and drain for 2 hours in the refrigerator. 2) Place the chopped cucumber in a tea towel and squeeze to remove the liquid; discard liquid.
1 medium cucumber, peeled, seeded, and finely chopped **Pinch kosher salt** **4 cloves garlic, finely minced** **1 tablespoon olive oil** **2 teaspoons red wine vinegar** **5 to 6 mint leaves, finely minced**	3) In a medium mixing bowl, combine the drained yogurt, cucumber, salt, garlic, olive oil, vinegar, and mint. 4) Serve as a sauce for gyros. 5) Store in the refrigerator in an airtight container for up to a week.

Gyro Meat
Difficulty: Medium **Prep Time:** 30 minutes **Inactive Prep Time:** 2 hours **Cook Time:** 1 hr 15 min **Yield:** 6 to 8 servings
Tzatziki Sauce
Difficulty: Easy **Prep Time:** 15 minutes **Inactive Prep Time:** 2 hours **Yield:** 1 1/2 cups

FRIED CHICKEN

Episode: Fry Hard II: The Chicken, EA1D02

1 broiler/fryer chicken, cut into 8 pieces **2 cups low fat buttermilk**	1) Place chicken pieces into a plastic container and cover with buttermilk. 2) Cover and refrigerate for 12 to 24 hours.
Vegetable shortening, for frying	3) Melt enough shortening (over low heat) to come just 1/8-inch up the side of a 12-inch cast iron skillet or heavy fry pan. 4) Once shortening liquefies raise heat to 350° F. Do not allow oil to go over 350° F. 5) Drain chicken in a colander.
2 tablespoons Kosher salt **2 tablespoons Hungarian paprika** **2 teaspoons garlic powder** **1 teaspoon cayenne pepper**	6) Combine salt, paprika, garlic powder, and cayenne pepper. Liberally season chicken with this mixture.
Flour, for dredging	7) Dredge chicken in flour and shake off excess. 8) Place chicken skin side down into the pan. Put thighs in the center, and breast and legs around the edge of the pan. The oil should come half way up the pan. 9) Cook chicken until golden brown on each side, approximately 10 to 12 minutes per side. More importantly, the internal temperature should be right around 180°. (Be careful to monitor shortening temperature every few minutes). 10) Drain chicken on a rack over a sheet pan. Don't drain by setting chicken directly on paper towels or brown paper bags. 11) If you need to hold the chicken before serving, cover loosely with foil but avoid holding in a warm oven, especially if it's a gas oven.

Difficulty: Easy **Prep Time:** 20 minutes **Cook Time:** 20 minutes **Yield:** 3 to 4 servings

40 CLOVES AND A CHICKEN

Episode: The Bulb of the Night, EA1D11

	1) Preheat oven to 350° F.
1 whole chicken (broiler/fryer) cut into 8 pieces Salt and pepper	2) Season chicken with salt and pepper.
1/2 cup plus 2 tablespoons olive oil	3) Toss with a 2 tablespoons olive oil and brown on both sides in a wide fry pan or skillet over high heat.
10 sprigs fresh thyme 40 peeled cloves garlic	4) Remove from heat, add oil, thyme, and garlic cloves. 5) Cover and bake for 1 1/2 hours. 6) Remove chicken from the oven, let rest for 5 to 10 minutes, carve, and serve.

Difficulty: Easy **Prep Time:** 10 minutes **Cook Time:** 1 hour 30 minutes **Yield:** 6 servings

BROILED, BUTTERFLIED CHICKEN

Episode: A Bird in the Pan, EA1A05

	1) Position the oven rack 8 inches from the flame/coil and turn broiler to high.
1 1/2 teaspoons black peppercorns **4 garlic cloves, minced** **1/2 teaspoon kosher salt**	2) Crack peppercorns with a mortar and pestle until coarsely ground. Add garlic and salt and work well.
1 lemon, zested	3) Add lemon zest and work just until you can smell lemon.
Extra virgin olive oil	4) Add just enough oil to form a paste.
Onions, carrots and celery cut into 3 to 4-inch pieces	5) Check out your refrigerator for onions, carrots and celery that are a little past their prime. Cut vegetables into pieces and place in a deep roasting pan.
3 to 4-pound broiler/fryer chicken	6) Place chicken on a plastic cutting board breast-side down. Using kitchen shears, cut ribs down one side of back bone and then the other and remove. 7) Open chicken like a book and remove the keel bone separating the breast halves by slicing through the thin membrane covering it, then by placing two fingers underneath the bone and levering it out. 8) Turn chicken breast-side up and spread out like a butterfly by pressing down on the breast and pulling the legs towards you. 9) Loosen the skin at the neck and the edges of the thighs. Evenly distribute the garlic mixture under the skin, saving 2 teaspoons for the jus.
Canola oil	10) Drizzle the skin with oil and rub in, being sure to cover the bird evenly. Drizzle oil on bone side of chicken as well. 11) Arrange bird in roasting pan, breast up, atop vegetables. 12) Place pan in oven being sure to leave the oven door ajar. Check bird in 10 minutes. 13) If the skin is a dark mahogany, hold the drumstick ends with paper towels and flip bone-side up. Cook 12 to 15 minutes or until the internal temperature reaches 165°. Juices must run clear. 14) Remove and place chicken into a deep bowl and cover loosely with foil. 15) Tilt pan so that any fat will pool at corner. Siphon this off with a bulb baster. (This fat is great in vinaigrettes).
1 cup red wine	16) Set pan over 2 burners set on high. De-glaze pan with a few shots of red wine and scrape brown bits from bottom using a carrot chunk held with tongs.
8 ounces chicken stock **2 to 3 sprigs thyme**	17) Add chicken stock, thyme, the remaining garlic paste and reduce briefly to make a jus. 18) Strain out vegetables and discard. 19) Slice chicken onto plates or serve in quarters. Sauce lightly with jus and serve.

Difficulty: Easy **Prep Time:** 30 minutes **Cook Time:** 30 minutes **Yield:** 4 to 6 servings

Notes:

CHICKEN KIEV

Episode: Flat is Beautiful II, EA1H03

8 tablespoons (1 stick) unsalted butter, room temperature **1 teaspoon dried parsley** **1 teaspoon dried tarragon**	1) Combine butter, parsley, tarragon, 1 teaspoon salt, and 1/4 teaspoon black pepper in the bowl of a stand mixer. 2) Place mixture on plastic wrap or waxed paper and roll into small log; place in freezer.
4 boneless, skinless chicken breast halves	3) Place chicken breasts, 1 at a time, between 2 pieces of plastic wrap. 4) Squirt chicken lightly with water and squirt the top of the plastic wrap as well. 5) Pound to no less than 1/8-inch thickness.
1 teaspoon kosher salt, plus extra for seasoning chicken **1/4 teaspoon freshly ground black pepper, plus extra for seasoning chicken**	6) Season each piece of chicken with salt and pepper.
2 large whole eggs, beaten with 1 teaspoon water **2 cups Japanese bread crumbs (panko), plus 1/4 cup for filling**	7) Lay 1 chicken breast on a new piece of plastic wrap and place 1/4 of the compound butter and 1 tablespoon bread crumbs in the center of each breast. 8) Using the plastic wrap to assist, fold in ends of breast and roll breast into a log, completely enclosing the butter; roll very tightly. Repeat with each breast. 9) Place chicken in refrigerator for 2 hours, or up to overnight. 10) Place egg and water mixture in 1 pie pan and 2 cups bread crumbs in a different pie pan. 11) Heat 1/2-inch of vegetable oil in a 12-inch sauté pan over medium-high heat until oil reaches 375 degrees F. 12) Dip each breast in the egg mixture and then roll in the bread crumbs.
Vegetable oil, for frying	13) Gently place each breast in oil, sealed-side down, and cook until golden brown, approximately 4 to 5 minutes on each side, until the internal temperature reaches 165 degrees F. 14) Remove to a cooling rack set in sheet pan and allow to drain for 5 to 10 minutes before serving.

Difficulty: Medium **Prep Time:** 35 minutes **Inactive Prep Time:** 2 hours **Cook Time:** 10 minutes **Yield:** 4 servings

CURRY CHICKEN POT PIE

Episode: Casserole Over, EA1F11

4 cups frozen vegetable mix, peas, carrots **1 to 2 tablespoons canola oil**	1) Preheat oven to 400 degrees F. 2) Toss frozen vegetables with canola oil and spread evenly onto a sheet pan. 3) Place into oven and cook until golden brown.
3 tablespoons butter **1 cup chopped onion** **1 cup chopped celery**	4) In a sauté pan heat 1 tablespoon of butter and sweat the onion and celery.
1 1/2 cups low sodium chicken broth **1/2 cup milk**	5) In another saucepan, heat the broth and milk. 6) Add 2 more tablespoons of butter to the celery mix and cook out the water.
3 tablespoons flour **1 teaspoon curry powder**	7) Add the flour and curry and cook for 1 to 2 minutes. 8) Whisk in the hot milk mixture and cook until thickened.
2 tablespoons dried parsley **1 teaspoon salt** **1/2 teaspoon fresh ground pepper**	9) Add the parsley, salt and pepper.
2 cups cubed cooked chicken	10) Toss the browned vegetables and the chicken.
1 package puff pastry	11) Pour into a shallow baking pan, or a large terra cotta pot base, lined with foil, and top with 6 to 8 circles of puff pastry. 12) Place into the oven and cook until puff pastry has browned and the mixture is hot and bubbly, about 25 minutes.

Difficulty: Easy **Prep Time:** 30 minutes **Cook Time:** 25 minutes **Yield:** 6 to 8 servings

COQ AU VIN

Episode: Cuckoo for Coq au Vin, EA1H18

Ingredients	Directions
24 to 30 pearl onions	1) Cut off the root end of each pearl onion and make an "x" with your knife in its place. 2) Bring 2 to 3 cups of water to a boil and drop in the onions for 1 minute. 3) Remove the onions from the pot, allow them to cool, and then peel. You should be able to slide the onions right out of their skin. Set aside.
4 chicken thighs and legs, or 1 (5 to 7-pound) stewing chicken, cut into serving pieces **Kosher salt and freshly ground black pepper**	4) Sprinkle the chicken on all sides with kosher salt and freshly ground black pepper.
1/4 to 1/2 cup all-purpose flour	5) Place the chicken pieces, a few at a time, into a large (1 or 2-gallon) sealable plastic bag along with the flour. 6) Shake to coat all of the pieces of the chicken. Remove the chicken from the bag to a metal rack.
2 tablespoons water **6 ounces salt pork, slab bacon, or lardon, cubed**	7) Add the 2 tablespoons of water to a large, 12-inch sauté pan over medium heat along with the salt pork. 8) Cover and cook until the water is gone, and then continue to cook until the salt pork cubes are golden brown and crispy, approximately 8 to 10 minutes. 9) Remove the salt pork from the pan and set aside. 10) In the same pan, using the remaining fat, add the pearl onions, sprinkle with salt and pepper, and sauté until lightly brown, approximately 8 to 10 minutes. Remove the onions from the pan and set aside. 11) Next, brown the chicken pieces on each side until golden brown, working in batches if necessary to not overcrowd the pan. 12) Transfer the chicken into a 7 to 8-quart enameled cast iron Dutch oven.
8 ounces button mushrooms, quartered **1 tablespoon unsalted butter**	13) Add the mushrooms to the same 12-inch sauté pan, adding the 1 tablespoon of butter if needed, and sauté until they give up their liquid, approximately 5 minutes. 14) Store the onions, mushrooms and pork in an airtight container in the refrigerator until ready to use.
2 (750-ml) bottles red wine, preferably pinot noir	15) Pour off any remaining fat and deglaze the pan with approximately 1 cup of the wine.
2 cups chicken stock or broth **2 tablespoons tomato paste** **1 medium onion, quartered** **2 stalks celery, quartered** **2 medium carrots, quartered** **3 cloves garlic, crushed** **6 to 8 sprigs fresh thyme** **1 bay leaf**	16) Pour this into the Dutch oven along with the chicken stock, tomato paste, quartered onion, carrots, celery, garlic, thyme, and bay leaf. 17) Add all of the remaining wine. Cover and refrigerate overnight. 18) The next day, preheat the oven to 325 degrees F. 19) Place the chicken in the oven and cook for 2 to 2 1/2 hours, or until the chicken is tender. Maintain a very gentle simmer and stir occasionally. 20) Once the chicken is done, remove it to a heatproof container, cover, and place it in the oven to keep warm. 21) Strain the sauce in a colander and remove the carrots, onion, celery, thyme, garlic, and bay leaf. 22) Return the sauce to the pot, place over medium heat, and reduce by 1/3. Depending on how much liquid you actually began with, this should take 20 to 45 minutes. 23) Once the sauce has thickened, add the pearl onions, mushrooms, and pork and cook for another 15 minutes or until the heated through. 24) Taste and adjust seasoning if necessary, remove from the heat, add the chicken and serve. 25) Serve over egg noodles, if desired.

Difficulty: Medium **Prep Time:** 1 hour **Inactive Prep Time:** 8 hours **Cook Time:** 4 hours **Yield:** 4 to 6 servings

Cook's Note: If the sauce is not thick enough at the end of reducing, you may add a mixture of equal parts butter and flour kneaded together. Start with 1 tablespoon of each. Whisk this into the sauce for 4 to 5 minutes and repeat, if necessary.

Notes:______________________________

GOOD EATS ROAST TURKEY

Episode: Romancing The Bird—A Good Eats Thanksgiving, EASP01

For the brine: **1 cup kosher salt** **1/2 cup light brown sugar** **1 gallon vegetable stock** **1 tablespoon black peppercorns** **1/2 tablespoon allspice berries** **1/2 tablespoon candied ginger**	1) Combine all brine ingredients in a stock pot and bring to a boil. 2) Stir to dissolve solids, then remove from heat, cool to room temperature refrigerate until thoroughly chilled.
1 gallon iced water	3) Early on the day of cooking, (or late the night before) combine the brine and ice water in a clean 5 gallon bucket.
1 (14-16 pound) frozen young turkey	4) Place thawed turkey breast side down in brine, cover, and refrigerate or set in cool area (like a basement) for 6 hours. 5) Turn turkey over once, half way through brining. 6) A few minutes before roasting, heat oven to 500°.
1 red apple, sliced **1/2 onion, sliced** **1 cinnamon stick** **1 cup water**	7) Combine the apple, onion, cinnamon stick and cup of water in a microwave safe dish and microwave on high for 5 minutes. 8) Remove bird from brine and rinse inside and out with cold water. Discard brine. 9) Place bird on roasting rack inside wide, low pan and pat dry with paper towels.
4 sprigs rosemary **6 leaves of sage**	10) Add steeped aromatics to cavity along with rosemary and sage.
Canola oil	11) Tuck back wings and coat whole bird liberally with canola (or other neutral) oil. 12) Roast on lowest level of the oven at 500° for 30 minutes. 13) Remove from oven and cover breast with double layer of aluminum foil, insert probe thermometer into thickest part of the breast and return to oven, reducing temperature to 350°. 14) Set thermometer alarm (if available) to 161°. A 14 to 16 pound bird should require a total of 2 to 2 1/2 hours of roasting. 15) Let turkey rest, loosely covered for 15 minutes before carving.

Difficulty: Easy **Prep Time:** 1 hour **Inactive Prep Time:** Overnight **Cook Time:** 3 hours **Yield:** 10 to 12 servings

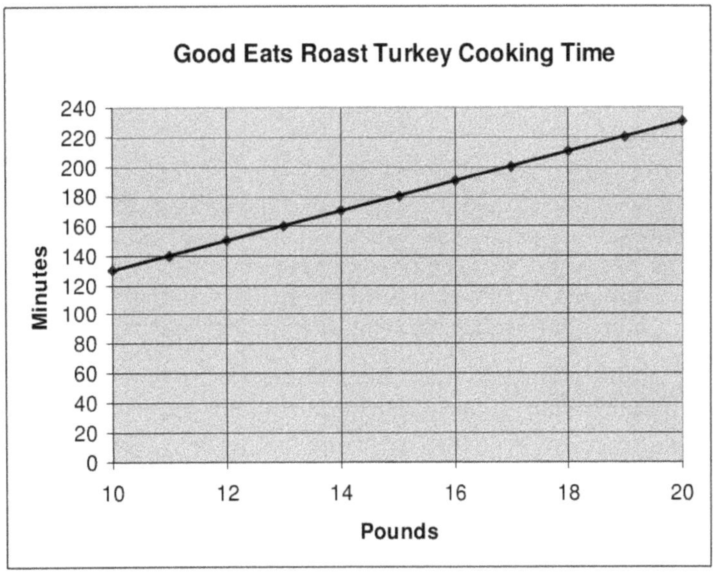

After taking times and temps of many brined turkeys by the Good Eats fans, we've come to the following equation for estimating the time it'll take to cook the Good Eats Roast Turkey above:

30 Minutes @ 500° + 10 Minutes/lb @ 350°

For example, if you have a 14 lb bird, then the total cooking time would be:

30 + (10*14) or
30 + 140 or
170 minutes or
2 hours, 50 minutes.

This is only an estimated time for planning purposes. Use your probe thermometer for cooking doneness per the recipe.

TURKEY WITH STUFFING

Episode: Stuff It, EA1H04

Special equipment: 1 re-usable organic cotton produce bag*	
1 (10 to 12-pound) turkey, with giblets removed	1) Preheat the oven to 400 degrees F. 2) Place the turkey into a deep, high-sided bowl on its end with the stuffing end up. Set aside.
1 quart chicken broth	3) Heat the chicken broth in the microwave in a large microwave-proof container.
2 ounces dried mushrooms	4) Place mushrooms in a glass bowl and pour heated broth over them. 5) Cover and allow to sit for 35 minutes.
1 cup chopped onion **1 cup chopped celery** **1 cup chopped green pepper** **1 tablespoon vegetable oil, plus extra for rubbing on turkey** **1 tablespoon kosher salt, plus extra for seasoning turkey**	6) In a large mixing bowl toss the onion, celery, and green pepper with the oil and salt. 7) Place the vegetables on a sheet pan and roast for 35 minutes.
3 cups Challah bread, cut into 1/2-inch cubes (from approximately 4 to 5 slices)	8) During the last 10 minutes of cooking, spread the cubed bread over the vegetables, return to the oven, and continue cooking. 9) Drain mushrooms, reserving 1 cup of liquid.
4 ounces unsweetened dried cherries, approximately 1 cup **2 ounces chopped pecans, approximately 1/2 cup** **2 whole eggs, beaten** **2 teaspoons dried rubbed sage** **2 teaspoons dried parsley** **1/2 teaspoon freshly ground black pepper, plus extra for seasoning chicken**	10) Chop the mushrooms and place in a large microwave-proof bowl with the vegetables and bread, reserved chicken stock, cherries, pecans, eggs, sage, parsley and black pepper. 11) Stir well in order to break up pieces of bread. Use your hands to combine, if necessary. 12) Heat the stuffing in a microwave on high power for 6 minutes. 13) While the stuffing is heating, rub the bird with oil. 14) Working quickly, place the stuffing into the cavity of the turkey to avoid losing heat. 15) Place the turkey into a roasting pan, on a rack, and season with salt and pepper. 16) Place the roasting pan on the middle rack of the oven. 17) Roast for 45 minutes and then reduce the heat to 350 degrees F and cook for another 60 to 75 minutes or until the bird reaches an internal temperature of 170 degrees F. Serve immediately.

Difficulty: Easy **Prep Time:** 45 minutes **Cook Time:** 2 hrs 30 min **Yield:** 4 to 6 servings

*Cook's Note: The bag is optional. Once the stuffing is made, you can place the stuffing into the bag and then place the bag into the cavity of the turkey.

TURKEY PICCATA

Episode: Flat is Beautiful II, EA1H03

1 whole turkey breast, approximately 1 1/2 to 2 pounds	1) Preheat oven to 200 degrees F. 2) Cut the turkey breast crosswise into 1/2-inch pieces. 3) Place pieces of turkey, 1 at a time, between 2 pieces of plastic wrap. 4) Squirt the meat lightly with water and squirt the top of the plastic wrap as well. 5) Pound to no less than 1/8 inch thickness.
Kosher salt **Freshly ground black pepper** **1/2 cup all-purpose flour**	6) Season both sides of meat with salt and pepper and then dredge in flour. Shake off the excess flour. Set aside.
2 tablespoons olive oil **6 tablespoons unsalted butter**	7) In a large sauté pan over medium to medium high heat, heat olive oil and 4 tablespoons butter. 8) Once hot, but not yet smoking, brown turkey scaloppini quickly, about 1 minute on each side, and remove to an ovenproof platter. Place in oven to keep warm.
2 tablespoons finely chopped shallots	9) Reduce the heat to low and add the shallots to the pan. Sauté for 1 to 2 minutes or until they begin to turn translucent.
1/2 cup white wine **1/3 cup freshly squeezed lemon juice**	10) Add wine and lemon juice to the pan and simmer until slightly reduced, about 2 minutes. 11) Add remaining 2 tablespoons butter and whisk to combine. 12) Season with salt and pepper, to taste, if necessary.
2 tablespoons freshly chopped parsley leaves	13) Pour sauce over turkey, sprinkle with parsley, and serve immediately.

Difficulty: Easy **Prep Time:** 35 minutes **Cook Time:** 10 minutes **Yield:** 4 servings

MIGHTY DUCK

Episode: What's Up Duck?, EA1B04

Ingredients	Directions
<u>Brine</u> **1/2 cup kosher salt** **1 pint pineapple orange juice** **15 whole black peppercorns** **1 bunch fresh thyme** **4 cloves garlic, smashed**	1) Combine all brine ingredients in a plastic container with a lid. 2) Place the lid on the container and shake to dissolve the salt.
1 (5 1/2 to 6 pound) frozen Long Island Duck, thawed	3) Remove the pop-up thermometer, liver, gizzards, and heart. 4) Cut off the wings. 5) Using kitchen shears, locate the spine at the base of the neck. Cut up the line of the backbone towards the neck cavity. 6) Turn the duck and cut straight towards the rear cavity. Remove the backbone. 7) Turn the duck over and cut straight down the middle of the breastbone, leaving 2 equal duck halves. 8) To separate the legs from the breast, flip your halves over so the flesh side is facing up at you. Using a knife, make a crescent shape cut between the leg and the breast. Lay your knife flat against the skin and make 3 marks in one direction and then in the other, making an X. Make sure that you are cutting through the skin and not the meat. 9) Line the inside of a plastic Lexan or a pot with a zip-top bag. 10) Place the duck quarters inside the bag, and pour the brine over the duck. 11) Seal the bag, ensuring that all air is removed from the bag. 12) Brine the duck for 2 to 2 1/2 hours in the refrigerator. 13) Bring 1 1/2 inches to 2 inches of water to a boil in a large pot. 14) Place a colander into the pot and line the sides of the colander with the duck. Do not stack the duck quarters on each other. 15) Cover and turn the heat to medium low. 16) Steam the duck for 45 minutes. 17) Set oven to 475° F. Place a large cast iron skillet into the oven. 18) Remove duck pieces from steamer and place legs, skin side down, into the hot skillet. 19) Place the skillet into the hot oven immediately and cook the leg quarters for 10 minutes. 20) Add the breasts, skin side down, and cook for 7 more minutes or until the duck takes on a deep mahogany color and the skin is very crisp. 21) Remove the duck from the skillet and rest under foil.
2 handfuls shredded chard **2 shallots, minced**	22) Add the chard and the shallots to the skillet. 23) Toss the chard in the fat until it barely wilts.
Dash sherry or balsamic vinegar	24) Season with the sherry or balsamic vinegar. 25) Serve the duck with the chard.

Difficulty: Easy

Yield: 2 to 4 servings

Notes:

Fish

CATFISH AU LAIT

Episode: Mission: Poachable, EA1C13

Ingredients	Directions
1 (12-ounce can) evaporated milk 1 teaspoon Old Bay or other "Crab Boil" seasoning 1/2 teaspoon freshly ground black pepper 1 1/2 teaspoon kosher salt 1/2 onion, thinly sliced	1) Combine the milk, Old Bay, pepper, salt, and onion in an electric skillet, cover, and bring to a simmer.
3 to 4 catfish fillets	2) Add the catfish to the liquid, spooning some of the liquid over the fillets. 3) Reduce the heat to low, around 140 to 145°, cover the skillet, and poach for 6 to 9 minutes.

Difficulty: Easy **Prep Time:** 15 minutes **Cook Time:** 9 minutes **Yield:** 3 to 4 servings

CHIMNEY TUNA LOIN

Episode: The Other Red Meat, EA1F01

Ingredients	Directions
1/2 cup dark soy sauce **1/2 cup honey** 1/4 cup dry wasabi powder	1) In a non-reactive bowl combine soy, honey, and wasabi powder. Reserve 1/4 cup for dipping sauce.
2 pounds tuna loin, cut into 2 pieces	2) Roll each piece of tuna in this mixture to coat evenly. 3) Marinate from 1 hour to overnight. 4) Remove the tuna from the marinade and discard the marinade.
1/2 cup sesame seeds	5) On a plate, lay the sesame seeds. Roll the tuna in the seeds to evenly coat.
2 tablespoons peanut oil	6) Fire up the chimney and top with a well-oiled grate. 7) Sear for 15 to 30 seconds per side or to desired temperature. 8) Remove to rack and rest for 3 minutes. 9) Cover with foil or plastic wrap to achieve carry over cooking. 10) Slice thinly and serve with the dipping sauce.

Difficulty: Easy **Prep Time:** 10 minutes **Cook Time:** 3 minutes **Yield:** 4 servings

CHIPS AND FISH

Episode: Fry Hard, EA1B10

	1) Heat oven to 200° F.
1 gallon safflower oil	2) Heat the safflower oil in a 5-quart Dutch oven over high heat until it reaches 320°.
4 large Russet potatoes	3) Using a V-slicer with a wide blade, slice the potatoes with the skin on. Place in a large bowl with cold water.
2 cups flour **1 tablespoon baking powder** **1 teaspoon kosher salt** **1/4 teaspoon cayenne pepper** **Dash Old Bay Seasoning**	4) In a bowl, whisk together the flour, baking powder, salt, cayenne pepper, and Old Bay seasoning.
1 bottle brown beer, cold	5) Whisk in the beer until the batter is completely smooth and free of any lumps. 6) Refrigerate for 15 minutes. Note: The batter can be made up to 1 hour ahead of time. 7) Drain potatoes thoroughly, removing any excess water. 8) When oil reaches 320°, submerge the potatoes in the oil. 9) Working in small batches, fry for 2 to 3 minutes until they are pale and floppy. 10) Remove from oil, drain, and cool to room temperature. 11) Increase the temperature of the oil to 375°. 12) Re-immerse fries and cook until crisp and golden brown, about 2 to 3 minutes. 13) Remove and drain on roasting rack.
Kosher salt	14) Season with kosher salt while hot and hold in the oven. 15) Allow oil to return to 350°.
1 1/2 pounds firm-fleshed whitefish (tilapia, pollock, cod), cut into 1-ounce strips **Cornstarch, for dredging**	16) Lightly dredge fish strips in cornstarch.
Malt Vinegar	17) Working in small batches, dip the fish into batter and immerse into hot oil. 18) When the batter is set, turn the pieces of fish over and cook until golden brown, about 2 minutes. 19) Drain the fish on the roasting rack. Serve with malt vinegar.

Difficulty: Easy

Yield: 4 servings

Alton Brown: Now, wet stuff does not like sticking to other wet … stuff. It's one of those universal axioms that keeps the galaxy from ripping itself to shred and dissolving into the void.

Marsha Brown: That's funny. I could have sworn that was gravity.

Alton Brown: That's one of them, too.

Good Eats, *Fry Hard*

Notes:____

PAN FRIED FISH

Episode: Hook, Line and Dinner, EA1A10

Ingredients	Directions
	1) Heat a heavy pan over medium high heat.
1 large or two small skin-on fish fillets, about 8 ounces (rainbow trout, small salmon, brown trout) **Kosher salt** **Ground black pepper**	2) Season fish on meat side with salt and pepper.
Flour for dredging	3) Lightly dredge fish in flour and shake off excess.
2 tablespoon Canola oil **3 tablespoons butter**	4) When pan is good and hot, add Canola oil followed immediately by 1 tablespoon butter. 5) As soon as foaming subsides, place fish in pan with the skin side down. 6) Jiggle pan for the first 10 seconds to keep the fish from sticking. 7) Cook until golden crust forms on meat. 8) Carefully turn fish away from you and again jiggle pan for the first few seconds. 9) Cook until skin turns golden brown. 10) Remove to a warm plate.
1 tablespoons capers, drained	11) Pour out the cooking fat, add remaining butter and quickly fry the capers.
1 lemon, juiced	12) Remove pan from the heat, add lemon juice to pan and swirl. 13) Pour sauce over the fish and serve.

Difficulty: Easy **Prep Time:** 15 minutes **Cook Time:** 15 minutes **Yield:** 2 servings

STRIPED BASS IN SALT DOME

Episode: Hook, Line and Dinner, EA1A10

	1) Heat oven to 450°. 2) Cover the bottom of a baking sheet large enough to hold the fish with parchment paper.
1 striped bass, 5 to 6 pounds, gills removed, fins trimmed	3) Rinse fish inside and out with cold water and drain. Dry with paper towels.
1 handful parsley **1 fennel bulb, (with stem) quartered** **Several sprigs thyme** **1 lemon, sliced thin** **1/2 orange, sliced thin**	4) Stuff body cavity with herbs and citrus, saving a few lemon slices for garnish. Set aside.
2 (3 pound) boxes of kosher salt **4 egg whites** **1/2 cup water**	5) Pour 1 box of salt into a large bowl, add egg whites and water, then the second box of salt. 6) Use your hands to work mixture to a mortar-like consistency. 7) Lay down a 1/2-inch thick bed for the fish to lay on with a 1-inch clearance on all sides. 8) Lay the fish on this bed and pile the remainder of the salt mortar on top. 9) Work into a smooth dome completely encasing the fish. (Don't worry if the head or tail poke out a little.) 10) Cook approximately 35 minutes. 11) Check for doneness by pushing the probe of an instant read thermometer through the salt into the fish. When temperature reaches 130°, remove from oven, and rest at room temperature for 5 minutes. 12) Open the fish at the table by hitting the dome several times with a small hammer and lifting off the slabs of salt. Brush away any stray salt. 13) Gently pull out dorsal (back) fin. 14) Using a fish knife or serrated pie server, make a single incision all the way down the back of the fish and around the gill plate. Then lift the skin off working from the head to the tail. 15) Remove meat from top side of fish, going down one side of the spine then the other. 16) Grasp the tail and remove the skeleton, (it should come up intact). The meat revealed below will slide right off the skin.
Olive oil	17) Sprinkle meat with a little virgin oil and lemon juice. Serve immediately.

Difficulty: Easy **Prep Time:** 25 minutes **Cook Time:** 40 minutes **Yield:** 8 servings

THE FRENCHMAN'S BASS

Episode: Mission: Poachable, EA1C13

1 pint Good Eats Court Bouillon (recipe in sauce section)	1) Bring the court bouillon to a simmer in a large saucepan.
4 (4-ounce) sea bass fillets	2) Add the fillets to the court bouillon, partially submerging them in the liquid. 3) Cover the pan with the lid and reduce heat. Poach the fish for 5 to 7 minutes.

Difficulty: Easy **Prep Time:** 18 minutes **Cook Time:** 7 minutes **Yield:** 4 servings

Notes:____

GRILLED SALMON STEAKS

Episode: Hook, Line and Dinner, EA1A10

	1) Prepare grill by lighting 4 quarts of charcoal (1 starter chimney's worth), or turning gas grill to medium-high.
4 salmon steaks 1-inch thick	2) Examine steaks for pin bones by rubbing fingers over surface of meat. If found, remove with bone tweezers or pliers reserved for culinary uses. 3) Using a sharp paring or boning knife, trim bones from the cavity side of the steak. 4) Trim the stomach flaps so that 1 side is missing about 2 inches of skin and the other, 1 inch of meat. 5) Roll the skinless section up into the hollow of the cavity, then wrap the other around the outside to form a round resembling a filet mignon. 6) Tie in place with 2 passes of butcher's twine. (Do not tie it too tight or fish will pop out during cooking.)
1 teaspoon whole cumin seed **1 teaspoon whole coriander seed** **1/2 teaspoon whole fennel seed** **1 teaspoon dry green peppercorns**	7) Combine cumin, coriander, fennel and peppercorns on a double thick piece of aluminum foil and toast over grill, shaking gently until seeds become fragrant. 8) Crush seeds in mortar and pestle or pour into spare pepper grinder.
Sea salt or kosher salt **Canola or olive oil to coat steaks**	9) Coat steaks lightly with oil, season with salt, then liberally grind toasted seeds on both sides of steaks. 10) Quickly wipe hot grill grate with a rag or towel dipped in a little Canola oil, then grill fish to medium rare, about 3 minutes per side. (Fish should be well colored on the outside and barely translucent at the center. 11) Serve steaks alongside simple salad dressed with "Veni, Vedi, Vinaigrette."

Difficulty: Easy **Prep Time:** 20 minutes **Cook Time:** 10 minutes **Yield:** 4 servings

ISLAND CEVICHE AND PICKLED ONIONS

Episode: Down and Out in Paradise, EASP02

1/2 pound pompano fillets, or other firm white fish fillet **1/2 pound bay scallops** **Vegetable oil, for coating** **Kosher salt and pepper**	1) Cut the fish into pieces resembling the size of the scallops. 2) Separately toss the seafood with a little oil and season with salt and pepper. 3) In a sauté pan over high heat, sear the fish and scallops, about 30 seconds on each side. The middle should still be raw. Work in batches so you don't overcrowd the pan.
3 ounces fresh lime juice, about 3 limes	4) Place seafood into a glass dish and coat with lime juice. Glass is best, as it won't react with the acid in the juice. 5) Marinate, refrigerated, overnight.
1 medium solo papaya, halved and seeded	6) Remove the flesh from 1/2 a papaya and cut into medium dice. 7) Slice the remaining 1/2 into long strips.
1 cup finely diced Vidalia onion **4 serrano peppers, seeded and diced** **1 small jalapeno, seeded and diced** **2 plum tomatoes, seeded and diced** **1/2 cup chopped cilantro** **2 ounces tomato juice** **1 tablespoon white wine Worcestershire sauce** **1/2 tablespoon capers** **1 tablespoon Mexican-style hot sauce** **Tortilla Chips, as accompaniment** **Pink Pickled Onions, recipe follows**	8) Next day, pour off the lime juice and gently fold the drained fish and scallop mixture together with remaining ingredients and diced papaya. 9) Serve with tortilla chips, sliced papaya, and Pink Pickled Onions.

Difficulty: Easy **Prep Time:** 20 minutes **Inactive Prep Time:** 12 hours **Cook Time:** 10 minutes **Yield:** 4 to 6 servings

Pink Pickled Onions

8 ounces champagne vinegar **1/2 cup sugar** **2 serrano chiles, seeded**	a) In a small saucepan, bring the vinegar, sugar, and chiles to a boil. Stir until sugar is dissolved. b) Remove from heat.
2 medium red onions, thinly sliced	c) In a plastic container, place the sliced onions and pour the liquid over them. d) Place the container in an ice bath to cool. e) Serve chilled with meats and seafood. These are also great on sandwiches.

Yield: about 2 cups

Notes:

SALMON TURNOVERS

Episode: Puff The Magic Pastry, EA1D07

	1) Preheat oven to 400° F.
Flour, for dusting	2) Lightly flour the countertop.
1 sheet puff pastry	3) Roll puff pastry so there are no seams. 4) Cut into 4 squares.
1 can boneless, skinless, salmon **1/2 cup sautéed mushrooms** **1 to 2 tablespoons sour pickle relish** **1 cup cooked white, brown or fried rice** **2 to 3 chopped scallions** **1 tablespoon parsley leaves, chopped** **Salt and pepper**	5) In a bowl, combine salmon, mushrooms, pickle relish, rice, scallions, parsley, salt, and pepper. 6) Place 1 tablespoon of filling in the center of each square.
1 egg beaten with 2 tablespoons water	7) Brush inside edges of puff pastry with egg wash and fold over to make a triangle. 8) Using a fork, seal the edges. 9) Poke a slit or two in the top of each turnover. 10) Brush tops with egg wash. 11) Bake in oven for 30 minutes or until golden brown.

Difficulty: Medium **Prep Time:** 15 minutes **Cook Time:** 30 minutes **Yield:** 4 servings

The Good Eats Custom Corrugated Vapor Colloid Applicator: (Cardboard Box Smoker)

a) Heavy-duty corrugated box (no interior painting)
b) Flap door
c) Electric hot plate
d) Small cast-iron skillet
e) Hardwood sawdust (no pressure-treated wood or plywood allowed)
f) Small battery-operated fan (optional)
g) 2 quarter-inch wooden dowels inserted through box in parallel fashion
h) Oven rack
i) target food (fish skin-side down)
j) Thermometers (although probe styles are shown, standard stem models may be used in a pinch)
k) Thermometer probes (one in the box, the other in the fish)

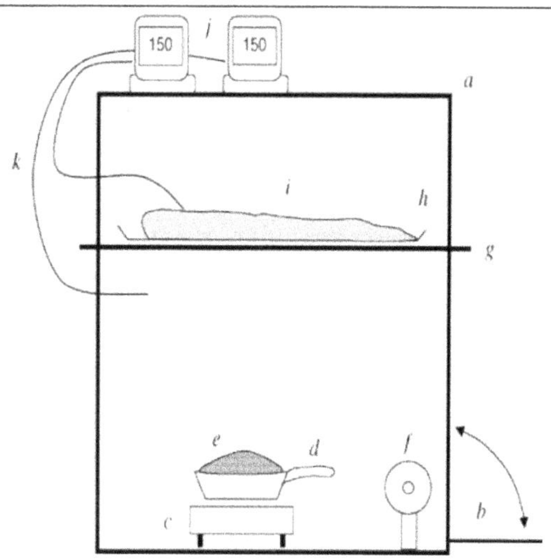

Figure 6: Cardboard Smoker

SMOKED SALMON

Episode: Where There's Smoke There's Fish, EA1D09

1 cup kosher salt **1/2 cup sugar** **1/2 cup dark brown sugar** **1 tablespoon crushed black peppercorns**	1) In a bowl, mix together salt, sugar, brown sugar and peppercorns.
2 large salmon fillets or sides, pin bones removed	2) Spread extra-wide aluminum foil a little longer than the length of the fish and top with an equally long layer of plastic wrap. 3) Sprinkle 1/3 of the rub onto the plastic. 4) Lay 1 side of the fish skin down onto the rub. 5) Sprinkle 1/3 of the rub onto the flesh of the salmon. 6) Place second side of salmon, flesh down onto the first side. 7) Use the remaining rub to cover the skin on the top piece. 8) Fold plastic over to cover then close edges of foil together and crimp tightly around the fish. 9) Place wrapped fish onto a plank or sheet pan and top with another plank or pan. 10) Weigh with a heavy phone book or a brick or two and refrigerate for 12 hours. 11) Flip the fish over and refrigerate another 12 hours. Some juice will leak out during the process so make sure there's a place for the runoff to gather. 12) Unwrap fish and rinse off the cure with cold water. 13) Pat salmon with paper towels then place in a cool, dry place (not the refrigerator) until the surface of the fish is dry and matte-like, 1 to 3 hours depending on humidity. 14) A fan may be used to speed the process. 15) Smoke fish over smoldering hardwood chips or sawdust, keeping the temperature inside the smoker between 150° F and 160° F until the thickest part of the fish registers 150°. 16) Serve immediately or cool to room temperature, wrap tightly and refrigerate for up to 3 days. 17) Cook's Note: trout, mackerel, and bluefish also smoke well.

Difficulty: Easy **Prep Time:** 24 hours 30 minutes **Cook Time:** 5 hours **Yield:** 20 to 30 portions depending on size of fish

BROILED SALMON WITH AB'S SPICE POMADE

Episode: Spice Capades, EA1G20

2 teaspoons canola oil **1 side of salmon (approximately 3 pounds), pin bones removed**	1) Rub sheet pan with the 2 teaspoons of oil and place side of salmon in pan.
1 1/2 teaspoons kosher salt **1 teaspoon fresh ground black pepper**	2) Salt and pepper salmon. Set aside.
1 tablespoon whole coriander, toasted **1 tablespoon whole fennel seed, toasted** **1 teaspoon whole cumin seed, toasted** **1 whole star anise pod** **2 teaspoons onion powder** **1 teaspoon garlic powder** **1/2 teaspoon cayenne pepper**	3) Add coriander, fennel seed, cumin seed, star anise, onion powder, garlic powder and cayenne pepper to a blender. 4) Turn blender on high and process until whole spices become powder.
1/3 cup canola oil	5) With blender running, pour in 1/3 cup canola oil and blend until well combined. 6) Stop blender to brush down sides of container, if necessary. 7) Brush salmon with spice mixture. 8) Allow salmon to sit at room temperature for 30 minutes. 9) Preheat oven to the high broiler setting. 10) Place salmon in the oven 6-inches from broiler. 11) Cook until salmon reaches an internal temperature of 131 degrees F. 12) This will take approximately 15 minutes, but will vary with different ovens. 13) Remove from oven and let rest for 10 minutes, and then serve immediately. Note that the internal temperature of the fish will a rise a little as carry-over cooking occurs.

Difficulty: Easy **Prep Time:** 15 minutes **Inactive Prep Time:** 40 minutes **Cook Time:** 15 minutes
Yield: 6 to 8 main course servings

MACADAMIA NUT CRUSTED MAHI MAHI

Episode: Sometimes You Feel Like A ..., EA1G14

5 ounces (about 1 1/4 cups) coarsely ground, roasted macadamia nuts **1/2 cup panko (Japanese-style bread crumbs)** **2 tablespoons all-purpose flour** **1/4 cup butter, melted**	1) Preheat oven to 425 degrees F. 2) In a medium bowl, stir together the nuts, panko, flour, and butter. Set aside.
Vegetable oil, for brushing foil	3) Place a piece of aluminum foil on a baking sheet and brush it liberally with vegetable oil.
4 (6 to 8-ounce) mahi mahi fillets **Kosher salt and pepper**	4) Place the mahi mahi on the foil and sprinkle each fillet with salt and pepper on both sides. 5) Bake for 5 minutes.
2 tablespoons coconut milk	6) Remove from the oven and brush each fillet with the coconut milk. 7) Divide the nut mixture among the tops of the 4 fillets, patting the mixture to spread and adhere to the fillets. 8) Return to the oven and bake for 5 to 10 minutes, or until the crust is golden brown. 9) Remove from the oven and allow to stand 10 minutes before serving.

Difficulty: Easy **Prep Time:** 10 minutes **Inactive Prep Time:** 10 minutes **Cook Time:** 15 minutes **Yield:** 4 servings

CLAMS ON THE HALF SHELL WITH FRESH MAYONNAISE

Episode: Send in The Clams, EA1D05

24 littleneck clams, steamed **Mayonnaise (recipe in the topping sections)**	1) Serve one teaspoon mayonnaise on top of chilled clams on the half shell. 2) For variations, add 1 tablespoon of any of the following ingredients: roasted garlic, basil chiffonade, chopped chipotle peppers, finely diced roasted red peppers, or prepared horseradish to one cup of mayonnaise.

Difficulty: Medium **Prep Time:** 20 minutes **Cook Time:** 5 minutes **Yield:** 4 to 6 servings

RADONSKY FOR THE NEW MILLENNIUM: Clams

Episode: Send in The Clams, EA1D05

24 Little Neck clams	1) Half shell the clams and set them aside.
1/4 cup flour **1/4 cup seasoned bread crumbs** **1 tablespoon Parmesan, grated** **1/4 teaspoon kosher salt** **1/4 teaspoon fresh pepper**	2) Mix the flour, bread crumbs, Parmesan, salt, and pepper.
3 tablespoons bacon fat	3) In a large pan over high heat, render the bacon fat. 4) Sprinkle a generous coating of the flour mixture over all the clams and carefully place them flesh side down, using a spoon, into the fat. 5) Cook for about two minutes and remove to serving plates flesh side up.
1 tablespoon chopped fresh parsley **Malt vinegar**	6) Top them with fresh parsley and malt vinegar.

Difficulty: Easy **Prep Time:** 10 minutes **Cook Time:** 5 minutes **Yield:** 4 servings

MOJO MOULIES: Mussels

Episode: Mussel Bound, EA1C02

Hardware: **8-quart nonreactive, stainless steel stockpot** **Metal colander or steamer insert** **2 tablespoons minced garlic** **1 large leek, cleaned, trimmed, and chopped** **Pinch kosher salt** **3 tablespoons olive oil**	1) In the stockpot, sweat the garlic, leeks, and salt in the olive oil until softened over medium-low heat.
20 mussels	2) Place the mussels in the colander and spray them with cold water to remove any excess dirt or grit. 3) Remove any beards with a pair of needle-nose pliers.
1 ripe tomato, seeded and chopped **1 1/2 cups white wine**	4) Add the chopped tomato and the wine to the stockpot and turn the heat to medium high, and bring to a simmer. 5) Insert the colander of mussels into the stockpot and cover. 6) After 3 minutes, check to see if the mussels have opened. If some are still closed, cover the pot, and cook for an additional 30 seconds. 7) Discard any unopened mussels. 8) Place the mussels in a serving bowl. 9) Remove 10 mussels from their shells and add them to the stockpot. 10) Using a stick blender or a bar blender, puree the mussels until the liquid is of a sauce-like consistency.
Chopped parsley	11) Pour the sauce over the mussels and garnish with chopped parsley. 12) Serve with a loaf of crusty bread.

Difficulty: Easy **Prep Time:** 10 minutes **Cook Time:** 15 minutes **Yield:** 2 to 4 servings

SQUID VICIOUS

Episode: Squid Pro Quo, EA1D13

1/2 pound squid tentacles and tubes	1) On a clean cutting board, remove the tentacles from the bodies of the squid and reserve. Make sure the tubes are cleaned out and split them open lengthwise so they look like a flat triangle. 2) Using a matte knife, lightly score the squid in a crosshatch pattern. 3) Cut each tube into four pieces of roughly equal size.
1 tablespoon soy sauce **2 teaspoons cornstarch**	4) In a bowl, combine 1 tablespoon of soy sauce with 1 teaspoon of cornstarch and toss the squid in it to coat. 5) Marinate while preparing for the rest of the dish.
1/2 cup miso broth (1/2 cup water mixed with 1 tablespoon miso paste) **1 teaspoon balsamic vinegar**	6) Combine the miso broth and balsamic vinegar with the remaining cornstarch.
2 teaspoons sesame oil	7) In a hot pan or wok, add the sesame oil and swirl to coat the pan. 8) Add the squid and cook for 30 to 40 seconds. It will curl up naturally and brown.
1/2 teaspoon thinly sliced garlic **1/4 teaspoon minced ginger** **2 dried arbol chiles**	9) Working quickly, add the garlic, ginger, and chiles. Allow them to fry for 10 to 15 seconds stirring constantly (they can burn fast).
1/3 cup medium dice sweet onion **1/4 cup torn-into-strips oyster mushrooms** **1/3 cup medium dice red bell pepper**	10) Add the onion, mushrooms, and bell pepper and sauté for another minute. 11) Pour in the stock mixture and simmer until the sauce begins to thicken.
Freshly ground white pepper **Rice, cooked**	12) Season with white pepper and additional soy sauce, if necessary. 13) Serve over rice.

Difficulty: Medium **Prep Time:** 25 minutes **Cook Time:** 5 minutes **Yield:** 2 entrée servings

Notes:

STUFFED LOBSTER

Episode: Crustacean Nation, EA1D05

Ingredients	Directions
	1) Preheat oven to 350° F.
2 (1 1/2-pound) lobsters	2) Place lobsters in pan and chill in freezer for 15 to 20 minutes. 3) Meanwhile, place 1 layer of river rocks in the bottom of a wide pot and fill with 1-inch of water. 4) Bring to a boil over high heat.
Fresh herbs: parsley, rosemary, thyme	5) Spread herbs across rocks, then quickly place lobsters on top. Cover and cook for 2 to 3 minutes. 6) Remove and place in ice bath to halt cooking. 7) Lay paper towels across a cutting board. 8) Bring one lobster to the board and using your chef's knife, cut the lobster straight down the center, from head to tail. 9) Remove tomalley and discard. 10) Remove legs and claws. 11) Using a rolling pin, roll over legs to extract the meat. 12) Roughly chop the meat. 13) Move claws to pan and roast for 4 minutes.
4 tablespoons of butter	14) Meanwhile, melt the butter in a large sauté pan over medium heat.
1/2 onion, diced	15) Add the onions and stir to coat.
1 teaspoon lemon zest 2 tablespoons sliced scallions	16) Follow with the lemon zest and scallions.
2 handfuls crumbled buttery crackers	17) Once onions are translucent add the leg meat. 18) Then add the crackers and toss, off the heat, until all the liquid has been absorbed. 19) Spoon filling into the open body cavities. 20) Brush tail meat with olive oil and place upright on the pan along with the claws. 21) Roast 10 to 14 minutes or until the stuffing browns and tail meat becomes opaque. 22) Crack claws and remove the meat.
Extra-virgin olive oil, for brushing and drizzling	23) Serve on top of stuffed lobster with extra-virgin olive oil on the side for dipping.

Difficulty: Easy **Prep Time:** 20 minutes **Cook Time:** 15 minutes **Yield:** 4 servings

Notes:

THE SHRIMP COCKTAIL

Episode: Crustacean Nation, EA1B07

Ingredients	Directions
32 shell-on (21 to 25 count) tiger shrimp	1) Using a pair of scissors or a serrated knife, make an incision down the backside of the shrimp, following the intestinal track. 2) Eviscerate shrimp and rinse under cool water leaving shells intact.
<u>For the brine:</u> **1/4 cup kosher salt** **1/4 cup sugar** **1 cup water** **2 cups ice**	3) Place cleaned shrimp into a bowl with brine and refrigerate mixture for 20 to 25 minutes.
<u>For the cocktail sauce:</u> **1 (14 1/2-ounce) can diced tomatoes, drained** **1/2 cup prepared chili sauce** **4 tablespoons prepared horseradish** **1 teaspoon sugar** **Few grinds fresh black pepper** **1/2 teaspoon kosher salt**	4) While shrimp are brining, place tomatoes, chili sauce, horseradish, sugar, pepper, and salt in food processor and blend until smooth. 5) Refrigerate cocktail sauce until ready to serve. 6) Place a baking sheet or broiler pan under oven broiler and preheat for 5 minutes. 7) Remove shrimp from brine and drain thoroughly. 8) Rinse the shrimp under cold water and dry on paper towels.
1 tablespoon olive oil **Sprinkle Old Bay seasoning**	9) In a large bowl, toss shrimp with olive oil and sprinkle with Old Bay seasoning, if desired. 10) Place shrimp onto a sizzling sheet pan and return to broiler immediately. 11) After 2 minutes, turn the shrimp with a pair of tongs. 12) Return the shrimp to broiler for 1 minute. 13) Transfer to a cold cookie sheet. Refrigerate immediately. 14) Once shrimp have chilled, arrange with cocktail sauce in a martini glass or as desired.

Difficulty: Easy **Prep Time:** 45 minutes **Inactive Prep Time:** 25 minutes **Cook Time:** x minutes **Yield:** 4 servings

Notes:____

COCONUT SHRIMP WITH PEANUT SAUCE

Episode: Down and Out in Paradise, EASP02

24 large (15 to 20 count) shrimp, peeled, deviened, and butterflied	1) Pat the shrimp dry with a paper towel.
1/2 cup cornstarch **1/4 teaspoon kosher salt** **1/4 teaspoon fresh ground white pepper** **1/4 teaspoon cayenne pepper**	2) In a small bowl combine cornstarch, salt, pepper, and cayenne.
4 egg whites	3) In a separate bowl, whisk the egg whites until foamy.
2 1/2 cups sweetened shredded coconut, or 2 1/2 cups shredded fresh coconut	4) In another bowl, place the coconut. 5) Coat the shrimp with the cornstarch and shake off any excess. 6) Dip into the egg white and then press into the coconut to get full coverage. Try to keep 1 hand dry, this will keep things a little cleaner.
Canola or peanut oil, for frying	7) In a large pan, heat the oil to 350° F and gently submerge the shrimp, 6 at a time. Fry for about 3 minutes or until golden brown. 8) Remove them to a rack to drain.
Peanut Sauce, recipe follows	9) Serve with Peanut Sauce.

Difficulty: Medium **Prep Time:** 25 minutes **Cook Time:** 15 minutes **Yield:** 4 to 6 servings

Peanut Sauce:

1/4 cup chicken stock **3 ounces unsweetened coconut milk** **1 ounce lime juice** **1 ounce soy sauce** **1 tablespoon fish sauce or 2 to 3 anchovies, ground** **1 tablespoon hot sauce** **2 tablespoons chopped garlic** **1 tablespoon chopped ginger**	1) In a food processor, puree the chicken stock, coconut milk, lime juice, soy sauce, fish sauce, hot sauce, chopped garlic, and ginger.
1 1/2 cups creamy peanut butter	2) Add the peanut butter and pulse to combine.
1/4 cup chopped cilantro	3) Fold in the cilantro and keep refrigerated until ready to serve. 4) Bring sauce to room temperature and serve with coconut shrimp.

Yield: about 2 cups

GARLIC SHRIMP CASSEROLE

Episode: Casserole Over, EA1F11

2 cups chicken stock **2 tablespoons cornstarch with 1 tablespoon water**	1) Preheat oven to 350 degrees F. 2) In a small saucepan, combine the chicken stock and the cornstarch slurry and bring to a simmer for 3 minutes.
1/2 cup heavy cream **1/2 teaspoon red pepper flakes**	3) Add the cream and the red pepper flakes.
1 pint leftover rice **2 pints leftover garlic shrimp**	4) In a foil lined terra cotta pot, pour the rice and add the leftover garlic shrimp. 5) Then pour the cream mixture over it.
3/4 cup toasted panko bread crumbs (Japanese bread crumbs)	6) Top with the toasted panko and place in the oven for 45 minutes. 7) Cool for 15 minutes before serving.

Difficulty: Easy **Prep Time:** 5 minutes **Inactive Prep Time:** 15 minutes **Cook Time:** 50 minutes **Yield:** 4 to 6 servings

SALT ROASTED SHRIMP

Episode: Eat This Rock!, EASP03

4 pounds rock salt	1) Divide salt evenly among 2 (9 by 13-inch) metal pans divide salt evenly. 2) Heat your oven to 400 degrees F and put the pans of salt into the oven to heat. 3) When the oven reaches 400 degrees F, allow the salt to continue heating for another 15 minutes.
1 pound jumbo shrimp (20 to 24 shrimp per pound), with heads on	4) After 15 minutes have passed, put the shrimp on top of the salt in 1 of the pans. Then cover with all of the salt in the second pan. The shrimp should be evenly and completely covered. 5) Roast for 8 minutes. 6) Remove from oven and check 1 shrimp for doneness. The shrimp should be opaque and white and pink in color. If not done, return to oven for 1 to 2 minutes. Serve immediately.

Difficulty: Easy **Prep Time:** 10 minutes **Cook Time:** 23 minutes **Yield:** 4 servings

SUSHI RICE

Episode: Wake Up Little Sushi, EA0907

2 cups sushi or short grain rice **2 cups water, plus extra for rinsing rice**	1) Place the rice into a mixing bowl and cover with cool water. 2) Swirl the rice in the water, pour off and repeat 2 to 3 times or until the water is clear. 3) Place the rice and 2 cups of water into a medium saucepan and place over high heat. 4) Bring to a boil, uncovered. 5) Once it begins to boil, reduce the heat to the lowest setting and cover. Cook for 15 minutes. 6) Remove from the heat and let stand, covered, for 10 minutes.
2 tablespoons rice vinegar **2 tablespoons sugar** **1 tablespoon kosher salt**	7) Combine the rice vinegar, sugar and salt in a small bowl and heat in the microwave on high for 30 to 45 seconds. 8) Transfer the rice into a large wooden or glass mixing bowl and add the vinegar mixture. 9) Fold thoroughly to combine and coat each grain of rice with the mixture. 10) Allow to cool to room temperature before using to make sushi or sashimi.

Difficulty: Easy **Prep Time:** 5 minutes **Inactive Prep Time:** 1 hour **Cook Time:** 10 minutes **Yield:** 4 cups

Notes:

CALIFORNIA ROLL

Episode: Wake Up Little Sushi, EA0907

Ingredients	Directions
Juice of 1/2 lemon **1 medium avocado, peeled, pitted, and sliced into 1/4-inch thick pieces**	1) Squeeze the lemon juice over the avocado to prevent browning. 2) Cover a bamboo rolling mat with plastic wrap.
4 sheets nori	3) Cut nori sheets in half crosswise. 4) Lay 1 sheet of nori, shiny side down, on the plastic covered mat.
1/2 batch sushi rice (recipe elsewhere)	5) Wet your fingers with water and spread about 1/2 cup of the rice evenly onto the nori.
1/3 cup sesame seeds, toasted	6) Sprinkle the rice with sesame seeds. 7) Turn the sheet of nori over so that the rice side is down.
1 small cucumber, peeled, seeded, and cut into matchstick-size pieces **4 crabsticks, torn into pieces**	8) Place 1/8 of the cucumber, avocado and crab sticks in the center of the sheet. 9) Grab the edge of the mat closest to you, keeping the fillings in place with your fingers, and roll it into a tight cylinder, using the mat to shape the cylinder. 10) Pull away the mat and set aside. 11) Cover with a damp cloth. 12) Repeat until all of the rice has been used. 13) Cut each roll into 6 pieces.
Pickled ginger, for serving **Wasabi, for serving** **Soy sauce, for serving**	14) Serve with pickled ginger, wasabi and soy sauce.

Difficulty: Medium **Prep Time:** 45 minutes **Inactive Prep Time:** 1 hour **Cook Time:** 20 minutes **Yield:** 8 appetizer servings

Some Japanese Terms and Phrases for Sushi

Konnichi-wa	Good afternoon!
Komban wa	Good evening!
Hashi	Chopsticks
Maki-zushi	Sushi made in a rice and seaweed roll, sliced into bite-size rounds.
Nigiri-zushi	Traditional sushi, fish or other food on top of bite-size balls of rice.
Temaki-zushi	"Hand roll," a sushi roll shaped very much like an ice-cream cone for eating out of hand.
Sashimi	Fresh raw seafood attractively sliced and displayed as a dinner dish.
Nori	Crisp and papery, blackish-green seaweed used to wrap maki-zushi.
Shoyu	Soy Sauce.
Wasabi	Hot green Japanese horseradish paste.
O Kudasai	"I would like." Say this after the word for the item you want, as in "Maguro O Kudasai" for "Tuna sushi, please."
Oma ka se	"Make me something good."
Kanpai!	"Here's to you!" toasting with sake.
Sumimasen	Pardon me.
Domo, Arigato or **Domo Arigato**	Thanks.
Arigato Gozaimashita	Thanks and so long!

FISH ROLL WITH COMPOUND BUTTER

Episode: Fit to be Tied, EA1F17

2 thin salmon fillets **3 flounder fillets**	1) On your counter top lay out a sheet of parchment paper and top it with a layer of plastic wrap. 2) Lay out your fillets of salmon, tails away from you. 3) Overlap the fillets of flounder about 1-inch over the tails of the salmon.
8 sea scallops	4) Then place the scallops on a metal skewer and set at the end of the flounder furthest from you.
1 tablespoon chopped fresh dill **1 tablespoon chopped fresh parsley** **Salt and pepper, for seasoning**	5) Sprinkle the herbs over the fish and season with salt and pepper. 6) Using the plastic wrap pull the fish towards you so that the plastic begins to pull the flounder over the scallops. Be sure not to roll the plastic into the fish roll. 7) Use a sheet pan to push the roll tightly as you pull the plastic toward you. The roll should be tight and you should be able to remove the sheet of plastic. 8) Then roll the fish in the parchment away from you so it is covered and can be place into the refrigerator. Refrigerate for 1 hour.
<u>Compound Butter:</u> **4 ounces butter (1 stick), at room temperature** **1 teaspoon dry parsley flakes** **1/4 teaspoon salt** **1/4 teaspoon fresh ground black pepper**	9) For Compound Butter: In a large bowl using a wooden spoon mix all ingredients. 10) Place the mixture on a piece of parchment and fold the parchment over itself. 11) Pull to form a roll and twist the ends. 12) Place in the freezer for 10 minutes to set up. 13) Slice into 1/4-inch rounds and remove the parchment.
Canola oil, for brushing	14) Preheat your broiler and place the oven rack 6-inches from the heating element. 15) Remove the metal skewer and slice the roulade into 3/4 to 1-inch rounds. 16) Place onto a broiler pan and brush each round with canola oil. 17) Put under the broiler for 3 to 6 minutes depending on how well done you like your fish. 18) Serve with 1 slice of compound butter on each fish roll.

Difficulty: Medium **Prep Time:** 25 minutes **Inactive Prep Time:** 70 minutes **Cook Time:** 6 minutes **Yield:** 9 servings

STEAMED ALASKA KING CRAB CLAWS

Episode: Crustacean Nation III: Feeling Crabby, EA1G01

6 Alaskan king crab claws, thawed **2 sprigs dill**	1) If necessary in order to fit in microwave, cut claws at joints. 2) Wrap 3 claws at a time in a damp paper towel, along with 1 sprig of dill, and then wrap in plastic wrap. 3) Place wrapped claws in microwave 1 package at a time and cook on high for 2 minutes. 4) Remove and unwrap carefully. Serve immediately.

Difficulty: East **Prep Time:** 5 minutes **Cook Time:** 6x minutes **Yield:** 2 servings

Notes:____

CRAB CAKES OR FRITTERS

Episode: Crustacean Nation III: Feeling Crabby, EA1G01

1 cup lump or backfin crabmeat **1 cup special crabmeat (small pieces white crabmeat)** **1/2 cup mayonnaise** **1/2 teaspoon freshly ground black pepper** **1/2 lemon, juiced**	1) If using a deep fryer, heat vegetable oil to 375 degrees F. 2) In a bowl combine the crabmeat, mayonnaise, pepper, and lemon juice. 3) Form into either 1-ounce balls for fritters or into 3-ounce cakes.
1 1/2 cups panko bread crumbs	4) Roll in the panko to evenly coat.
Vegetable oil, for frying	5) Deep-fry the fritters in until golden brown, about 5 to 7 minutes or pan-fry the cakes in 1 to 2 inches of 375 degree F vegetable oil until golden brown and flip to brown on the other side about 3 to 4 minutes per side. 6) Drain both on a tray lined with paper towels. Serve immediately.

Difficulty: Easy **Prep Time:** 15 minutes **Cook Time:** 7 minutes **Yield:** 4 to 6 cakes, 16 fritters

BAKED OYSTERS BROWNEFELLER

Episode: Shell Game, EA1H02

6 tablespoons unsalted butter	1) Preheat oven to 425 degrees F. 2) Melt butter in a 12-inch sauté pan over medium-low heat.
3/4 cup finely chopped onion **3/4 cup finely chopped celery** **1 teaspoon kosher salt, divided**	3) Increase the heat slightly and add the onion, celery, and 1/2 teaspoon kosher salt; sweat for 5 to 7 minutes.
1 tablespoon minced garlic	4) Add garlic and cook for an additional 1 to 2 minutes.
1 (14-ounce) can artichoke hearts, drained and finely chopped **1 cup Japanese (panko) bread crumbs** **2 teaspoons finely chopped lemon zest** **1/2 teaspoon freshly ground black pepper** **1 teaspoon dried oregano**	5) Reduce the heat to low and add the artichoke hearts, bread crumbs, lemon zest, remaining 1/2 teaspoon kosher salt, pepper, and oregano. 6) Continue cooking for 2 to 3 more minutes. Remove from the heat and set aside.
4 cups rock salt	7) Place the 4 cups rock salt on a sheet pan with sides and spread evenly.
24 oysters on the half shell, with their liquor	8) Set oysters atop the salt and divide the bread crumb mixture evenly among them. 9) Place in oven and bake for 10 to 12 minutes. 10) Bread crumbs should be lightly browned. Serve immediately.

Difficulty: Medium **Prep Time:** 45 minutes **Cook Time:** 25 minutes **Yield:** 4 servings

BIG CHEESE SQUEEZE

Episode: For Whom The Cheese Melts, EA1B02

Ingredients	Directions
	1) Find 2 heavy skillets that will nest together. Two (10-inch) cast iron skillets are ideal. Heat them over high heat.
2 slices of bread, cut thin (as far as bread selection goes, all I'll say is the bigger the loaf the bigger the sandwich) **1 teaspoon (or more) smooth Dijon mustard**	2) Meanwhile, spread mustard on one slice of bread.
1 cup Grated cheese (This is the soul of the thing, so use the good stuff. We like a semi-hard, semi-soft combo like smoked gouda and Gruyere or Fontina with a young Asiago. If you're a purist, go for the Cheddar, but make it sharp and aged if possible. **Fresh Black Pepper**	3) Distribute the cheese evenly over the mustard, season with fresh black pepper and top with second piece of bread.
Good quality olive oil for spritzing.	4) Spritz the bread surface that's staring up at you with olive oil using either a Misto or a pump sprayer. A light coat will do, don't soak. 5) When the pans are hot enough to vigorously sizzle a drop of water, remove them from the heat and place the sandwich, top-side down in the middle of one pan. (If your pans are a different size, this would be the smaller one.) 6) Spritz the slice now facing you, as well as the bottom of the other skillet. 7) Lay the skillet right on top of the sandwich. If the top pan isn't cast iron, weigh it down with a brick, can, or something of similar heft. 8) Wait patiently, crack a beer. When you hear the first bit of cheese run out and sizzle on the pan, it's done. This will take anywhere from 3 to 5 minutes. 9) Carefully remove the top skillet, (you may need to coax it off with a spatula, but I doubt it). Just look at it. It's perfect...better than mom's. (No reason to tell her.) 10) Remove to a plate, count to 10 and slice it in half. 11) Take a bite. 12) Take another. So they lost ... there's always next year.

CUBAN SANDWICH

Episode: SandwichCraft, EA1H01

Ingredients	Directions
4 hoagie rolls	1) Slice the bread horizontally in half, leaving 1 edge intact.
2 tablespoons yellow mustard	2) Lay the bread open and spread each side with the mustard.
1/4 pound baked ham, thinly sliced **1/4 pound roast pork, thinly sliced** **1/4 pound provolone cheese, thinly sliced** **10 thin dill pickle slices, approximately 2 whole pickles**	3) Divide the ingredients evenly among the slices of roll. Start with the ham followed by the pork, cheese, and dill pickles. 4) Bring the tops and bottoms together. 5) Heat your panini maker or sandwich press.
1 tablespoon unsalted butter, room temperature	6) Butter each side of the press. 7) Place the sandwiches inside, press down and grill until the cheese is melted and the bread is flat and browned, approximately 10 minutes. 8) If you don't have a sandwich press, you can heat 6 fireplace bricks wrapped in foil, in a 500 degrees F oven for 1 hour and then press the sandwich between them for 10 minutes. Serve warm.

Difficulty: Easy **Prep Time:** 10 minutes **Cook Time:** 10 minutes **Yield:** 4 servings

PAN BAGNAT

Episode: SandwichCraft, EA1H01

1 tablespoon red wine vinegar **1/2 teaspoon Dijon mustard** **1/2 teaspoon kosher salt** **1/4 teaspoon freshly ground black pepper**	1) In a small mixing bowl, whisk together the red wine vinegar, mustard, salt, and pepper.
3 tablespoons olive oil	2) While continuing to whisk, gradually add the olive oil. Whisk until an emulsion forms. Set aside.
1 baguette, approximately 16 to 18 inches long	3) Slice the baguette horizontally into 2 pieces. 4) Tear out some of the soft bread in the center of each side, making a slight well in the bread.
12 ounces canned tuna packed in oil or water, drained and crumbled **1 small green pepper, sliced into rings** **1 small red onion, sliced into rings** **2 hard-boiled eggs, sliced** **1 cup chopped kalamata olives** **1 tomato, thinly sliced**	5) Place the tuna, green pepper, red onion, hard-boiled eggs, olives, and tomato on the bottom side of the bread in that order. 6) Drizzle the vinaigrette over the vegetables, top with the second piece of bread, and wrap tightly in plastic wrap. 7) Let stand at room temperature for 2 hours before serving. 8) Cut into 4 sandwiches and serve.

Prep Time: 25 minutes **Inactive Prep Time:** 2 hours **Yield:** 4 sandwiches

Soup

BIRD TO THE LAST DROP: Vegetable Soup

Episode: Behind the Bird, EA1C14

2 quarts vegetable stock **1 turkey carcass**	1) Combine the vegetable stock and the turkey carcass in a large soup pot over low heat and bring to a simmer. 2) Cover and simmer for 1 hour.
1 (10-ounce) box frozen mixed vegetables **1/2 cup rice** **2 cups cooked turkey, cubed** **1 teaspoon Old Bay seasoning** **2 teaspoons dried thyme** **Salt and pepper, to taste**	3) Add the remaining ingredients to the stock. 4) Cover and simmer for an additional 20 minutes. 5) Remove the bones before serving.

Difficulty: Easy **Prep Time:** 10 minutes **Cook Time:** 1 hour 20 minutes **Yield:** 6 servings

CLAM CHOWDER

Episode: Send in The Clams, EA1D05

Ingredients	Directions
3 ounces salt pork, finely diced	1) In a heavy-bottomed saucepot, render the salt pork until just crisp. Remove and discard.
1 1/2 cups small diced yellow onion	2) Sweat the onion in the pork fat until tender.
6 cups small diced baking potatoes, like russets **2 cups milk** Kosher salt and freshly ground pepper	3) Add the potatoes and cover with milk. 4) Bring to a boil and let simmer until potatoes are soft. 5) Season with salt and pepper.
1 (6.5 ounce) can clams, drained, juice reserved	6) In a separate pot, fitted with a steamer basket, bring the reserved clam juice to a boil.
12 Little Neck clams	7) Add clams and cover. 8) Steam for three minutes until all clams are open. 9) Remove the clams as they open and transfer to a bowl. 10) Add the steaming juices to the pot with the chowder. 11) Using a stick blender puree to desired consistency. Adjust seasonings. 12) Finely chop the drained canned clams. 13) Fold into the chowder.
Chopped fresh parsley, for garnish **Sour cream, for garnish** **Grape tomatoes, halved, for garnish**	14) Serve with steamed clams, parsley, sour cream and grape tomatoes, as garnish.

Difficulty: Medium **Prep Time:** 20 minutes **Cook Time:** 20 minutes **Yield:** 4 large servings

CHICKEN NOODLE SOUP

Episode: True Brew IV: Take Stock, EA1G11

Ingredients	Directions
4 cups chicken stock, home made or store bought (see Chicken Stock recipe)	1) Bring stock to boil for 2 minutes in a large, non-reactive stockpot with lid on, over high heat.
3/4 cup diced onion **3/4 cup diced celery** **1 tablespoon minced garlic**	2) Add onion, celery, and garlic. 3) Lower heat and simmer for 2 minutes.
2 ounces dried egg noodles, cooked to al dente	4) Add noodles and cook 5 more minutes.
1/2 teaspoon finely chopped fresh tarragon leaves **2 teaspoons finely chopped fresh parsley leaves**	5) Remove from heat and add herbs and salt and pepper, to taste.
Lemon halves, for serving	6) Serve with lemon halves and add squeeze of lemon juice if desired.

Difficulty: Easy **Prep Time:** 30 minutes **Cook Time:** 7 minutes **Yield:** 4 1/2 cups soup

Notes:

FRENCH ONION SOUP

Episode: A Bowl of Onion, EA1A09

10 sweet onions (like Vidalias) or a combination of sweet and red onions	1) Trim the ends off each onion then slice from end to end. 2) Remove peel and finely slice into half moon shapes.
3 tablespoons butter	3) Set electric skillet to 300° and add butter.
1 teaspoon salt	4) Once butter has melted add a layer of onions and sprinkle with a little salt. Repeat layering onions and salt until all onions are in the skillet. Do not try stirring until onions have sweated down for 15 to 20 minutes. After that, stir occasionally until onions are dark mahogany and reduced to approximately 2 cups. This should take 45 minutes to 1 hour. Do not worry about burning.
2 cups white wine	5) Add enough wine to cover the onions and turn heat to high, reducing the wine to a syrup consistency.
10 ounces canned beef consume **10 ounces chicken broth (low sodium, fat free*)** **10 ounces apple cider (unfiltered is best)** **Bouquet garni; thyme sprigs, bay leaf and parsley**	6) Add consume, chicken broth, apple cider and bouquet garni. 7) Reduce heat and simmer 15 to 20 minutes. 8) Place oven rack in top 1/3 of oven and heat broiler.
1 loaf country style bread	9) Cut country bread in rounds large enough to fit mouth of oven safe soup crocks. 10) Place the slices on a baking sheet and place under broiler for 1 minute.
Kosher salt **Ground black pepper** **Splash of Cognac (optional)**	11) Season soup mixture with salt, pepper and cognac. 12) Ladle soup into crocks leaving one inch to the lip.
1 cup Fontina or Gruyere cheese, grated	13) Place bread round, toasted side down, on top of soup and top with grated cheese. 14) Broil until cheese is bubbly and golden, 1 to 2 minutes.

Difficulty: Easy **Prep Time:** 15 minutes **Cook Time:** 1 hour 45 minutes **Yield:** 8 servings

*Mentioned in the show

LEFTOVER BAKED POTATO SOUP

Episode: This Spud's For You Too, EA1D11

3 tablespoons butter **1 1/2 cups finely diced leeks** **1 1/2 tablespoons minced garlic**	1) In a large saucepot, over high heat melt the butter and add the leeks and garlic. 2) Cook over medium heat until they are translucent.
6 cups chicken stock, hot	3) Add the hot stock and whisk to combine.
4 large leftover baked potatoes, halved. pulp scooped out and put through a ricer **1 1/2 cups buttermilk** **1/2 cup sour cream** **1/2 cup freshly grated Parmesan**	4) In a separate bowl, whisk together the riced potatoes, buttermilk, sour cream, and grated Parmesan. 5) Add this mixture to the soup stirring constantly.
2 1/2 teaspoons kosher salt **1 teaspoon freshly ground pepper**	6) Season with salt and pepper.
2 tablespoons Sherry vinegar	7) Remove from the heat and add the Sherry vinegar.
1/4 cup minced chives	8) Ladle into bowls and garnish with chives.

Difficulty: Easy **Prep Time:** 15 minutes **Cook Time:** 20 minutes **Yield:** 4 servings

PAPAYA SOUP

Episode: Down and Out in Paradise, EASP02

1 cup sugar **1 cup water**	1) In a small saucepot combine the sugar and water, and cook over low heat until sugar is dissolved.
2 lemons, zested and juiced **3 limes, juiced and strained**	2) Pour into a bowl containing the lemon and lime juice.
3 papayas, peeled, seeded, and small diced **3 tablespoons thinly sliced candied ginger** **2 tablespoons chiffonade fresh mint leaves**	3) Add the papaya, candied ginger, and mint.
1 cup raspberries **1 cup blackberries**	4) In a separate bowl toss raspberries and blackberries. 5) Place papaya mixture into each serving bowl. 6) In the center place a spoonful of mixed berries and garnish with lemon zest.

Difficulty: Easy **Prep Time:** 20 minutes **Cook Time:** 5 minutes **Yield:** 4 servings

SQUASH SOUP

Episode: Art of Darkness, EA1D08

	1) Preheat the oven to 400° F.
6 cups (about 2 large squash) seeded 2-inch wide chunks butternut squash **Melted butter, for brushing** **1 tablespoon kosher salt, plus 1 teaspoon** **1 teaspoon freshly ground white pepper, plus 1/2 teaspoon**	2) Brush the flesh of the squash with a little butter and season with 1 tablespoon salt and 1 teaspoon freshly ground white pepper. 3) On a sheet pan lay the squash flesh side up. 4) Roast for about 30 to 35 minutes or until the flesh is nice and soft.
3 cups chicken or vegetable stock **4 tablespoons honey** **1 teaspoon minced ginger**	5) Scoop the flesh from the skin into a pot and add the stock, honey, and ginger. 6) Bring to a simmer and puree using a stick blender.
4 ounces heavy cream	7) Stir in the heavy cream and return to a low simmer.
1/4 teaspoon nutmeg	8) Season with salt, pepper, and nutmeg.

Difficulty: Easy **Prep Time:** 10 minutes **Cook Time:** 40 minutes **Yield:** 4 servings

Notes:______________________________

GARDEN VEGETABLE SOUP

Episode: Soup's On, EA1H12

Ingredients	Directions
4 tablespoons olive oil	1) Heat the olive oil in large, heavy-bottomed stockpot over medium-low heat.
2 cups chopped leeks, white part only (from approximately 3 medium leeks) **2 tablespoons finely minced garlic** **Kosher salt**	2) Once hot, add the leeks, garlic, and a pinch of salt and sweat until they begin to soften, approximately 7 to 8 minutes.
2 cups carrots, peeled and chopped into rounds (approximately 2 medium) **2 cups peeled and diced potatoes** **2 cups fresh green beans, broken or cut into 3/4-inch pieces**	3) Add the carrots, potatoes, and green beans and continue to cook for 4 to 5 more minutes, stirring occasionally.
2 quarts chicken or vegetable broth	4) Add the stock, increase the heat to high, and bring to a simmer.
4 cups peeled, seeded, and chopped tomatoes **2 ears corn, kernels removed** **1/2 teaspoon freshly ground black pepper**	5) Once simmering, add the tomatoes, corn kernels, and pepper. 6) Reduce the heat to low, cover, and cook until the vegetables are fork tender, approximately 25 to 30 minutes.
1/4 cup packed, chopped fresh parsley leaves	7) Remove from heat and add the parsley and lemon juice.
1 to 2 teaspoons freshly squeezed lemon juice	8) Season, to taste, with kosher salt. Serve immediately.

Difficulty: Medium **Prep Time:** 40 minutes **Cook Time:** 45 minutes **Yield:** 6 to 8 servings

BULGUR GAZPACHO

Episode: Ill Gotten Grains, EA1G07

Ingredients	Directions
1 cup water **1 cup tomato puree**	1) Bring the water and 1/2 the tomato puree to a boil.
3/4 cup bulgur	2) Pour over the bulgur and cover for 20 minutes. 3) Fluff with a fork.
2 tablespoons balsamic vinegar **1 garlic clove, minced** **1/2 teaspoon ground cumin** **1 1/2 teaspoons salt** **1 1/4 teaspoons Louisiana hot sauce** **4 scallions, sliced** **1 cup roughly chopped tomatoes** **1 cup cucumbers, peeled, seeded, and diced** **3/4 cup green bell pepper, small dice** **3 tablespoons chopped cilantro leaves**	4) Combine remaining ingredients and toss with the bulgur. 5) Chill for 1 hour before serving.

Difficulty: Easy **Prep Time:** 25 minutes **Inactive Prep Time:** 1 hour **Cook Time:** 20 minutes **Yield:** 6 servings

GRAPE GAZPACHO

Episode: Soup's On, EA1H12

1 small cucumber, seeded and chopped (approximately 1 cup) 1 Granny Smith apple, peeled, cored, and chopped (approximately 1 cup) 1 cup chopped tomatillos (approximately 3 medium tomatillos)	1) Place half of the cucumbers, apples, and tomatillos into the bowl of a food processor.
1 pound seedless green grapes (approximately 3 cups) 1 cup chopped walnuts, toasted 1 cup plain yogurt 1 cup white grape juice 1 teaspoon rice wine vinegar 6 large mint leaves	2) Add all of the grapes, walnuts, yogurt, grape juice, vinegar, and mint. 3) Pulse 9 to 10 times. 4) Combine with the remaining half of the cucumber, apple, and tomatillo.
Kosher salt	5) Season with salt, to taste. 6) Chill for 2 hours in the refrigerator before serving. 7) Serve as an appetizer or soup course.

Difficulty: Easy **Prep Time:** 15 minutes **Inactive Prep Time:** 2 hours **Yield:** 4 servings

Pasta

FRESH PASTA

Episode: Use Your Noodle Too, EA1F15

3 cups all-purpose flour 2 large eggs 3 tablespoons water 1 teaspoon olive oil 1/2 teaspoon salt	<u>By Hand:</u> 1) On a clean surface make a well with the flour. 2) In a measuring cup mix the eggs, water and oil and salt. 3) Pour the wet mixture slowly into the flour and mix with your 2 fingers until all of the wet is incorporated. 4) Do not force the dough to take all of the flour. 5) If you are going to use a pasta machine to roll out the dough you may at this point form the dough into a disk and cover with plastic wrap. 6) Place in the refrigerator for 1 hour to rest. 7) If you going to roll this by hand you should knead the dough on a floured work surface for 8 to 10 minutes.
	<u>By Food Processor:</u> 1) In the bowl of your food processor combine the flour and salt and pulse 2 to 3 times. 2) In a liquid measuring cup whisk the eggs, water and oil. 3) While pulsing the machine pour this mixture in a continuous stream and continue running the machine until the dough begins to pull away from the sides of the bowl. 4) Follow directions above for hand rolling or machine.

Difficulty: Easy **Prep Time:** 5 minutes **Cook Time:** 3 to 5 minutes **Yield:** 4 to 6 servings

PASTA: Spaghetti

Episode: Use Your Noodle, EA1A11

3 quarts water **1 tablespoon kosher salt**	1) Place water in large lidded pot, add salt and bring to a rolling boil.
16 ounces dried spaghetti noodles	2) Add spaghetti, fanning it into the water so that each strand makes contact. 3) Using a wooden spoon or tongs, gently bend noodles to submerge. 4) Cover pot and return to a rolling boil, reducing heat to medium-high. 5) Stir occasionally.
3 tablespoons extra-virgin olive oil **2 to 3 cloves of garlic, minced fine**	6) Pour 3 tablespoons of good quality extra virgin olive oil into the bottom of a wide serving bowl along with garlic. 7) In 4 minutes, start tasting. When done, a string of spaghetti should be springy when pulled on. 8) To the tooth, there should be some resistance but not so much that the pasta sticks in the teeth. 9) As soon as pasta is done, drain immediately in a large colander (lidded models are the best). Shake pasta to stop cooking but don't shake dry. And no rinsing. 10) Add pasta to serving bowl and toss to coat.
Optional Toppings **Capers, Sun dried tomatoes, Red pepper, Olives, Walnuts, Hard cheeses like Asiago and Parmesan, Soft or veined cheeses like gorgonzola or chevre, Canned Artichokes, Smoked oysters, Black pepper**	11) Quickly divide into individual bowls and toss with various toppings.

Yield: 4 servings

RAVIOLI

Episode: Use Your Noodle Too, EA1F15

1/4 recipe Alton Brown's Meatloaf, (elsewhere in this tome) **1 tablespoon balsamic vinegar** **3 tablespoons grated Parmesan** **1/2 teaspoon dry oregano** **Fresh pasta dough, recipe follows** **1 egg mixed with 1 teaspoon water (egg wash)**	1) In a bowl, combine the meatloaf, balsamic vinegar, Parmesan, and oregano, mix well, and set aside 2) Using the fresh pasta recipe (see below), roll out your dough either by hand or by machine. 3) After you have rolled the pasta out into sheets, cut the sheet into an even amount of squares. 4) Using a teaspoon fill the center of half with the filling. 5) Brush around the filling with the egg wash and place the remaining squares on top. 6) Press down around the seal to push out any air bubbles. 7) In half a gallon of rapidly boiling salted water add the ravioli in batches. Remove to a strainer.
For the browned butter for 10 raviolis: **2 tablespoons butter**	8) In a separate pan over medium heat place the butter until it just starts to brown. Toss in 10 ravioli until coated.
1 tablespoon sliced sage	9) Sprinkle in the sage and toss again to evenly distribute.

Difficulty: Medium **Prep Time:** 20 minutes **Cook Time:** 10 minutes **Yield:** 4 servings

TORTELLINI

Episode: Use Your Noodle Too, EA1F15

1/2 cup ricotta cheese **1/4 cup grated Parmesan** **2 tablespoons chopped spinach** **1 egg** **1/4 teaspoon fresh ground black pepper** **1 pinch freshly grated nutmeg** **Fresh pasta**	1) In a bowl combine all ingredients, except for the pasta and egg wash. 2) Using the fresh pasta recipe (see below), roll out your dough either by hand or by machine. 3) Cut into 3 or 4- inch rounds with a round cookie cutter. 4) Place 1/4 teaspoon into the center of each round.
1 egg mixed with 1/2 teaspoon water	5) Brush egg wash (on the bottom half of the round and fold over to seal. 6) Fold back around your finger and turn down the edge to form a tortellini. 7) In half a gallon of rapidly boiling salted water add the tortellini in batches. 8) Cook for 3 to 5 minutes, or until they float to the surface. Remove to a strainer to drain.

Difficulty: Medium **Prep Time:** 25 minutes **Cook Time:** 5 minutes **Yield:** 6 to 8 servings

STOVE TOP MAC-N-CHEESE

Episode: Use Your Noodle II, EA1D10

1/2 pound elbow macaroni	1) In a large pot of boiling, salted water cook the pasta to al dente and drain.
4 tablespoons butter	2) Return to the pot and melt in the butter. Toss to coat.
2 eggs **6 ounces evaporated milk** **1/2 teaspoon hot sauce** **1 teaspoon kosher salt** **Fresh black pepper** **3/4 teaspoon dry mustard** **10 ounces sharp cheddar, shredded**	3) Whisk together the eggs, milk, hot sauce, salt, pepper, and mustard. 4) Stir into the pasta and add the cheese. 5) Over low heat continue to stir for 3 minutes or until creamy.

Difficulty: Easy **Prep Time:** 10 minutes **Cook Time:** 25 minutes **Yield:** 6 to 8 servings

Notes:______________________________

BAKED MACARONI AND CHEESE

Episode: Use Your Noodle II, EA1D10

	1) Preheat oven to 350° F.
1/2 pound elbow macaroni	2) In a large pot of boiling, salted water cook the pasta to al dente.
3 tablespoons butter **3 tablespoons flour** **1 tablespoon powdered mustard**	3) While the pasta is cooking, in a separate pot, melt the butter. 4) Whisk in the flour and mustard and keep it moving for about five minutes. Make sure it's free of lumps.
3 cups milk **1/2 cup yellow onion, finely diced** **1 bay leaf** **1/2 teaspoon paprika**	5) Stir in the milk, onion, bay leaf, and paprika. 6) Simmer for ten minutes and remove the bay leaf.
1 large egg	7) Temper in the egg.
12 ounces sharp cheddar, shredded	8) Stir in 3/4 of the cheese.
1 teaspoon kosher salt **Fresh black pepper**	9) Season with salt and pepper. 10) Fold the macaroni into the mix and pour into a 2-quart casserole dish. 11) Top with remaining cheese.
Topping: **3 tablespoons butter** **1 cup panko bread crumbs**	12) Melt the butter in a sauté pan and toss the bread crumbs to coat. 13) Top the macaroni with the bread crumbs. 14) Bake for 30 minutes. 15) Remove from oven and rest for five minutes before serving. Remember to save leftovers for fried Macaroni and Cheese.

Difficulty: Easy **Prep Time:** 20 minutes **Cook Time:** 45 minutes **Yield:** 6 to 8 servings

NEXT DAY MAC AND CHEESE "TOAST"

Episode: Use Your Noodle II, EA1D10

Leftover baked macaroni and cheese, refrigerated for at least overnight	1) Cut refrigerated macaroni and cheese into slices or bite size pieces.
1 cup all-purpose flour **1 teaspoon salt** **1 teaspoon pepper** **1 teaspoon cayenne**	2) Season the flour with salt, pepper and cayenne. 3) Dredge each piece through the flour and gently tap off excess.
1 egg beaten with 2 ounces water **1 cup panko bread crumbs**	4) Dip in the egg wash and then coat with the bread crumbs. Allow them to rest for 5 minutes so the crust can set.
Oil for deep frying, preheated to 375°	5) Very carefully drop into the oil and fry until golden brown. 6) Remove to a baking sheet fitted with a rack and rest for 2 minutes before serving.

Difficulty: Easy **Prep Time:** 20 minutes **Inactive Prep Time:** overnight **Cook Time:** 4 minutes **Yield:** varies with amount

STEAMED COUSCOUS

Episode: Ill Gotten Grains, EA1G07

2 cups couscous	1) Place couscous in a fine strainer and rinse under cold running water.
Pinch salt	2) Dump couscous onto a sheet pan, sprinkle with salt, and let stand until grains swell, about 10 minutes. 3) Break up lumps with your fingers. 4) Partially fill a large steamer pot or stockpot with 1-inch water. Bring water to simmer.
1/2 cup cold water	5) Place damp tea towel in steamer or colander and add couscous. 6) Fold towel over couscous. Steam, covered, over simmering water for 15 minutes. 7) Pour couscous onto large, rimmed baking sheet and sprinkle with 1/2 cup cold water. 8) Toss with slotted spatula until cool and the water is absorbed.
Olive oil, for spraying hands	9) Spritz hands with olive oil and spread out couscous, breaking up any lumps as you go. 10) Set aside for 5 minutes. 11) Refill pot with enough water to make 1-inch again. 12) Return couscous to colander or steamer and steam, covered, for 10 minutes.

Difficulty: Easy **Prep Time:** 10 minutes **Cook Time:** 30 minutes **Yield:** 4 to 5 cups

PIZZA PIZZAS

Episode: Flat Is Beautiful, EA1C11

2 tablespoons sugar **1 tablespoon kosher salt** **1 tablespoon pure olive oil** **3/4 cup warm water** **2 cups bread flour (for bread machines)** **1 teaspoon instant yeast** **Cooking Spray**	1) Place the sugar, salt, olive oil, water, 1 cup of flour, yeast, and remaining cup of flour into the mixer's work bowl 2) Using the paddle attachment, start the mixer on low and mix until the dough just comes together, forming a ball. 3) Lube the hook attachment with cooking spray. 4) Attach the hook to the mixer and knead for 15 minutes on medium speed. 5) Tear off a small piece of dough and flatten into a disc. 6) Stretch the dough until thin. 7) Hold it up to the light and look to see if the baker's windowpane, or taut membrane, has formed. If the dough tears before it forms, knead the dough for an additional 5 to 10 minutes. 8) Roll the pizza dough into a smooth ball on the countertop. 9) Place into a stainless steel or glass bowl.
2 teaspoons olive oil	10) Add 2 teaspoons of olive oil to the bowl and toss to coat. 11) Cover with plastic wrap and refrigerate for 18 to 24 hours. 12) Place the pizza stone or tile onto the bottom of a cold oven and turn the oven to its highest temperature, about 500° F. If the oven has coils on the oven floor, place the tile onto the lowest rack of the oven. 13) Split the pizza dough into 2 equal parts using a knife or a dough scraper. 14) Flatten into a disk onto the countertop and then fold the dough into a ball. 15) Wet hands barely with water and rub them onto the countertop to dampen the surface. 16) Roll the dough on the surface until it tightens. 17) Cover one ball with a tea towel and rest for 30 minutes. 18) Repeat the steps with the other piece of dough. 19) If not baking the remaining pizza immediately, spray the inside of a zip-top bag with cooking spray and place the dough ball into the bag. Refrigerate for up to 6 days.
Flour, for dusting the pizza peel	20) Sprinkle the flour onto the peel and place the dough onto the peel. 21) Using your hands, form a lip around the edges of the pizza. 22) Stretch the dough into a round disc, rotating after each stretch. Toss the dough in the air if you dare. 23) Shake the pizza on the peel to be sure that it will slide onto the pizza stone or tile. (Dress and bake the pizza immediately for a crisp crust or rest the dough for 30 minutes if you want a chewy texture.)
Olive oil, for the pizza crust	24) Brush the rim of the pizza with olive oil. 25) Spread the pizza sauce evenly onto the pizza.
<u>Toppings</u> **1 1/2 ounces pizza sauce** **1/2 teaspoon each chopped fresh herbs such as thyme, oregano, red pepper flakes, for example** **A combination of 3 grated cheeses such as mozzarella, Monterey Jack, and provolone**	26) Sprinkle the herbs onto the pizza and top with the cheese. 27) Slide the pizza onto the tile and bake for 7 minutes, or until bubbly and golden brown. 28) Rest for 3 minutes before slicing.

Difficulty: Medium **Prep Time:** 24 hours **Cook Time:** 45 minutes **Yield:** 2 pizzas

Notes:____

RAMEN SHRIMP POUCH

Episode: The Pouch Principal, EA1G08

Special equipment: **4 (18-inch) squares aluminum foil**	
2 packages Ramen noodles	1) Preheat oven to 400 degrees F. 2) Divide ramen noodles evenly in center of each of the 4 pieces of aluminum foil.
1/2 cup dried mushrooms, chopped **20 large raw shrimp, peeled and deveined** **1/2 cup finely chopped onion** **1/2 cup sliced scallions** **1/2 teaspoon red pepper flakes** **1/2 teaspoon kosher salt**	3) Stack the following ingredients on top of noodles, in this order: mushrooms, shrimp, onions, scallions, red pepper flakes, and salt. 4) Pull sides and corners of pouch up to form a small basket shape leaving an opening at the top to pour in liquid.
1 quart vegetable broth **1/2 cup mirin** **1/4 cup soy sauce** **4 teaspoons sesame oil**	5) In small bowl, combine vegetable broth, mirin, soy sauce, and sesame oil. 6) Distribute liquid evenly among packs. 7) Press foil together, leaving a small opening to allow steam to escape. 8) Place on cookie sheet and bake in oven for 15 minutes. Serve immediately.

Difficulty: Easy **Prep Time:** 15 minutes **Cook Time:** 15 minutes **Yield:** 4 servings

STONE FRUIT POUCHES

Episode: The Pouch Principal, EA1G08

2 cups crushed gingersnaps	1) Heat coals of grill or fire pit. 2) Cut 8 (18 by 18-inch) squares of aluminum foil. 3) Lay down double thickness of foil and divide gingersnaps evenly among the 4 squares.
4 apricots, pit removed and cut into eighths **4 plums, pit removed and cut into fourths**	4) Divide fruit evenly and place on top of gingersnaps.
4 tablespoons unsalted butter	5) Dot with butter.
2 tablespoons plus 2 teaspoons sugar **Pinch salt** **4 teaspoons lime zest**	6) In small bowl mix sugar, salt, and lime zest.
2 limes, juiced **4 teaspoons brandy**	7) Sprinkle sugar mixture evenly over fruit, drizzle with juice and brandy and seal packets. 8) Once **coals** are ash covered, lay packets over them and cover with lid of grill. If cooking in a **fire pit** carefully try to partially bury packets in hot coals. 9) Cook for 10 minutes. 10) Remove from heat and open carefully, as steam inside packet is very hot. 11) Serve on plates as is or spoon into shallow bowls and top with *crème fraiche* or ice cream.

Difficulty: Easy **Prep Time:** 15 minutes **Cook Time:** 10 minutes **Yield:** 4 servings

Notes:____

RED SNAPPER EN PAPILLOTE

Episode: The Pouch Principal, EA1G08

1 cup couscous	1) Preheat oven to 425 degrees F. 2) Rinse couscous in fine mesh strainer, under cold water, lay out on parchment lined baking sheet and sprinkle with pinch of salt. Set aside. 3) Cut parchment paper into 15 by 48-inch sheet. 4) Fold in 1/2 and lay on baking/cookie sheet.
1 (2-pound) whole red snapper, cleaned, head on	5) Unfold and lay snapper diagonally on sheet pan on top of 1 layer of parchment.
2 teaspoons salt, plus pinch for couscous **1/2 teaspoon freshly ground black pepper**	6) Salt and pepper fish, inside and out.
1 small bunch fresh oregano **1 small bunch fresh parsley** **1 whole lemon, thinly sliced** **1 cup thinly sliced red onion**	7) Place herbs inside cavity of fish along with 1/2 of lemon, and 1/2 of red onion. 8) Arrange couscous next to fish on all sides.
2 teaspoons minced garlic **1 cup halved grape tomatoes** **1 cup drained and quartered artichoke hearts**	9) Put garlic, and remaining lemon and red onion on fish and lay tomatoes and artichoke hearts around outside of couscous, creating somewhat of a wall.
1/2 cup white wine **1 tablespoon butter**	10) Pour wine over fish and dot with butter. 11) Fold over edges of parchment paper, stapling if necessary, to create and almost airtight seal. 12) Bake in oven for 30 minutes. 13) Carefully open and serve (be aware of bones in the fish).

Difficulty: Easy **Prep Time:** 25 minutes **Cook Time:** 30 minutes **Yield:** 4 servings

SALMON FILLET EN PAPILLOTE WITH JULIENNE VEGETABLE

Episode: The Pouch Principal, EA1G08

1/3 cup julienned fennel bulb **1/3 cup julienned leeks, white part only** **1/3 cup julienned carrots** **1/3 cup julienned snow peas**	1) Take a 15 by 36-inch piece of parchment paper and fold in 1/2 like a book. 2) Draw a large 1/2 heart on paper with fold of paper being the center of the heart. 3) Cut out heart and open. 4) Lay fennel, leeks, carrots, and snow peas on parchment in center to 1 side of fold.
1 teaspoon salt **1/8 teaspoon freshly ground black pepper** **1/8 teaspoon whole coriander seed, ground fine**	5) Mix together salt, pepper, and ground coriander. 6) Sprinkle vegetables with 1/2 of salt, pepper, and coriander.
1 (8-ounce) salmon fillet, pin bones removed	7) Lay salmon on top of vegetables and season with remaining salt, pepper and coriander.
1 orange cut into wedges with white, pithy membrane removed **1 tablespoon dry vermouth**	8) Top with the orange wedges and sprinkle with vermouth. 9) Fold other side of heart over fish and starting at top of heart shape, fold up both edges of parchment, overlapping folds as you move along. 10) Once you reach the end tip, twist several times to secure tightly. 11) Place on microwave safe plate and cook for 4 minutes, on high in microwave, or until fish reaches 131 degrees. 12) Open parchment carefully and serve for a complete meal.

Difficulty: Easy **Prep Time:** 25 minutes **Cook Time:** 5 minutes **Yield:** 1 serving

SPLIT PEA BURGERS

Episode: Give Peas a Chance, EA0902

1 tablespoon olive oil, plus 1 to 2 additional tablespoons for sautéing	1) Heat 1 tablespoon olive oil in a large (4 to 6-quart) saucepan over medium heat.
1/2 cup chopped onion **1/2 cup chopped bell pepper** **Kosher salt and freshly ground black pepper**	2) Add the onion and bell pepper along with a generous pinch of salt. 3) Sweat for 5 minutes or until the onions are soft.
2 teaspoons minced garlic **4 ounces mushrooms, sliced**	4) Add the garlic and mushrooms and continue to cook for another 4 minutes.
3 cups vegetable broth **1 cup dry split peas, picked and rinsed** **1/2 cup dry brown rice** **1 teaspoon ground coriander** **1 teaspoon ground cumin**	5) Add the broth, peas, rice, coriander and cumin. Increase the heat to high and bring to a boil. 6) Decrease heat to low, cover and cook at a simmer for 1 hour or until the rice and peas are tender. 7) Remove from the heat and gently pour the mixture into the bowl of a food processor and process until just combined.* Do not puree.
3/4 cup plain dry bread crumbs, plus 1/4 cup for coating	8) Pour this mixture into a bowl and stir in the 3/4 cup of bread crumbs. 9) Season, to taste, with salt and freshly ground pepper. 10) Refrigerate for 30 minutes. 11) Shape the mixture into patties and dredge on each side in the remaining 1/4 cup of bread crumbs. 12) Heat 1 tablespoon of olive oil in a medium sauté pan over medium heat. 13) Add 2 burgers at a time and sauté until brown on each side, approximately 3 to 4 minutes per side. 14) To grill, cook on high for 3 to 4 minutes per side as well. Serve immediately.

Difficulty: Medium **Prep Time:** 35 minutes **Inactive Prep Time:** 30 minutes **Cook Time:** 1 hr 15 min **Yield:** 8 5-oz burgers

*When blending hot liquids: Remove liquid from the heat and allow to cool for at least 5 minutes. Transfer liquid to a blender or food processor and fill it no more than halfway. If using a blender, release one corner of the lid. This prevents the vacuum effect that creates heat explosions. Place a towel over the top of the machine, pulse a few times then process on high speed until smooth.

Notes:______________________________

FILLET O'FU

Episode: Tofuworld, EA1C01

1 (19-ounce) block firm tofu	1) Slice the block of tofu into 4 equal portions. 2) Place the slices on paper towels and fold the towels over in both directions to cover the tofu. 3) Place a baking sheet on top of the tofu and weigh it down with a 28-ounce can of tomatoes for 1 hour.
2 tablespoons sherry vinegar **2 tablespoons Worcestershire sauce** **Few dashes of hot pepper sauce**	4) Combine the sherry vinegar, Worcestershire sauce, and hot pepper sauce and place the tofu into the marinade. Marinate for 15 minutes on each side.
1/2 cup all-purpose flour **2 eggs**	5) Place the flour into a shallow dish and the eggs into another. 6) Lightly beat the eggs.
Canola oil to cover skillet by 1/8-inch	7) Heat the canola oil in the skillet over medium-high heat. 8) Remove tofu from marinade and drain on paper towels to remove any excess marinade. 9) Lightly dredge the tofu in the flour, knocking off any excess flour and slide into the eggs until completely, but thinly, coated on both sides. 10) Slide tofu gently into the hot oil and fry for 2 minutes until golden brown and delicious. 11) Flip the tofu using the tongs, and cook for another 2 minutes.

Difficulty: Easy **Prep Time:** 1 hour 20 minutes **Cook Time:** 5 minutes **Yield:** 2 servings

VEGETABLE CURRY

Episode: Spice Capades, EA1G20

1 (1-pound) bag mixed frozen vegetables	1) Poke several holes in the bag of frozen vegetables and microwave on high for 2 to 3 minutes or until thawed. Set aside.
2/3 cup plain yogurt **1 teaspoon cornstarch**	2) In medium mixing bowl, whisk together yogurt and cornstarch. Set aside.
2 tablespoons vegetable oil	3) Heat oil in a 10-inch, non-reactive sauté pan over medium-high heat.
1 teaspoon cumin seeds **1/2 teaspoon fennel seeds** **1/2 teaspoon mustard seeds**	4) Add cumin seeds, fennel seeds and mustard seeds, cover pan with a splatter screen, and cook, stirring occasionally, until they begin to pop.
1 teaspoon ground turmeric **1/2 teaspoon onion powder** **1/2 teaspoon freshly ground coriander** **1/8 teaspoon freshly ground cinnamon** **2 medium cloves garlic, crushed** **3 dried red chiles, stems and seeds removed if less heat is desired**	5) Once they begin to pop, turn the heat down to medium, and add turmeric, onion powder, coriander, cinnamon, garlic, and chiles. 6) Sauté until garlic turns golden brown in color, approximately 3 to 5 minutes.
1/4 teaspoon sugar **1/2 teaspoon kosher salt** **Black pepper, optional**	7) Gently add the vegetables, sugar, salt and pepper, if desired, and cook for 3 to 5 minutes, or until vegetables are heated through. 8) Remove vegetables from heat, pour into bowl with yogurt mixture, and stir to combine. 9) Remove chiles if desired, and serve immediately.

Difficulty: Easy **Prep Time:** 10 minutes **Cook Time:** 15 minutes **Yield:** 2 main course servings or 4 as side dish

VEGETARIAN STEAMED DUMPLINGS

Episode: Wonton Ways, EA1H05

1/2 pound firm tofu	1) Preheat the oven to 200 degrees F. 2) Cut the tofu in half horizontally and lay between layers of paper towels. 3) Place on a plate, top with another plate, and place a weight on top (a 14-ounce can of vegetables works well). Let stand 20 minutes. 4) After 20 minutes, cut the tofu into 1/4-inch cubes and place in a large mixing bowl.
1/2 cup coarsely grated carrots **1/2 cup shredded Napa cabbage** **2 tablespoons finely chopped red pepper** **2 tablespoons finely chopped scallions** **2 teaspoons finely minced fresh ginger** **1 tablespoon chopped cilantro leaves** **1 tablespoon soy sauce** **1 tablespoon hoisin sauce** **2 teaspoons sesame oil** **1 egg, lightly beaten** **1 teaspoon kosher salt** **1/4 teaspoon freshly ground black pepper**	5) Add the carrots, cabbage, red pepper, scallions, ginger, cilantro, soy sauce, hoisin, sesame oil, egg, salt, and pepper. Lightly stir to combine.
Bowl of water, plus additional water for steamer **35 to 40 small wonton wrappers**	6) To form the dumplings, remove 1 wonton wrapper from the package, covering the others with a damp cloth. 7) Brush the edges of the wrapper lightly with water. 8) Place 1/2 rounded teaspoon of the tofu mixture in the center of the wrapper. 9) Shape as desired. 10) Set on a sheet pan and cover with a damp cloth. Repeat procedure until all of the filling is gone. 11) Using a steaming apparatus of your choice, bring 1/4 to 1/2-inch of water to a simmer over medium heat.
Non-stick vegetable spray, for the steamer	12) Spray the steamer's surface lightly with the non-stick vegetable spray to prevent sticking. 13) Place as many dumplings as will fit into a steamer, without touching each other. 14) Cover and steam for 10 to 12 minutes over medium heat. 15) Remove the dumplings from the steamer to a heatproof platter and place in oven to keep warm. 16) Repeat until all dumplings are cooked.

Difficulty: Medium **Prep Time:** 50 minutes **Cook Time:** 12 minutes **Yield:** 35 to 40 dumplings

Notes:____

Other

AB'S BEEFY BROTH

Episode: Pressure, EA1D03

	1) Place pressure cooker over high heat.
Vegetable oil Salt and pepper, to taste 3 pounds combined beef shank and oxtail pieces	2) Oil and salt the oxtail and shank pieces then sear in batches.
2 onions, quartered 2 ribs celery, halved 2 carrots, halved 3 cloves garlic 1 bunch parsley 1 teaspoon black peppercorns 2 quarts water	3) Add remaining ingredients and cover with water, being careful not to fill above the cooker's "maximum fill" line. (If your pressure cooker does not have a water line, fill the pot 2/3 full). 4) Bring to a boil and skim off any foam that gathers at the surface. 5) Cover and lock lid. 6) Once pressure builds up inside the cooker, reduce the heat so that you barely hear hissing from the pot. 7) Cook for 50 minutes. 8) Release pressure using your cookers release device (read that manual) or cool the cooker by running cold water over the lid for 5 minutes. 9) Carefully opening the lid and strain squeezing the solids before feeding to the compost pile, or the dogs. 10) Strain through a fine sieve or several layers of cheesecloth. 11) Season and serve or use as a base for other soup recipes.

Difficulty: Easy **Prep Time:** 10 minutes **Cook Time:** 1 hour **Yield:** 4 to 6 servings

CHICKEN STOCK

Episode: True Brew IV: Take Stock, EA1G11

4 pounds chicken carcasses, including necks and backs 1 large onion, quartered 4 carrots, peeled and cut in 1/2 4 ribs celery, cut in 1/2 1 leek, white part only, cut in 1/2 lengthwise 10 sprigs fresh thyme 10 sprigs fresh parsley with stems 2 bay leaves 8 to 10 peppercorns 2 whole cloves garlic, peeled 2 gallons cold water	1) Place chicken, vegetables, and herbs and spices in 12-quart stockpot. 2) Set opened steamer basket directly on ingredients in pot and pour over water. 3) Cook on high heat until you begin to see bubbles break through the surface of the liquid. 4) Turn heat down to medium low so that stock maintains low, gentle simmer. 5) Skim the scum from the stock with a spoon or fine mesh strainer every 10 to 15 minutes for the first hour of cooking and twice each hour for the next 2 hours. 6) Add hot water as needed to keep bones and vegetables submerged. 7) Simmer uncovered for 6 to 8 hours. 8) Strain stock through a fine mesh strainer into another large stockpot or heatproof container discarding the solids. 9) Cool immediately in large cooler of ice or a sink full of ice water to below 40 degrees. 10) Place in refrigerator overnight. 11) Remove solidified fat from surface of liquid and store in container with lid in refrigerator for 2 to 3 days or in freezer for up to 3 months. 12) Prior to use, bring to boil for 2 minutes. Use as a base for soups and sauces.

Difficulty: Easy **Prep Time:** 30 minutes **Inactive Prep Time:** 8 hours **Cook Time:** 6 hours **Yield:** 5 quarts

GOOD EATS COURT BOUILLON

Episode: Mission: Poachable, EA1C13

1 1/2 cups water **1/2 cup white wine** **1 lemon, juiced** **1 onion, chopped** **1/2 celery rib, chopped** **1 garlic clove, chopped finely** **1 teaspoon black peppercorns** **4 to 5 sprigs fresh thyme** **1 bay leaf**	1) Combine all ingredients in a saucepan and bring to a boil over high heat. 2) Reduce the heat and simmer for 8 minutes. 3) Strain or use chunky the first time, then strain through a fine mesh and either refrigerate for up to 3 days or freeze for up to 2 months. Either way, be sure to bring to a boil before reusing.

Difficulty: Easy **Prep Time:** 20 minutes **Cook Time:** 8 minutes **Yield:** 2 cups

HAGGIS

Episode: Oat Cuisine, EA1D06

1 sheep stomach	1) Rinse the stomach thoroughly and soak overnight in cold salted water.
1 sheep liver **1 sheep heart** **1 sheep tongue**	2) Rinse the liver, heart, and tongue. 3) In a large pot of boiling, salted water, cook these parts over medium heat for 2 hours. 4) Remove and mince. Remove any gristle or skin and discard.
1/2 pound suet, minced **3 medium onions, minced** **1/2 pound dry oats, toasted**	5) In a large bowl, combine the minced liver, heart, tongue, suet, onions, and toasted oats.
1 teaspoon kosher salt 1/2 teaspoon ground black pepper **1 teaspoon dried ground herbs**	6) Season with salt, pepper, and dried herbs. 7) Moisten with some of the cooking water so the mixture binds. 8) Remove the stomach from the cold salted water and fill 2/3 with the mixture. 9) Sew or tie the stomach closed. 10) Use a turning fork to pierce the stomach several times. This will prevent the haggis from bursting. 11) In a large pot of boiling water, gently place the filled stomach, being careful not to splash. 12) Cook over high heat for 3 ours. 13) Serve with mashed potatoes, if you serve it at all.

Difficulty: Expert **Prep Time:** 30 minutes **Inactive Prep Time:** 12 hours **Cook Time:** 5 hours **Yield:** Depends...Good Luck

Notes:____

REFRIGERATOR PIE

Episode: The Egg Files II: Man with a Flan, EA1C03

1cup heavy cream or half-and- half **2 eggs**	1) In a nonreactive, stainless steel bowl, combine the cream or half-and-half and the eggs. 2) Whisk until combined thoroughly.
2 pinches kosher salt **Freshly grated nutmeg**	3) Add the salt and the nutmeg. 4) Whisk to combine.
1 frozen 9-inch pie crust **Any one of the following combinations:** **a) Cooked spinach, cheddar cheese, cubed cooked ham** **b) Bacon, sautéed leeks, and Gruyere cheese** **c) Cooked spinach, canned artichoke hearts, and Parmesan cheese** **d) Roasted chicken, goat cheese, and sun-dried tomatoes** **e) Blanched asparagus and smoked salmon** **f) Port Salut and Spam**	5) Refrigerator Pie Rules: a) Heat oven to 350° F. b) Evenly distribute the pie fillings in the pie crust. c) Do not overfill the crust with the filling ingredients. d) Do not pour too much royale into the crust. The eggs will expand upon cooking. 6) Bake the pie until it is firm to the touch like set Jell-O, about 45 minutes. 7) Cool the pie for at least 15 minutes before slicing.

Difficulty: Easy **Prep Time:** 15 minutes **Cook Time:** 45 minutes **Yield:** 1 refrigerator pie

*Cook's Note: If you want to make more than one pie, whip up the first 4 ingredients in a blender multiplying the amount by the number of pies you want.

PEAR WALNUT WONTONS

Episode: Wonton Ways, EA1H05

1/4 cup water **1/4 cup sugar**	1) In a small saucepan over medium heat, bring water and sugar to a simmer, stirring occasionally, until sugar is dissolved.
1 vanilla bean, scraped **1 tablespoon orange liqueur**	2) Remove from the heat and stir in vanilla bean scrapings and orange liqueur.
6 ounces dried pears, roughly chopped	3) Place pears in the bowl of a food processor and process until finely chopped, stopping to scrape down the bowl if necessary. 4) Add the sugar syrup and pulse just until combined.
1.25 ounces walnuts, toasted and finely chopped	5) Transfer the pears to a bowl and stir in the walnuts. 6) Place the mixture in the refrigerator to cool completely, approximately 1 hour. The filling may be made up to 1 day ahead of time.
25 to 30 wonton wrappers **Bowl of water, for sealing wontons**	7) Heat oil in a 6-quart Dutch oven to 360 degrees F.
1/2 gallon vegetable or peanut oil, for frying	8) To form the dumplings, remove 1 wonton wrapper from the package, covering the others with a damp cloth. 9) Brush the edges of the wrapper lightly with water. 10) Place 1 teaspoon of the pear mixture in the center of the wrapper. 11) Fold over the edges, seal, and shape as desired. 12) Set on a sheet pan and cover with a damp cloth. 13) Repeat procedure until all of the filling is gone. 14) Gently place the wontons in the oil, 7 to 8 at a time. 15) Fry until golden, approximately 2 minutes. 16) Remove to a cooling rack set in a sheet pan lined with newspaper and let cool at least 5 minutes before serving.

Difficulty: Medium **Prep Time:** 35 minutes **Inactive Prep Time:** 1 hour **Cook Time:** 15 minutes **Yield:** 25 to 30 wontons

Notes:____

PRESSURE COOKER CHILI

Episode: The Big Chili, EA1H07

3 pounds stew meat (beef, pork, and/or lamb) **2 teaspoons peanut oil** **1 1/2 teaspoons kosher salt**	1) Place the meat in a large mixing bowl and toss with the peanut oil and salt. Set aside. 2) Heat a 6-quart heavy-bottomed pressure cooker over high heat until hot. 3) Add the meat in 3 or 4 batches and brown on all sides, approximately 2 minutes per batch. 4) Once each batch is browned, place the meat in a clean large bowl.
1 (12-ounce) bottle of beer, preferably a medium ale	5) Once all of the meat is browned, add the beer to the cooker to deglaze the pot. 6) Scrape the browned bits from the bottom of the pot.
1 (16-ounce) container salsa **30 tortilla chips** **2 chipotle peppers canned in adobo sauce, chopped** **1 tablespoon adobo sauce (from the chipotle peppers in adobo)** **1 tablespoon tomato paste** **1 tablespoon chili powder** **1 teaspoon ground cumin**	7) Add the meat back to the pressure cooker along with the salsa, tortilla chips, chipotle peppers, adobo sauce, tomato paste, chili powder, and ground cumin and stir to combine. 8) Lock the lid in place according to the manufacturer's instructions. 9) When the steam begins to hiss out of the cooker, reduce the heat to low, just enough to maintain a very weak whistle. Cook for 25 minutes. 10) Remove from the heat and carefully release the steam. Serve immediately.

Difficulty: Medium **Prep Time:** 15 minutes **Cook Time:** 35 minutes **Yield:** 4 servings

SALAD

Green Salad

BACON VINAIGRETTE WITH GRILLED RADICCHIO

Episode: Scrap Iron Chef - Bacon Challenge, EA1D12

1/4 cup extra-virgin olive oil **1/4 cup cider vinegar** **2 tablespoons bacon drippings** **1 tablespoon dark brown sugar** **1 tablespoon prepared mustard** **1 teaspoon salt** **1 teaspoon freshly ground pepper**	1) In a small non-reactive bowl combine all ingredients except radicchio. 2) Whisk until emulsion is formed and reserve at room temperature.
2 heads radicchio, quartered	3) Place quartered radicchio onto a hot grill or grill pan. Cook on each side for approximately 2 minutes per side. You are looking to achieve slightly wilted edges. 4) Remove from the grill and place onto a plate. 5) Cover with a stainless steel bowl and allow steam to continue cooking radicchio for 5 minutes. 6) Drizzle vinaigrette over radicchio wedges and serve immediately.

Difficulty: Easy **Prep Time:** 10 minutes **Cook Time:** 10 minutes **Yield:** 8 servings

HAIL CAESAR SALAD

Episode: Salad Daze, EA1A04

	1) Heat oven to 350°.
1 loaf day old Italian bread	2) Cut 1/2 to 3/4-inch croutons from the loaf of bread and place on a baking sheet and put into the oven until dry but not browned.
3 garlic cloves, mashed **9 tablespoons extra virgin olive oil** **1/4 teaspoon plus 1 pinch kosher salt**	3) Use a mortar and pestle to mash the garlic with 4 tablespoons of oil and 1/4 teaspoon kosher salt. 4) Strain the oil into a skillet over medium heat. 5) Add the dried croutons and fry, tossing constantly until all of the oil is absorbed and the croutons turn gold. Set aside.
2 Cups water	6) Bring 2 cups water to a boil in a small saucepan.
2 eggs	7) Add the eggs and cook for 1 minute. 8) Chill in ice water to halt cooking. Set aside.
2 heads romaine lettuce, inner leaves only	9) In a very large bowl, tear lettuce and toss with 3 tablespoons of olive oil.
7 grinds black pepper	10) Sprinkle with the remaining kosher salt and the black pepper. 11) Add the remaining olive oil. Toss well.
1 lemon, juiced **6 drops Worcestershire sauce**	12) Add the lemon juice and Worcestershire sauce. 13) Break in the eggs. Toss until a creamy dressing forms.
1/4 cup grated Parmesan cheese	14) Toss in Parmesan cheese and serve with croutons.

Difficulty: Easy **Prep Time:** 20 minutes **Yield:** 6 to 8 servings

NO GUILT CAESAR

Episode: Tofuworld, EA1C01

2 ounces cubed Parmesan	1) Starting on the lowest speed, chop the cheese cubes in the blender jar until it settles into the bottom of the jar, gradually increasing the speed.
2 cloves garlic	2) Add the garlic down the chute and chop until minced.
2 tablespoons Dijon mustard **11/2 teaspoons white wine vinegar** **11/2 teaspoon Worcestershire sauce** **Pinch kosher salt** **Pinch freshly ground black pepper** **1 cup silken soft tofu**	3) Next, add the mustard, white wine vinegar, Worcestershire sauce, salt and pepper and tofu to the blender and blend until smooth.
2 tablespoons extra-virgin olive oil	4) While the blender is running, drizzle olive oil down the middle of the vortex that has formed. 5) Add more or less of the olive oil and blend until it reaches salad dressing consistency.

Difficulty: Easy **Prep Time:** 10 minutes **Yield:** 1 cup

PARSLEY SALAD

Episode: Herbal Preservation, EA1G19

4 ounces (about 2 quarts) Italian parsley	1) Wash and dry the parsley. Pick the leaves, and set aside. Discard the stems.
2 tablespoons fresh lemon juice **2 tablespoons lemon zest** **6 tablespoons walnut oil** **2 teaspoons dark sesame oil** **1 teaspoon honey** **Salt and freshly ground pepper**	2) In a large bowl, whisk together the lemon juice, zest, walnut oil, sesame oil, honey, and salt and pepper, to taste.
3 tablespoons toasted sesame seeds	3) Add the parsley and sesame seeds and toss to combine. 4) Allow the salad to sit for at least 30 minutes before serving so that flavors meld.

Difficulty: Easy **Prep Time:** 15 minutes **Inactive Prep Time:** 30 minutes **Yield:** 4 servings

Other Salads

ARTICHOKE PASTA SALAD

Episode: The Choke's On You, EA1F02

4 cups cooked bow tie pasta, cooled **2 tablespoons red wine vinegar** **3 tablespoons herb oil (recipe in topping section)** **1 cup grape tomatoes, split** **2 tablespoons thinly sliced fresh basil** **1 tablespoon chopped fresh oregano** **1 cup roughly chopped roasted chicken** **1 cup roughly chopped marinated artichokes** **Salt** **Freshly ground black pepper**	1) In a large bowl toss all of the ingredients. Serve or store in the refrigerator until ready to serve.

Difficulty: Easy **Prep Time:** 10 minutes **Cook Time:** 12 minutes **Yield:** 4 servings

IT'S A WONDERFUL WALDORF

Episode: Apple Family Values, EA1B03

2 Ginger Gold apples (Fuji will substitute) 1 Red Delicious apple	1) Cut apples in half and remove the core with a melon baller. 2) Chop apples into medium-sized pieces, leaving skin on.
3 tablespoons cider vinegar	3) In a bowl, toss apples with the cider vinegar.
1 cup prepared mayonnaise	4) Fold in mayonnaise thoroughly.
1 pinch kosher salt Cracked black pepper	5) Season with salt and pepper to taste.
3/4 cup toasted walnuts, crushed 1 cup golden raisins 2 teaspoons curry powder 2 stalks celery, thin bias cut 1/3 cup fresh mint, chiffonade 1/2 red onion, julienned	6) Fold in walnuts, raisins, curry powder, celery, mint and onion. Adjust seasoning. 7) Refrigerate for at least 1 hour to allow flavors to incorporate.
1 head romaine lettuce, heart only	8) To serve, arrange 2 leaves of romaine lettuce per plate and spoon salad on top.

Difficulty: Easy **Prep Time:** 15 minutes **Yield:** 4 to 6 servings

MA MAE'S CONGEALED CHRISTMAS SALAD

Episode: Food Network Stars: Family Traditions, SPFSSP01

1 small package orange flavored gelatin* 1 small package lemon flavored gelatin* 2 1/2 cups boiling water	1) Sprinkle the gelatins in a 9 by 13 glass-baking dish and slowly stir in the boiling water. 2) Cool to room temperature, then refrigerate approximately 30 minutes or just until gelatin begins to set. (If the gelatin sets, you won't be able to stir in the goodies.)
1 small can pineapple bits with juice 1/2 cup toasted, chopped pecans 1 can whole cranberry sauce	3) Meanwhile, in a medium size bowl, combine the canned pineapple and its juice, with the pecans and the whole cranberry sauce. 4) Add mixture to slightly thickened gelatin and stir until thoroughly combined. 5) Return to refrigerator until firmly set. 6) Cover with plastic wrap until ready to serve.

Yield: 10 portions

*Don't substitute with low-sugar or sugar-free. Neither will set properly.

Alton's Herbal BIG 10

The Top 10 Herbs AB Thinks We Need to Know About

From the Episode "Herbal Preservation"

1. Chives	6. Oregano
2. Mint	7. Basil
3. Thyme	8. Tarragon
4. Dill	9. Sage
5. Rosemary	10. Parsley

COLD-FASHIONED POTATO SALAD

Episode: This Spud's For You Too, EA1D11

2 1/2 pounds red potatoes, large diced	1) Place potatoes into a large heavy-bottomed pot. 2) Cover with cold water and place over medium heat. 3) Cover the pot and bring to a boil. 4) Immediately reduce heat and remove lid. 5) Gently simmer until potatoes are fork tender. 6) Drain and place into an ice bath to cool. 7) Remove skin by rubbing with a tea towel. 8) Slice potatoes into rounds and place into a zip top bag.
3 tablespoons cider vinegar	9) Add the vinegar and toss to coat all of the potatoes. 10) Place the bag into the refrigerator overnight.
3/4 cup mayonnaise (homemade if possible) 1 teaspoon mustard powder 1/4 cup chopped parsley 1 tablespoon chopped fresh tarragon 1/2 tablespoon very thinly sliced garlic 3 tablespoons fine chopped cornichons 1/2 cup small dice red onion 1/2 cup thinly sliced celery	11) In a large mixing bowl, combine the mayonnaise, mustard, parsley, tarragon, garlic, cornichons, onions, and celery.
1 teaspoon kosher salt 1/2 teaspoon freshly ground black pepper	12) Once evenly combined, add the potatoes and season with salt and pepper. 13) Let the salad chill in the refrigerator for at least an hour before serving.

Difficulty: Medium **Prep Time:** 35 minutes **Inactive Prep Time:** 9 hours **Cook Time:** 15 minutes **Yield:** 4 to 6 servings

TBL PANZELLA

Episode: Tomato Envy, EA1F06

Vinaigrette 1/4 cup red wine vinegar 1/4 teaspoon salt 1/4 teaspoon pepper 3 tablespoons olive oil 1 tablespoon chiffonade mint 1 tablespoon chiffonade basil	Mix all ingredients well.
4 cups French bread cut into 1-inch cubes and dried overnight 6 slices bacon, cooked, chopped, drippings reserved	1) Toss bread cubes in the bacon drippings.
2 cups halved grape tomatoes 2 tablespoons oil, for searing	2) Sear the halved grape tomatoes in 2 tablespoons of oil, cut side down, until caramelized about 5 minutes, set aside.
2 cups halved yellow pear tomatoes or roughly chopped heirloom tomatoes	3) Combine red wine vinegar, salt and pepper in a bowl, slowly whisk in olive oil in a thin stream until emulsified.
2 cups chopped romaine lettuce	4) Combine all tomatoes, bread, bacon, and lettuce and dress with vinaigrette, toss well, garnish with mint and basil and serve.

Difficulty: Easy **Prep Time:** 20 minutes **Cook Time:** 15 minutes **Yield:** 4 to 6 servings

Notes:____

BROWN RICE SALAD

Episode: Do the Rice Thing, EA1H19

6 slices bacon	1) In a 10-inch sauté pan over medium heat, fry the bacon until crisp. 2) Drain, crumble, and set aside. Reserve 1 tablespoon of the bacon fat.
1/2 cup diced red onion	3) Add the red onion to the pan and cook until translucent, approximately 5 to 6 minutes.
1/2 cup white wine vinegar 1/2 cup chicken broth 2 teaspoons Dijon mustard 1 teaspoon sugar 1 teaspoon kosher salt, plus a pinch 1/2 teaspoon freshly ground black pepper	4) Add the vinegar, chicken broth, mustard, sugar, salt, and pepper to the pan and stir to combine.
1 recipe Baked Brown Rice (recipe elsewhere)	5) Add the bacon back to the pan along with the rice and cook, stirring occasionally, until the liquid is absorbed, approximately 7 to 10 minutes.
1 tablespoon chopped fresh dill	6) Stir in the dill. Allow to cool slightly before serving.

Difficulty: Easy **Prep Time:** 10 minutes **Cook Time:** 1 hour 20 minutes **Yield:** 4 servings

HOT MELON SALAD

Episode: Melondrama, EA1H01

1 1/2 tablespoons olive oil 1 small red onion, sliced into thin rounds	1) Heat a large sauté pan or wok over high heat. 2) Once the pan is hot, add the olive oil, followed by the onion, and sauté for 1 to 2 minutes, moving the pan continually.
16 ounces medium-diced melon, approximately 2 cups	3) Add the melon and sauté for another 1 to 2 minutes or until the melon starts to take on color.
1 tablespoon fresh basil, cut into chiffonade 1/2 teaspoon kosher salt 1/2 teaspoon freshly ground black pepper	4) Add the basil, salt, and pepper and continue to cook for another minute.
2 teaspoons red wine vinegar	5) Add the vinegar to the pan and toss to combine.
2 ounces feta cheese, crumbled 1 tablespoon pine nuts, toasted	6) Pour mixture onto a serving platter, sprinkle with the cheese and pine nuts, and serve immediately.

Difficulty: Easy **Prep Time:** 15 minutes **Cook Time:** 6 minutes **Yield:** 4 first-course servings

MARINATED CRAB SALAD

Episode: Crustacean Nation III: Feeling Crabby, EA1G01

1 cup olive oil 1 cup red wine vinegar 2 large garlic cloves, minced 1 1/2 teaspoons salt 1/2 teaspoon freshly ground black pepper 1/2 cup chopped parsley, leaves 1/4 cup chopped fresh tarragon	1) In a non-reactive bowl combine the oil, vinegar, garlic, salt, pepper, parsley, and tarragon.
1/2 pound cooked lump or back fin crabmeat 1/2 pound cooked special crabmeat	2) Add the crab and place in the refrigerator. 3) Toss every hour for 4 hours.
6 cups mixed greens 4 to 6 lemon wedges	4) Serve on a bed of mixed greens and squeeze a lemon wedge over right before eating.

Difficulty: Easy **Prep Time:** 20 minutes **Cook Time:** 4 hours **Yield:** 4 to 6 servings

HONEY MUSTARD DRESSING

Episode: Pantry Raid IV: Comb Alone, EA1D13

5 tablespoons medium body honey (sourwood is nice) **3 tablespoons smooth Dijon mustard** **2 tablespoons rice wine vinegar**	1) Combine all ingredients in a bowl and whisk until smooth. Serve as a dressing or a dip.

Difficulty: Easy **Prep Time:** 5 minutes **Yield:** 4 to 6 servings

MILLION ISLAND DRESSING

(a.k.a. Thousand Island Dressing)

Episode: Good Milk Gone Bad, EA1F04

1 cup plain yogurt **2 tablespoons vegetable oil** **2 tablespoons tomato sauce** **2 teaspoons lemon juice** **2 teaspoons mustard powder** **2 teaspoons sugar** **1 teaspoon salt** **1/2 teaspoon ground black pepper**	1) In a bowl combine yogurt, vegetable oil, tomato sauce, lemon juice, mustard powder, sugar, salt, and pepper. 2) Whisk together until blended.
1/2 cup finely chopped onion **1 tablespoon sweet relish** **1 tablespoon finely chopped green olives** **1 jalapeno, finely chopped**	3) Add onion, sweet relish, olives, and jalapeno and whisk to combine evenly. 4) Chill 1 hour.

Difficulty: Easy **Prep Time:** 20 minutes **Yield:** 2 cups

VENI VEDI VINAIGRETTE

Episode: Salad Daze, EA1A04

2 ounces red wine vinegar **2 teaspoons Dijon mustard** **2 garlic cloves, mashed** **1/4 teaspoon of kosher salt**	1) Place red wine vinegar, Dijon mustard, garlic and salt in a glass or metal container with a tight fitting lid and shake to combine
3/4 cup olive oil	2) Add olive oil and shake vigorously, until dressing emulsifies and thickens to the consistency of cream. 3) Let dressing sit for 1 hour at room temperature before straining out garlic and serving. 4) Dressing can be refrigerated, but should be brought to room temperature and shaken again before serving.

Difficulty: Easy **Prep Time:** 5 minutes **Yield:** 1 cup

Yield: 1 cup Prep Time: 5 minutes Cooking Time: 0 minutes

WHEAT BERRY TAPANADE

Episode: Ill Gotten Grains, EA1G07

3 cloves garlic, minced **1 cup pitted and finely chopped Kalamata olives** **1 teaspoon salt** **1/2 teaspoon Dijon mustard** **1 cup fully cooked wheat berries**	1) In a bowl combine all ingredients. 2) Serve with crusty bread, on a salad or on its own.

Difficulty: Easy **Prep Time:** 20 minutes **Yield:** 4 to 6 servings

Notes:____

SIDE DISHES

Artichokes

BROILED CHOKES

Episode: The Choke's On You, EA1F02

	1) Preheat oven to broil setting.
8 whole artichokes	2) Cut the top 1/4 off the choke and snap off the outer leaves until you reach pale green, soft leaves. 3) Using a spoon, remove the hairy choke from the center and discard.
Acidulated water: 6 cups water with juice of 4 lemons 1/4 cup olive oil	4) Immediately plunge in acidulated water to avoid discoloration. 5) Repeat with remaining artichokes. 6) Drain the artichokes and spin to dry.
2 teaspoons kosher salt 1 teaspoon fresh ground pepper	7) Toss in a bowl with oil, and season with salt and pepper. 8) Lay the chokes out on a sheet pan lined with foil and place on the lower rack of the oven, and broil for 5 to 6 minutes. 9) Flip the artichokes and return to the oven for 3 minutes.
Herb oil, optional (recipe in topping section)	10) Eat as they are or marinate in herb oil for up to 2 days.

Difficulty: Easy **Prep Time:** 15 minutes **Cook Time:** 12 minutes **Yield:** 4 servings

Yield: 4 servings Prep Time: 15 minutes Cook Time: 12 minutes Difficulty: Easy

Beans

BLACK BEAN SALAD

Episode: Pantry Raid III: Cool Beans, EA1C12

1/2 celery stalk 1/2 carrot A few sprigs fresh thyme A few sprigs fresh parsley 1 bay leaf	1) Tie the celery, carrot, thyme, parsley, and bay leaf into a bundle using cotton butcher's twine.
2 cups dried black beans 1/2 onion	2) Place the beans, bundle, and onion into a pot.
Water	3) Add just enough water to barely cover the beans. 4) Bring to a simmer, partially cover, and cook for 1 to 2 hours until beans are barely tender.
2 teaspoons kosher salt	5) After 30 minutes, add the salt to the beans. 6) Occasionally check on the beans and add water to cover the beans, if needed. 7) When beans are just barely tender, drain them and remove the carrot bundle.
1/3 cup extra virgin olive oil 1/3 cup lime juice 1 red onion, minced A handful fresh cilantro, chopped 1 teaspoon ground cumin 1 teaspoon chili powder	8) Toss the beans while hot with the olive oil, lime juice, onion, cilantro, cumin, and chili powder.
Kosher salt and pepper, to taste	9) Chill thoroughly and season with salt and pepper.

Difficulty: Easy **Prep Time:** 15 minutes **Cook Time:** 2 hours **Yield:** 4 servings

THE ONCE AND FUTURE BEANS

Episode: Pantry Raid III: Cool Beans, EA1C12

	1) Heat oven to 250° F.
1 pound dried Great Northern beans	2) Soak beans in a plastic container overnight in just enough cold water to submerge them completely.
1 pound bacon, chopped 1 onion, chopped 2 jalapeños, chopped	3) Place a cast iron Dutch oven over medium heat and stir in the bacon, onion, and jalapeños until enough fat has rendered from the bacon to soften the onions, about 5 minutes.
1/4 cup tomato paste 1/4 cup dark brown sugar 1/4 cup molasses	4) Stir in the tomato paste, dark brown sugar, and molasses. 5) Drain the beans and reserve the soaking liquid. 6) Add the drained beans to the Dutch oven.
Vegetable broth	7) Place the soaking liquid in a measuring cup and add enough vegetable broth to equal 4 cups of liquid. 8) Add the liquid to the Dutch oven and bring to a boil over high heat.
1/4 teaspoon cayenne pepper 1 teaspoon black pepper 2 teaspoons kosher salt	9) Add in cayenne, black pepper and salt. Give them a stir and cover with the lid. 10) Place the Dutch oven in the oven for 6 to 8 hours, or until the beans are tender.

Difficulty: Easy **Prep Time:** 30 minutes **Cook Time:** 8 hours **Yield:** 6 servings

Beets

BEET SLAW

Episode: Salad Daze II: The Long Arm of the Slaw, EA1F12

<u>Vinaigrette:</u> 1/4 cup red wine vinegar 2 tablespoons honey 1/2 teaspoon black pepper 1/4 teaspoon salt	1) In a small bowl combine the red wine vinegar, honey, black pepper, and salt.
1/4 cup olive oil	2) Slowly, while whisking add the oil until the mixture is emulsified.
4 cups beets, boiled until tender, through a rouet, and pressed in paper towels 2 cups jicama, peeled and cut into sticks 3 cups fennel, cored, halved, and sliced with mandoline 1/4 cup grated onion 1 Asian pear, halved, cored, and sliced with a mandoline	3) Combine all fruits and vegetables and let drain in a colander.
6 ounces goat cheese, crumbled 2 tablespoons lemon juice	4) Combine vegetables and dressing then toss with the lemon juice and goat cheese.

Difficulty: Easy **Prep Time:** 35 minutes **Cook Time:** 45 minutes **Yield:** 6 to 8 servings

Notes:____________________

BEET GREEN GRATIN

Episode: Beet It, EA1F16

1 tablespoon butter	1) Preheat the oven to 375 degrees F. 2) Melt the butter in a saucepan.
12 ounces sliced mushrooms 2 cloves garlic, minced	3) Add the mushrooms and garlic and sweat.
1 pound beet greens, cleaned and picked	4) Add the beet greens and mix well.
Kosher salt and fresh ground black pepper	5) Remove pan from heat. Season with salt and pepper.
4 egg yolks, beaten 1 cups ricotta 1/2 cup grated Parmesan 1/2 teaspoon salt	6) In a separate bowl, combine the egg yolks, ricotta, Parmesan cheese, and salt. 7) Combine everything and put into a lightly oiled 9 by 11-inch baking dish.
3/4 cup crumbled crackers (recommended: Ritz crackers)	8) Top with the crumbled crackers and bake for 30 minutes covered. 9) Uncover and bake for an additional 15 minutes.

Difficulty: Easy **Prep Time:** 25 minutes **Cook Time:** 50 minutes **Yield:** 6 to 8 servings

Broccoli

BROCCOLI CASSEROLE

Episode: Casserole Over, EA1F11

1/2 cup mayonnaise 1/2 cup plain yogurt 1 1/4 cup shredded sharp cheddar cheese 1/3 cup blue cheese dressing 2 eggs 1/2 teaspoon salt 1 1/2 teaspoon fresh ground black pepper Flavor Pack from Ramen	1) Preheat oven to 350 degrees F. 2) In a bowl combine mayonnaise, yogurt, cheddar cheese, blue cheese dressing, eggs, salt, pepper, and flavor pack from noodles.
6 cups broccoli, peeled stems and heads, chopped and blanched in salted water 12 ounces sliced mushrooms, Sautéed in 1 tablespoon butter 1 package chicken flavored Ramen noodles, broken up	3) In a separate bowl combine broccoli, mushrooms, and broken noodles then toss together wet mixture and vegetables to evenly coat. 4) Place in an 8 by 8-inch baking dish that has been sprayed with non-stick cooking spray and cook for 45 minutes covered. 5) Then remove cover and bake for additional 15 minutes to brown. 6) Cool for 15 minutes before serving.

Difficulty: Easy **Prep Time:** 25 minutes **Cook Time:** 1 hour **Yield:** 6 to 8 servings

Notes:

Cabbage

HOME OF THE BRAISE

Episode: Head Games, EA1C10

2 tablespoons canola oil	1) Heat the canola oil in a pan over medium heat.
1 Granny Smith apple, peeled, cored, and cubed	2) Add the apple to the pan and cook until lightly browned.
1 pint unfiltered apple juice **1/4-teaspoon caraway seeds** **1 1/2 teaspoons kosher salt** **Freshly ground black pepper** **1/2 head of red cabbage, shredded**	3) Increase the heat to high and add the apple juice, caraway seeds, salt, pepper and cabbage to the pan. 4) Cover the pan and shake to toss the cabbage to coat. 5) Reduce the heat to low and cook for 20 minutes.

Difficulty: Easy **Prep Time:** 30 minutes **Cook Time:** 30 minutes **Yield:** 4 servings

SHRED, HEAD, BUTTER AND BREAD

Episode: Head Games, EA1C10

	1) Fill your largest pot 3/4 full with water and bring to a boil on high heat.
1/2 stick unsalted butter **1/2 cup pulverized, seasoned croutons**	2) Melt the butter and croutons in a skillet.
2 pinches dry mustard **1 teaspoon caraway seeds**	3) Add the mustard and caraway seeds and stir over medium heat until the butter browns and smells nutty. 4) Remove the skillet from the heat, but leave dressing in the pan.
1 tablespoon kosher salt **1 tablespoon sugar**	5) Add the salt and sugar to the boiling water and cook until dissolved.
1 small head cabbage, shredded	6) Place the cabbage in the boiling water and cook for 2 minutes exactly. 7) Drain the cabbage in the bowl of the salad spinner or colander. 8) Spin the cabbage to remove any excess water. 9) Add the cabbage to the butter-crumb dressing and toss to coat thoroughly.

Difficulty: Easy **Prep Time:** 20 minutes **Cook Time:** 10 minutes **Yield:** 4 servings

ASIAN SLAW

Episode: Salad Daze II: The Long Arm of the Slaw, EA1F12

Dressing: **1 (3-inch) piece ginger, grated fine** **1/2 cup rice wine vinegar** **1 tablespoon soy sauce** **1 lime, juiced** **2 tablespoons sesame oil** **1/2 cup peanut butter**	1) In a small bowl, or food processor combine ginger, vinegar, soy sauce, lime juice, oil, and peanut butter.
1 head Napa cabbage, sliced thin **1 red bell pepper, julienne fine** **1 yellow bell pepper, julienne fine** **2 serrano chiles, minced fine** **1 large carrot, grated fine with a peeler** **3 green onions, cut on the bias, all of white part and half of the green** **2 tablespoons chiffonade cilantro** **2 tablespoons chiffonade mint** **1/2 teaspoon ground black pepper**	2) In a large bowl, combine all other ingredients and then toss with dressing. You can save some of the dressing to dress noodles that can be added to this dish along with stir fried pork to make an entire meal.

Difficulty: Easy **Prep Time:** 20 minutes **Yield:** 4 to 6 servings

COLESLAW

Episode: Salad Daze II: The Long Arm of the Slaw, EA1F12

1/2 head green cabbage, thinly sliced **1/2 head red cabbage, thinly sliced** **Kosher salt, as needed**	1) Generously salt the cabbage and drain in colander for 3 hours. 2) Rinse thoroughly and dry.
1/2 cup buttermilk **2 fluid ounces plain yogurt** **2 fluid ounces mayonnaise** **1 tablespoon pickle juice** **1 teaspoon dry mustard** **1 tablespoon chives, chopped** **1/2 teaspoon fresh ground black pepper**	3) In a separate bowl, combine all of the ingredients except the cabbage and carrot. 4) Whisk to combine evenly.
1 carrot, thinly sliced	5) Toss the cabbage and carrot with the dressing.

Difficulty: Easy **Prep Time:** 30 minutes **Inactive Prep Time:** 3 hours 30 minutes **Yield:** 8 to 10 servings

MARINATED SLAW

Episode: Salad Daze II: The Long Arm of the Slaw, EA1F12

1/2 head Napa cabbage, shredded, salted, and rinsed **2 red bell peppers, thinly sliced** **2 green bell peppers, thinly sliced**	1) Toss the cabbage and peppers and place into a strainer resting over a bowl to drain for 2 hours. 2) Then place into a mason jar.
3/4 cup apple cider vinegar **1 tablespoon mustard seed** **1 teaspoon celery seed** **1 cup sugar**	3) In a small saucepan, bring the vinegar, sugar, mustard seed, and celery seed to a boil. 4) Pour over the cabbage and the peppers. 5) Store in the refrigerator for 3 days before serving.

Difficulty: Easy **Prep Time:** 10 minutes **Inactive Prep Time:** 3 days **Cook Time:** 5 minutes **Yield:** 8 servings

SAUERKRAUT

Episode: Eat This Rock!, EASP03

5 pounds green cabbage, shredded **3 tablespoons pickling salt** **1 tablespoon juniper berries** **2 teaspoons caraway seeds**	1) In large mixing bowl, mix cabbage thoroughly with salt, juniper berries, and caraway seeds, using hands or tongs. If using your hands, make sure that they are very clean prior to mixing. 2) Let stand for 10 minutes. 3) Pack cabbage mixture down into a large plastic food container.
1 quart water, in a sanitized glass jar	4) Top with a lid smaller than the opening of the container and place a glass jar filled with the quart of water on top of the lid. 5) Place in cool area overnight (65 to 70 degrees F). 6) In a day, the cabbage should have given up enough liquid to be completely submerged. The jar serves as a weight to keep the cabbage submerged and away from air. 7) Check cabbage every other day for approximately 2 weeks and skim the surface of scum, if necessary. 8) Let stand for 4 weeks. 9) Transfer to an airtight container and store in the refrigerator for up to 6 months.

Difficulty: Medium **Prep Time:** 15 minutes **Inactive Prep Time:** 4 weeks **Yield:** 12 cups

Notes:________________________________

Carrots

CARROT SLAW

Episode: A Taproot Orange, EA1H16

2 pounds carrots, approximately 12 to 15 medium	1) Wash the carrots and peel, if necessary. 2) Using a vegetable peeler, cut the carrots into wide noodle-shaped strips.
1/2 cup mayonnaise **Pinch kosher salt** **1/3 cup sugar** **1/2 cup canned, crushed pineapple, drained thoroughly of all liquid** **1/2 cup raisins** **2 teaspoons curry powder** **1 teaspoon minced garlic** **Pinch celery seed and/or caraway seed, optional**	3) In a large mixing bowl whisk together the mayonnaise, salt, sugar, pineapple, raisins, curry powder, garlic, and celery seed and/or caraway seed, if using. 4) Add the carrots and toss to combine. 5) Serve immediately or refrigerate for 1 hour to serve cold.

Difficulty: Easy **Prep Time:** 12 minutes **Yield:** 4 servings

GLAZED CARROTS

Episode: A Taproot Orange, EA1H16

1 pound carrots, approximately 7 medium, peeled and cut on the bias 1/4-inch thick **1 ounce (2 tablespoons) unsalted butter** **Heavy pinch kosher salt** **1 cup good-quality ginger ale**	1) In a 12-inch sauté pan over medium heat, combine the carrots, butter, salt and ginger ale. 2) Cover and bring to a simmer. 3) Once simmering, remove the lid, stir, and reduce the heat to low. Cover again and cook for 5 minutes.
1/2 teaspoon chili powder	4) Remove the lid, add the chili powder and increase the heat to high. 5) Cook, tossing occasionally, until the ginger ale is reduced to a glaze, approximately 4 to 5 minutes.
1 tablespoon chopped fresh parsley leaves	6) Pour into a serving dish and sprinkle with the parsley. Serve immediately.

Difficulty: Easy **Prep Time:** 10 minutes **Cook Time:** 15 minutes **Yield:** 4 servings

GLAZED BABY CARROTS

Episode: Beet It, EA1F16

20 baby beets, scrubbed **2 cups apricot juice**	1) In a large sauté pan, add the beets and the apricot juice. 2) Cover and cook on medium high for 10 minutes.
3 tablespoons white balsamic vinegar **2 tablespoons honey**	3) Add the vinegar and honey and cook for another 10 minutes. 4) Pull off of the heat and keep covered for an additional 5 minutes.

Difficulty: Easy **Prep Time:** 10 minutes **Inactive Prep Time:** 5 minutes **Cook Time:** 20 minutes **Yield:** 4 to 8 servings

Corn

BETTER THAN GRANNIE'S CREAMED CORN

Episode: Ear Apparent, EA1B09

1/2 onion, diced **1 tablespoon butter** **2 pinches kosher salt**	1) In a saucepan over medium heat, sweat the onion in butter and salt until translucent. 2) In a large mixing bowl, place a paper bowl in the middle of the bowl.
8 ears fresh corn	3) Resting the cob on the bowl in a vertical position remove only the tops of the kernel with a knife, using long smooth downward strokes and rotating the cob as you go. 4) After the cob has been stripped, use the dull backside of your knife to scrape any remaining pulp and milk off the cob. 5) Add the corn and pulp mixture to the saucepan and cook over medium high until the juice from the corn has tightened.
1 sprig fresh rosemary, bruised	6) Add the rosemary.
1 tablespoon sugar **1/4 teaspoon turmeric**	7) Sprinkle the corn with the sugar and turmeric. 8) Stir constantly for about 2 minutes.
2 tablespoons yellow cornmeal	9) Sprinkle the cornmeal onto the corn, using a whisk to combine well.
1 cup heavy cream	10) Add the heavy cream and cook until the corn has softened, about 2 to 3 minutes. 11) Remove the rosemary.
Fresh ground black pepper	12) Season with freshly ground black pepper.

Difficulty: Easy **Prep Time:** 10 minutes **Cook Time:** 10 minutes **Yield:** 3 cups

CREAMED CORN CORNBREAD

Episode: Ear Apparent, EA1B09

	1) Preheat oven to 425°. 2) Place a 10-inch cast iron skillet into the oven.
2 cups yellow cornmeal **1 teaspoon kosher salt** **1 tablespoon sugar** **2 teaspoons baking powder** **½ teaspoon baking soda**	3) In a bowl, combine the cornmeal, salt, sugar, baking powder, and baking soda. Whisk together to combine well.
1 cup buttermilk **2 eggs** **1 cup creamed corn**	4) In a large bowl, combine the buttermilk, eggs, and creamed corn, whisking together to combine thoroughly. 5) Add the dry ingredients to the buttermilk mixture and stir to combine. 6) If the batter will not pour, add more buttermilk to the batter.
2 tablespoons canola oil	7) Add 2 tablespoons canola oil to the cast iron skillet. 8) Pour the batter into the skillet. 9) Bake until the cornbread is golden brown and springs back upon the touch, about 20 minutes.

Difficulty: Easy **Prep Time:** 15 minutes **Cook Time:** 20 minutes **Yield:** 8 servings

Notes:________________________________

SWEET CORN BREAD PUDDING

Episode: Romancing The Bird—A Good Eats Thanksgiving, EASP01

	1) Heat oven to 350°.
1/2 onion, diced fine 1 ounce unsalted butter 1/2 teaspoon thyme 1/2 teaspoon rosemary	2) Sweat onions with butter and herbs in a oven safe skillet until translucent.
1 fifteen ounce can creamed style sweet corn 1 cup heavy cream 2 eggs 1 teaspoon baking powder 1/2 cup yellow cornmeal, whole grain, stone ground 1/2 cup shredded parmesan cheese 1 teaspoon kosher salt Ground black pepper to taste	3) Combine corn, cream, eggs, baking powder, corn meal, parmesan, salt, and pepper in a large mixing bowl.
2 cups French bread, cubed	4) Add cubed bread and fold to combine. 5) Pour batter into skillet, right on top of the onion mixture. 6) Bake 50 minutes, or until set. 7) Cool slightly before serving.

Difficulty: Easy **Prep Time:** 55 minutes **Cook Time:** 40 minutes **Yield:** 6 to 8 servings

Eggplant

BABA GHANNOUJ

Episode: Deep Purple, EA1D07

1 eggplant	1) Pierce some holes in the skin of the eggplant (to avoid explosion) and grill over medium-high heat turning every 7 minutes, until the skin is blackened and the body is nice and soft. Total time for grilling is about 30 minutes. 2) If you do not have a grill you can roast your eggplant in a 375 degree F oven for about 30 minutes. 3) Remove eggplant from the grill and let cool. 4) Once the eggplant is cool enough to handle, peel away the skin and discard. 5) Place the eggplant flesh in a colander and drain for 10 minutes.
2 cloves garlic 2 ounces fresh lemon juice 2 tablespoons tahini 1/2 bunch parsley, leaves only	6) In a food processor, combine garlic, lemon juice, tahini and parsley and pulse to combine. 7) Add the eggplant flesh.
Salt and pepper	8) Season with salt and pepper and pulse to combine. 9) Adjust the flavor with more Tahini or lemon juice if you prefer. 10) If it's bitter, some sugar or honey will help. Research shows that the white variety of plant is sweeter in flavor.

Difficulty: Easy **Prep Time:** 10 minutes **Cook Time:** 30 minutes **Yield:** 1 cup

EGGPLANT PASTA

Episode: Deep Purple, EA1D07

2 medium-large eggplants	1) Peel each eggplant leaving 1-inch of skin at the top and bottom unpeeled. 2) Slice the eggplant thinly lengthwise, about 1/4-inch thick.
Kosher salt, for purging	3) Evenly coat each slice with the salt and purge on a sheet pan fitted with a rack for 30 minutes. 4) Rinse with cold water and roll in paper towels to dry. 5) Slice the pieces into thin strips to resemble pasta.
4 tablespoons olive oil	6) In a large sauté pan heat the oil.
1 teaspoon garlic, minced **1/2 teaspoon chile flakes**	7) Add the garlic and chili flakes and toast. 8) Add the eggplant "pasta" and toss to coat.
4 small tomatoes, seeded and chopped	9) Add the tomatoes and cook for 3 minutes.
1/2 cup cream	10) Add the cream and increase heat to thicken sauce.
4 tablespoons basil chiffonade **1/4 cup freshly grated Parmesan**	11) Finally add the basil and Parmesan and toss to combine.
Freshly ground pepper	12) Season with pepper, no salt needed as the eggplant will have residual salt from the purge. 13) Serve immediately.

Difficulty: Expert **Prep Time:** 40 minutes **Cook Time:** 10 minutes **Yield:** 4 servings

EGGPLANT STEAKS

Episode: Deep Purple, EA1D07

1/4 cup Worcestershire sauce **1/4 cup thick steak sauce** **1/2 cup olive oil** **2 tablespoon honey** **2 teaspoons apple cider vinegar**	1) In a small bowl whisk together the Worcestershire, steak sauce, olive oil, honey, and apple cider vinegar.
Kosher salt and fresh ground pepper	2) Season with salt and pepper.
8 (1/2-inch) eggplant slices, purged with salt	3) Pat your eggplant dry with paper towels. 4) With a pastry brush apply the sauce to both sides of the eggplant. 5) Place eggplant rounds onto a sheet tray fitted with a rack. 6) Place the tray under the broiler for until eggplant is nicely browned, approximately 2 minutes. 7) Turn slices over and place back under broiler to brown the other side.
1 cup grated Parmesan **3 tablespoons chopped parsley, optional**	8) Generously sprinkle freshly grated Parmesan over all of the slices. 9) Place back under the broiler for 1 minute to nicely brown the cheese. 10) Serve plain or sprinkle with freshly chopped herbs.

Difficulty: Easy **Prep Time:** 20 minutes **Cook Time:** 10 minutes **Yield:** 4 servings

Notes:____

VANILLA LIME PINEAPPLE SKEWERS

Episode: Dis-Kabob-Ulated, EA0903

8 (12-inch) metal skewers	
1 vanilla bean **8 ounces dark brown sugar, approximately 1 cup firmly packed** **1/2 cup freshly squeezed lime juice** **Pinch kosher salt**	1) Split open the vanilla pod and scrape out the pulp, and add the pod and the pulp to a small saucepan along with the brown sugar, lime juice, and salt. 2) Whisk together and place the mixture over medium high heat and bring to a boil, stirring just until the sugar has dissolved. 3) Remove from the heat and allow to sit for 2 hours before using. 4) Remove the vanilla pod. 5) Once cool, place the syrup in a squeeze bottle or other sealable container. Store in the refrigerator. 6) Preheat grill on high.
1 whole pineapple	7) Peel and remove the core from the pineapple. Cut the pineapple into eighths, lengthwise, and remove any prickly brown eyes. 8) Thread the pieces of pineapple onto the skewers lengthwise. 9) Coat the skewered pineapple on all sides with the syrup. 10) Grill on all sides until golden brown, approximately 4 minutes per side, 12 minutes total, or until the pineapple is tender. 11) Serve with any remaining sauce.

Difficulty: Easy **Prep Time:** 20 minutes **Inactive Prep Time:** 2 hours **Cook Time:** 12 minutes **Yield:** 4 servings

FROZEN STRAWBERRIES

Episode: Strawberry Sky, EA1F03

1 quart strawberries, de-stemmed	1) Wash strawberries and place in a paper towel-lined colander. 2) Cover with another paper towel and place in the refrigerator for 4 hours.
1 (3 pound) block dry ice	3) Break your dry ice into small pieces, and toss with berries in a large bowl. 4) Place into a container and cover with a towel. 5) Place this in a cooler for 25 to 30 minutes. 6) Remove berries and put into sealable bags and store in the freezer.

Difficulty: Easy **Prep Time:** 10 minutes **Inactive Prep Time:** 4 hour 30 minutes **Yield:** 1 quart frozen berries

VLAD'S VERY GARLICKY GREENS

Episode: The Bulb of the Night, EA1D11

5 to 7 cloves garlic, peeled, plus 2 cloves garlic, one sliced, one minced	1) Place sauté pan over medium heat and then lightly crush 5 to 6 garlic cloves.
Enough olive oil to cover the bottom of a wide sauté pan	2) When the pan is hot, add just enough oil to cover the bottom of the pan and add the garlic. 3) Cook, stirring frequently until golden brown (3 to 5 minutes).
4 big handfuls greens (baby mustard, turnip, chard), picked and roughly shredded	4) Remove from the oil. At this point, the greens can be quickly sautéed for a mild garlic flavor. 5) If you're looking for something a little stronger, thinly sliver 1 clove and add it to the pan stirring constantly (burned garlic is not Good Eats, nor is anything that touches it). 6) Once the slivers turn golden, add the greens and toss to coat with the hot oil.
Salt and freshly ground black pepper	7) Season with salt and pepper as soon as the greens start to wilt and plate immediately. 8) If you're looking for even more garlic flavor, finely mince a clove of garlic and toss it into the greens during the last 30 seconds of cooking and toss the greens to distribute. 9) Keep the pan and the greens moving constantly, if you can. 10) Serve as a side dish or toss with pasta and serve as a main course.

Difficulty: Medium **Prep Time:** 10 minutes **Cook Time:** 5 minutes **Yield:** 4 servings

> **"... last but not least, [add] two smashed and chopped cloves of garlic. Now, why garlic? Hey, garlic don't need no reason."**
>
> Alton Brown, Good Eats, *Pork Fiction*

Notes:

MUSTARD GREEN GRATIN

Episode: Field of Greens, EA1H20

1 pound stemmed mustard greens	1) Preheat the oven to 375 degrees F. 2) Remove any large stems from the greens and wash them thoroughly; do so in a sink with at least 5 inches of water. 3) Moving the leaves around in the water and allowing them to sit for a few minutes to allow the sand or dirt to fall to the bottom of the sink. 4) Once clean, roughly chop the greens. You should have 1 pound finished greens once they are stemmed. (Weigh the greens after stemming, but before washing.) 5) After washing the greens, place them in a salad spinner to thoroughly dry them.
1 tablespoon unsalted butter, plus extra for baking dish	6) Butter a 9 by 11-inch or 2 1/2-quart baking dish and set aside.
3 whole eggs, beaten 10 ounces ricotta cheese 2 ounces grated Parmesan (approximately 1/2 cup) 1/2 teaspoon kosher salt, plus extra for garlic and mushrooms 1/4 teaspoon freshly ground black pepper	7) In a large mixing bowl whisk together the eggs, ricotta, Parmesan, salt, and pepper. Set aside. 8) In a large, 13 by 11-inch roasting pan set over 2 burners on medium heat, melt the butter in 1 corner of the pan.
2 cloves garlic, minced 12 ounces mushrooms, sliced	9) Add the garlic, mushrooms, and a pinch of salt and cook until the mushrooms give up their liquid, approximately 5 to 6 minutes. 10) Add the greens and cook until they are wilted, approximately 3 to 4 minutes. The greens will reduce to less than 1/4 of their original volume and begin to look like thawed, frozen spinach. 11) Remove the pan from the heat. 12) Add the greens to the egg and cheese mixture and stir to thoroughly combine.
1 cup crushed round butter crackers	13) Pour into the prepared baking dish, top with the crackers, place on the middle rack of the oven and bake for 35 to 40 minutes. 14) Allow to cool for 5 minutes and serve.

Difficulty: Easy **Prep Time:** 25 minutes **Cook Time:** 50 minutes **Yield:** 4 TO 6 servings

POT O'GREENS

Episode: Field of Greens, EA1H20

1 quart water 1 1/2 pounds smoked turkey legs	1) Place the water and turkey legs in an 8-quart pot over medium-high heat. 2) Cover, bring to a boil, and allow to simmer for 10 minutes.
2 pounds stemmed collard or turnip greens	3) In the meantime, remove any large stems from the greens and wash them thoroughly; do so in a sink with at least 5 inches of water. Moving the leaves around in the water and allowing them to sit for a few minutes to allow the sand or dirt to fall to the bottom of the sink. 4) Once clean, chop pieces in half. You should have 2 pounds of greens once they are stemmed. (Weigh the greens after stemming, but before washing.)
1 teaspoon salt, plus extra if desired 1 teaspoon sugar	5) Once the turkey legs have simmered for 10 minutes, add the greens, salt and sugar, reduce the heat to low, cover, and allow to simmer gently for 45 minutes or until the greens are tender. 6) Move the greens around every 10 to 15 minutes. 7) Taste and season with additional salt, if desired. Serve immediately.

Difficulty: Easy **Prep Time:** 10 minutes `**Cook Time:** 55 minutes **Yield:** 4 servings

LEMON SESAME GLAZED GREENS

Episode: Field of Greens, EA1H20

1 to 1 1/4 pounds stemmed hearty greens, mustard greens, or kale	1) Remove any large stems from the greens and wash them thoroughly; do so in a sink with at least 5 inches of water. 2) Moving the leaves around in the water and allowing them to sit for a few minutes to allow the sand or dirt to fall to the bottom of the sink. 3) Once clean, roughly chop the greens. You should have 1 to 1 1/4 pounds finished greens once they are stemmed. (Weigh the greens after stemming, but before washing.) 4) Heat a large 13 by 11-inch roasting pan set over 2 burners on medium heat.
1 tablespoon olive oil	5) Once hot, add the olive oil.
2 cloves garlic, minced 1 lemon, zested 2 teaspoons freshly squeezed lemon juice 1 tablespoon honey 1 1/2 teaspoons kosher salt 1/4 teaspoon freshly ground black pepper	6) Add the garlic, lemon zest, lemon juice, honey, salt, and pepper and stir to combine. 7) Add the greens and sauté for 4 to 5 minutes, tossing continually.
1/2 teaspoon red pepper flakes 1 tablespoon sesame seeds	8) Add the red pepper flakes and the sesame seeds. 9) Toss to combine. Adjust seasoning, if needed. Serve immediately.

Difficulty: Easy **Prep Time:** 15 minutes **Cook Time:** 7 minutes **Yield:** 4 servings

Notes:______________________________

CPSIA information can be obtained
at www.ICGtesting.com
Printed in the USA
LVHW062018220223
740172LV00015B/1038